W9-ABI-575

*Colette and the Fantom Subject
of Autobiography*

Reading
WOMEN
Writing

a series edited by Shari Benstock and Celeste Schenck

Reading Women Writing is dedicated to furthering international feminist debate. The series publishes books on all aspects of feminist theory and textual practice. *Reading Women Writing* especially welcomes books that address cultures, histories, and experiences beyond first-world academic boundaries. A full list of titles in the series appears at the end of this book.

COLETTE

and the Fantom Subject
of Autobiography

Jerry Aline Flieger

Cornell University Press

ITHACA AND LONDON

First published 1992 by Cornell University Press.

International Standard Book Number 0-8014-2692-8 (cloth)
International Standard Book Number 0-8014-9980-1 (paper)
Library of Congress Catalog Card Number 91-55557

Printed in the United States of America

Reprinted by permission of Farrar, Straus, and Giroux, Inc. and Martin Secker and Warburg Ltd.: Excerpts from *Break of Day* by Colette, copyright © 1961, 1989 by Martin Secker and Warburg. Excerpts from *Earthly Paradise* by Colette, copyright © 1966 by Farrar, Straus, and Giroux, Inc. Excerpts from *My Mother's House and Sido* by Colette, copyright © 1953, 1981 by Farrar, Straus, and Giroux, Inc. Excerpts from *The Pure and the Impure* by Colette, copyright © 1966, 1967 by Farrar, Straus, and Giroux, Inc.

Librarians: Library of Congress cataloging information appears on the last page of the book.

⊗ The paper in this book meets the minimum requirements of the American National Standard for Information Sciences–Permanence of Paper for Printed Library Materials, ANSI Z39.48-1984.

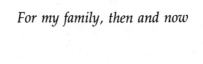

For my family, then and now

Contents

Preface

In his essay "Creative Writers and Daydreaming" (1908), one of the earliest examples of psychoanalytic literary theory, Freud maintains that all works of fiction are veiled acts of wish fulfillment, spawned by the writer's desire and somehow reflecting the writer's past history, the return of the repressed. The writer's imagination "creates for itself a situation which is to emerge in the future, representing the fulfillment of the wish—this is the daydream or phantasy, which now carries in it traces both of the occasion which engendered it and of some past memory. So past, present and future are threaded, as it were, on the string of the wish that runs through them all" (*Standard Edition* 9: 146). In this simple formulation, Freud suggests that all fiction is autobiographical, reflecting the writer's experience, and haunted by shades of the writer's past.

Freud is also responsible for the corollary discovery concerning narrative: all autobiography is fictional. The work of psychoanalytic therapy, the talking cure, is after all verbal work, in which the analysand tells his or her own story, creating a life narrative with a highly fictionalized first-person protagonist, and exposing this imaginary self to a listening analyst whose attention in turn helps shape the story that is told and retold.

No writer better exemplifies the cross-pollination between fiction and autobiography, past and present, than does Colette. Her tales deploy the writing "I" as heroine and create a textual identity in the process, a fantom who both is and is not the historical woman herself. By her own account, this process of self-discovery is made through fictional explorations, the telling of tales peopled by beloved ghosts—maternal, paternal, erotic—summoned from the depths of the writer's memory, active and latent, conscious and unconscious. This book is one reader's attempt to give chase to the fantom subject of autobiography who calls herself "Colette."

In writing this work on "what woman wants" as she writes, I am also inevitably deploying my own ghosts and fulfilling my own "wishes," conscious and unconscious. I would like to acknowledge the presence of one ghostwriter who has shaped my work: the figure of my grandmother, Emily Green. Throughout my childhood she told me tales of her girlhood on a vast farm in West Virginia, tales in large part inspired by the figure of her mother, Serena. More important, she worked countless hours writing down these stories, evoking her own childhood ghosts and her own mythological childhood landscape. These tales, which haunt me still, were in turn transcribed by my mother and transmitted to me and my brothers. Unfortunately, when my grandmother died, her manuscripts were lost—as so many women's manuscripts have been.

These missing works about my grandmother's childhood and family have undoubtedly had a great deal to do with the fascination that Colette's accounts of *her* childhood have always exerted on me. In particular, I am moved by Colette's account of her own father's "missing works," the empty pages the Captain never succeeded in filling, "the mirage of a writer's career," blank volumes discovered after his death. Colette in turn ghostwrites these volumes, filling empty pages as her father's spirit urges her to do, creating haunting works dedicated to her parents. Like Colette's own writing, my reading of her ghost story has been shadowed and encouraged by an intergenerational throng of others.

Jerry Aline Flieger

New Brunswick, New Jersey

*Colette and the Fantom Subject
of Autobiography*

Now fills the air so many a haunting shape,
That no one knows how best to escape.
—*Faust* (V, 2), epigraph to Freud's
The Psychopathology of Everyday Life

1

Fictional Autobiography:
The Spectral Subject

> I cannot do better than use the plural pronoun and
> take my place modestly among the crowd.
> —*My Apprenticeships*

Rereading Colette

Colette's life is an open book. If very few other writers have inspired as much biographical commentary and even prurient curiosity, it is perhaps in part because so much of Colette's work appears to be straightforward autobiographical statement, written in the first person and citing real people and places; indeed even the most fictional of her works often seem to be *romans à clef*, asking to be deciphered.[1] Colette's writing thus unfolds at the boundary between life and the literary text.

But in spite of the amount of attention devoted to her life and work, until recently Colette seems to have remained an underappreciated literary figure.[2] For decades, to be sure, she has been the *grande dame* of French letters, touted as the great feminine storyteller of the *Belle Epoque*, author of charming tales of female adolescence and titillating stories of bohemian life (the cover of a recent paper edition blazons, "She knows a woman's heart and

---

[1]Noteworthy biographical works on Colette that give information on the models for her fictional characters include Michèle Sarde's *Colette: Free and Fettered*, trans. Richard Miller (New York: William Morrow, 1980); Joan Hinde Stewart's *Colette* (Boston: G. K. Hall, 1983); Margaret Crosland's *Colette: The Difficulty of Loving* (New York: Dell, 1973); Joanna Richardson's *Colette* (London, Methuen, 1983); and Herbert R. Lottman's *Colette: A Life* (Boston: Little, Brown, 1991).

[2]For an annotated bibliography on Colette to 1978, see Elaine Marks's contribution in *A Critical Bibliography of French Literature*, ed. Douglas W. Alden and Richard A. Brooks (Syracuse, N.Y.: Syracuse University Press, 1980), vol. 6, 579–716.

mind, body and soul"). She has also been praised for her sensuous depictions of nature and her entertaining portraits of domestic animals. Yet although acknowledged as a peerless stylist, Colette has only relatively recently begun to receive the kind of serious theoretical reading long granted to such a figure as Proust, that other celebrated *Belle Epoque* poet of society and memory. (Even the best-known French theorists of *l'écriture féminine* have largely neglected her work, perhaps because she has always been accepted by the literary establishment.) We should perhaps begin then by forgetting what we know about Colette—taking a cue from Freud and lending a kind of "free-floating attention" to her text.

While some feminist critics have already undertaken a reevaluation of Colette's writing—drawing upon psychoanalytic, sociological, and linguistic concepts to analyze the role of gender in her work—they too have often tended to focus on the autobiographical axis of her writing, in order to examine her experience working within and against the constraints of patriarchal society.[3] As important as the feminist critic's emphasis on the life of the woman writer may be in the analysis of sexual politics, however, such an emphasis may risk relegating the text itself to the status of artifact, evidence about patriarchal society. And it is after all the textualized "Colette," the fictionalized persona, who motivates our curiosity about the real-life woman who produced the work.

Of course a textual focus need not (indeed should not) neglect biography, but it will necessarily foreground issues such as the gender of Colette's *textual* persona and the modernity of that textual voice, which at times bears a striking resemblance to that of other great moderns such as Proust and Woolf. For Colette is a pioneer in techniques that anticipate the genre of "fictional autobiography" prominent today:[4] the modernity of her work is mani-

---

[3]An early work that performs this kind of serious and seminal reading, however, is Elaine Marks's *Colette* (New Brunswick, N.J.: Rutgers University Press, 1960); more recent studies of particular merit include Joan Hinde Stewart's *Colette* and Nicole Ward Jouve's *Colette* (Bloomington: Indiana University Press, 1987). See also the Lacanian, sociological, and semiotic approaches in the special Colette issue of *Women's Studies* 8.3 (1981).

[4]What I call "fictional autobiography" is a quintessential modern genre that Co-

fest in the use of interior monologue and oblique characterization; the organization of autobiographical narratives by random associative memory (here she is a co-pioneer with Proust and with Breton); and in the tendency to intertwine herself with her own fictions, playing a game of hide-and-seek with her reader and creating a highly original brand of ironic humor in the process. Any rereading of this too-well-read author needs to pay attention to the intellectual importance of her contribution to the modern novel, forgetting the all-too-familiar notions about her femininity, spontaneity, and charm. For in addition to being profoundly modern, Colette's texts are often disturbing, unsettling, even uncanny in Freud's sense of the term, suggesting that perhaps more is at stake in rereading Colette than the rehabilitation of an undervalued writer.

I suggest that a combination of psychoanalytic and feminist perspectives may prove helpful in reconsidering the radicality of Colette's work and its uncanny impact on the reader. In weaving these approaches we will inevitably encounter the question of the nature and specificity of women's writing—if Colette is not simply "feminine," is she nonetheless a "woman writer"? Might her work answer the riddle that has haunted intellectual history in our century, first as the recurring refrain of psychoanalysis (what *does* woman want?) and more recently as the enigma of feminist criticism (just what is a woman writer)? Rereading Colette means confronting these two questions—woman's nature, and her desire—at the crossroads, at their intersection: What does woman (as writer, as subject of her text) want?

---

lette helped to invent—where an ostensibly true story has been reworked and rearranged, even peopled with fictional characters. In France, Gide, Proust, and Radiguet are also early pioneers of the genre, which more recently has been practiced by Alain Robbe-Grillet, Marcel Roche, Michel Tournier, and Marguerite Duras. Other prominent international figures associated with fictional autobiography are Mario Vargas Llosa, Luisa Valenzuela, Christa Wolf, and Philip Roth (who is notorious for inventing characters and situations in such works as *The Facts: A Novelist's Autobiography* [New York: Penguin, 1978]). A recent postmodern twist on fictional autobiography is found in Paul Auster's *City of Glass* (in *The New York Trilogy* [New York: Penguin, 1990]), where the main character adopts a false identity, posing as a detective, and taking on the author's real name (Paul Auster). He even pays a visit to the "real" Auster to discuss problems encountered in solving a case.

The Faces of Autobiography

At least three kinds of Colette's autobiographical writing need to be differentiated for purposes of this book. While recognizing that these categories overlap, I want first to differentiate between "impressionist memoir," "autobiographical fiction," and "fictional autobiography," and then to turn to a close examination of the third category, which will serve as my focus here. For it is in fictional autobiography that the narrating "I" is most elusive, a textual fantom of sorts.

Of these three kinds of writing it is perhaps the impressionist memoir (in the vein of *The Blue Lantern, Evening Star, Journal for Myself*[5]) that bears the least resemblance to the conventional autobiography. In fact, like all of Colette's works, these texts defy classification: they have something of the *mémoire intime* (written in middle or old age, these are recollections of a life well lived); yet at moments the intimate tone recalls the tradition of confessional writing, from Rousseau to Gide. But they also derive from the time-honored tradition of the French essay, and they have a great deal in common with the works of the classical *moralistes* as well, where the writer wryly observes society from her writing table. Thus however intimate, these reflections are not true autobiography, any more than an essay by Montaigne or a letter by Mme de Sévigné is autobiography. Colette's lyric recollections are perhaps most like the feminine diary, which recounts daily incidents and reflects on them with free flights of associative fantasy, and where the "I" is often an observer and dreamer, rather than an involved actor. In any case, these entertaining musings (on society, fashion, music, friendship) are not narrative. Less autobiographical than anecdotal, these idiosyncratic reveries are composed of reflection rather than plot, peopled by acquaintances rather than characters. (I might add that many of the vignettes of *My Apprenticeships*, while more straightforwardly autobiographical and narrative than the other works I include in this category, anticipate the impressionist memoirs in both style and subject matter.)

The remaining two categories—"autobiographical fiction" and "fictional autobiography"—are equally difficult to pin down and

---

[5]The last two works have been published in English as *Recollections*, trans. David Le Vay (New York: Macmillan, 1986).

even harder to sort out. Autobiographical fiction—represented by such works as *The Vagabond*, *Chéri*, and the *Claudine* series, which make ample use of autobiographical material but do not identify the protagonist as the author—is perhaps the more familiar of these two categories, belonging to a long literary tradition in which the author draws from her own life experience to shape her work. But in Colette, even this relatively straightforward category is complicated: for actual people from Colette's own life often appear in these works of fiction *without* a change of name, in delightful entanglements of imagination and reality. To cite one particularly rich example: in *Claudine at School*, the heroine meets the most famous actress of the day, Polaire—who, in real life, has built her reputation on playing none other than the fictional "Claudine," the admirer she meets in the novel. This is a hall of mirrors: for we recall that the real Colette and Polaire were alter egos of sorts, whom Colette's husband, Willy, paraded around dressed as twins, as a publicity stunt to promote the *Claudine* series. All costumes were straight out of the *Claudine* series, Colette's books, signed by Willy, who at first took credit for them. This whole *mise-en-abîme* is a text in itself, a tangle of cross-reflections and uncanny resemblance.

The sorting out of Colette's work is further complicated by the author herself, who often intercedes to underscore the autobiographical nature of her works of fiction and the fictional nature of what seems to be autobiography. In *Break of Day*, for instance, Colette writes that her novels ("if I dare to call them novels") are love stories from her own life: "In them I called myself Renée Néré or else, prophetically, I introduced a Léa."[6] But even while admitting the autobiographical base of these works, Colette insists that they are fiction. Noting her readers' confusion about these novels, which they may mistake for fact, Colette comments wryly on her literary "seductions":

These involuntary conquests have nothing to do with a time of life. We must look for their origin in literature—and this is where my responsibility begins. I write this humbly and conscientiously. When readers take to writing an author, especially to

---

[6]Colette, *Break of Day*, trans. Enid McLeod (New York: Farrar, Straus, and Giroux, 1979), 16. Hereafter *BD*.

a woman author, they don't easily lose the habit. Vial, who has only known me for two or three summers, must still be trying to find me in two or three of my novels—if I dare call them novels. There are still young girls—too young to notice the dates of editions—who write to tell me they have read the Claudine books in secret and that they will look for my answer at the *poste restante* . . . if indeed they do not give me an assignation in a teashop. (*BD* 63)[7]

This is a fascinating passage, a mixture of "conscientious and humble" reflection on the responsibility of the writer to the public she seduces, and outright fabrication, resorting to the very tricks of the trade that are ostensibly being criticized. For this passage contains a reference to the invented character Vial, whom the writer seems to pass off as real in this "conscientious" soul-searching about the reaction of the public to her *Claudine* novels. These meditations on the reader-writer bond may offer juicy food for thought; but they are also an exercise in artifice that ought not to be taken at face value. The writer seems to want to have it both ways: she insists on the verisimilitude of her "autobiographical" writing, owning up to her responsibility in engendering a dangerous cathexis on the part of the reader, even while she smiles at the reader's naïveté in confusing Colette and Claudine. So it is very hard indeed to draw the line between the writer and her fictional alter egos, and to know just how far to go in believing the narrator's abundant confessions. Even to begin to discuss this work we have to invent new terms to reflect the complicit mirroring of fiction and reality, chiasmic terms like "autobiographical fiction" and "fictional autobiography."

But as this crafty confession from *Break of Day* suggests, it is perhaps the mode that I call "fictional autobiography"—tales in the first person where "Colette" herself is identified as the narrator (*The Pure and the Impure, My Mother's House, Sido, Break of Day*)—that is the most opaque of the writer's autobiographical masks. For as the writer herself insists (again in *Break of Day*), these confessions, however transparent they may seem, continue to veil the author's essential self:

---

[7]Because Colette frequently uses suspension points (three dots) in her work, throughout this book I have placed ellipses, indicating that I have omitted something from a quotation, within brackets [. . .].

No other fear, not even that of ridicule, prevents me from writing these lines which I am willing to risk will be published. Why should I stop my hand from gliding over this paper to which for so many years I've confided what I know about myself, what I've tried to hide, what I've invented and what I've guessed? At no time has the catastrophe of love, in all its phases and consequences, formed a part of the true intimate life of a woman. (BD 62)

In spite of their daring disclosures, *all* of Colette's works—novels and autobiographies alike—remain works of fiction in a sense, where "guesses" and "inventions" are in the company of the most candid confessions, and where the creation itself seems to harbor its own secrets, propelled by forces the writer herself does not fully understand. Indeed, this admission of a compulsive desire that moves the writing along ("Why should I stop my hand from gliding over this paper") provides the uncanny suggestion that Colette's own unconscious is the ghostwriter of these texts.

Even more interesting is Colette's own disclaimer of the kind of full disclosure that these novels seem to provide; she asserts that even the most truthful autobiographical accounts do not tell all, the essential woman being something other than the sum of her love affairs, a ghostly essence dwelling in shadows too deep for the author herself to fathom:

Why do men—writers or so-called writers—still show surprise that a woman should so easily reveal to the public love-secrets and amorous lies and half-truths? By divulging these, she manages to hide other important and obscure secrets which she herself does not understand very well. The spotlight, the shameless eye which she obligingly operates, always explores the same sector of a woman's life, that sector tortured by bliss and discord round which the shades are thickest. (BD 62)

Almost in passing Colette hints at a problem inherent in all autobiography: however anguished or sincere, confessional writing never tells the whole story. Still, in the epigraph to *Break of Day*, she challenges her readers to delve for the truth behind the veneer of fiction, or at least to wait "patiently" for the dispelling of her ghostly doubles: "Do you imagine I am portraying myself?

Have patience; this is only my model." But the reader's patience will go unrewarded; Colette's text demonstrates that there is no final stratum of truth in the palimpsest of her work. (Here Colette even anticipates the poststructuralist/postmodern sensibility, which emphasizes that autobiography is a muting of the subject, veiled in an always plural account of "truth."[8])

In other words, Colette's position in these works is shifty: in the case of her novels, she warns against taking fiction at face value, since it is interwoven with fact; conversely, in the case of her autobiographical works, she warns us not to take "fact" at face value, since it is interwoven with fiction. Autobiographical fiction, fictional autobiography—so many turns of the screw, so many ghost stories, so many lures for the unsuspecting reader.

Even while recognizing the provisional character of these distinctions, I want to focus here on the notion of fictional autobiography: those ostensibly true stories that include invented characters and rearranged chronologies, but where "Colette" herself is the "I" in the center of the storm. Specifically, this book concerns itself with the works about Colette's childhood (*Sido, My Mother's House*) as a perspective from which to read the later fictional autobiographies (*Break of Day, The Pure and the Impure*). Of course much has been written concerning the autobiographical character of Colette's novels, but I want to suggest that the other side of the phenomenon, the fictional character of the autobiographies, is perhaps the most intriguing aspect of this enigmatic work. Indeed at the very moment when "Colette" seems to offer herself up to the reader's scrutiny, putting herself in the spotlight, a certain part of her "true nature" retains its elliptical reserve, enveloped in shadow, evading even the gaze of the conscious "I" who writes the tale: Colette's most apparently lucid work is ghostwritten by the fantom subject of autobiography.

---

[8]For one such fascinating essay on the fictional nature of autobiography, see Shoshana Felman, "Paul de Man's Silence," *Critical Inquiry* 15 (Summer 1989): 704–44. In this essay, Felman discusses (734ff.) the ramifications of de Man's statement that "autobiography veils a defacement of the mind of which it is itself the cause" (quoted from *The Rhetoric of Romanticism* [New York: Columbia University Press, 1984], 81). Another important poststructuralist text on the autobiographical nature of theory is Jacques Derrida's "Coming into One's Own," in *Psychoanalysis and the Question of the Text*, ed. Geoffrey Hartman (Baltimore and London: Johns Hopkins University Press, 1978), which I discuss in chapter 6.

Psychoanalysis and the Literary Text:
Looking for a Textual Unconscious

It is not in the illuminated zone
that the darkest plots are woven.
—*Break of Day*

How may we best approach this elusive work, which refuses to be classified, and in which the "I" is most concealed precisely where it is most candidly revealed? Finding a balance between a textual and a biographical approach is important for all gender-related theories of reading, but this balance is perhaps even more critical in reading an "autobiographical" writer like Colette. For if the text is read primarily as a documentation of social conditions (in the manner of some feminist criticism), or as a symptom of an author's neuroses (in the manner of some psychobiography), the autobiographical axis will assume more importance than the fictional axis, with a consequent loss of literary pleasure. If on the other hand the text's aesthetic characteristics are foregrounded with little reference to the real writing woman (in the manner of some poststructuralist criticism), we risk losing an understanding of the work as work, either in the psychoanalytic sense (dream-work, mourning-work, joke-work) or in the social sense, which recognizes that literature is communication and that it has an ideological valence in even the least polemical of texts.

Moreover, Colette's peculiar position in her fictional auto-biography imposes special conditions on the reader. Even if we wanted to do so, it would be impossible to exclude the author as historical person from this reading, since "Colette" confronts us on every page as the "I" of the first person. And her real life is intriguing, reflecting adventures and crises of particular interest to women readers: the fascination with powerful swashbuckling men who were unfaithful to her, the affairs with other women and with younger men, the struggle for independence, the enduring ties with her mother. Reading about these experiences, it is virtually impossible not to become an interested party—judging or cheering on that "I" in her lifelong struggle to become "Colette."

And since we are cathected to the persona of Colette—believers in her story (even sometimes, as she suggests, "seduced" by her narrating persona), it becomes of some import to us whether she is telling the truth, the whole truth, and nothing but the truth. Our belief in the narrator, or even our "willing suspension of disbelief" (Coleridge's term for the willful loan of fascinated attention that allows us to derive pleasure from works of imagination) has to be reexamined when the narrating "I" plays coquettishly with her readers, warning us not to believe everything we read ("do you imagine I am portraying myself?"). For when Colette alerts us that the reading of her apparent "autobiography" as fact is risky sport, she interjects a disturbing cat-and-mouse quality into the literary pact, refusing to play her conventional part in that transaction, reminding us not to get too involved—even while she lures us into doing so, by her "revealing" confessions.

Indeed fictional autobiography, for Colette, might be considered a kind of "autofiction," the result of a creative act that crafts a textual or narrative persona, but that finally reveals few facts about the biographical person. Colette's fictional autobiography gives rise to a complex play among text, writer, and reader: here the writing subject is a self-made woman, fabricated by the transaction of writing itself, which has a great deal in common with the transference in psychoanalysis (the analysand's "love" for the analyst, her cathexis to and belief in the analyst). Like the skillful psychotherapist, Colette elicits something like this transference, this confidence and cathexis, both by proclaiming her candor and by exercising the seductive wiles of her craft, eliciting belief. And like the analyst, the author refuses to respond completely to our desires, to give all the answers, to play the role we have assigned her. But at the same time, Colette occupies a position similar to that of the narrating patient: she is like the analysand who tells her story to the onlooking analyst—in an effort at persuasion that is also a call for love—eliciting in her turn the countertransference, the analyst's fascinated involvement with the patient's narrative, "his" stake in the imaginary configurations of her tale. In this position, Colette recalls Freud's (and Breuer's) most seductive patients—Dora, Emma, Anna O.—staging a peep show designed at once to entice the reading analysts of her tale and to throw them off the track ("By divulging these [secrets], she manages to hide other important and obscure secrets" *BD* 62). Throughout these autofictions, we may catch only fleeting glimpses of the veiled face of this woman, a written self shadowed by a throng of unconscious others, her ghosts and desires. This is Salome's dance of seduction, which seems among other things to restage the flirtatious maneuvers of analysis, the ballet of transference and countertransference, where analyst and analysand trade places as seducer and seduced.

The question of the listener's fascinated belief or absorption in the teller's tale is a familiar one, recalling an ongoing quarrel between psychoanalysis and feminism (to what degree should the analyst believe the subject's tale of seduction?). The case of Dora taught Freud the price of too much absorption in the analysand's story (for as Freud learned with Dora, the analyst's involvement with the narrating subject may compromise the outcome of the treatment); the case history of the writer "Colette" raises some analogous questions about the reader's involvement with the narrated text. Indeed, because so many of the issues raised by Colette's writing are also issues central to psychoanalysis, a Freudian perspective promises to enliven and illuminate our encounter with the fantom subject who calls herself "Colette."[9]

Precisely because psychoanalysis functions on the boundary between life and fiction—at the juncture between theory and practice, biography and interpretation—it challenges the boundaries between fiction and reality. And just as the act of analysis aims to reveal the profoundly fictional nature of one's own self-image (the domain of Lacan's Imaginary register of "misrecognition" [*méconnaissance*]), the act of textual analysis may reveal the profoundly fictional nature of all autobiography, in which a desiring subject (the author) creates and exhibits a self-effigy (an Imaginary alter ego) for the complicit reader (the Symbolic other), the outsider who witnesses the fantasy.

Psychoanalysis and Criticism: Literature as Circuit of Desire

But what kind of psychoanalytic reading is most appropriate for Colette's text? Freud's own pioneering efforts offer us many para-

---

[9]In other words, we are in search of a "textual unconscious" in Colette. The term is borrowed from Jean Bellemin-Noël's *Vers l'inconscient du texte* (Paris: Presses Universitaires de France, 1979).

digms: analysis of character, author, reader, theme/motif; the reading of literature as allegory for the functioning of the psyche; even the reading of the psyche itself for clues to the poet's secret, seeking to discover how poetic processes wield their magic.[10] All of these approaches may be brought to a reading of Colette, because her work provides a creative intersection between the real and the imagined, relying upon a play between what is said and what is left out.

My own reading is influenced by all of these approaches, and by the field of psychobiography as well (also pioneered by Freud, in his study of Leonardo da Vinci[11]); I am more concerned, however, with the psychobiography of the textual "Colette" than with the life history of her real counterpart. For although much has been made of the limitations of psychobiographical criticism— which may tell us more about the author's neurosis than about her creation—psychobiography may open new possibilities in the field of feminist theory. As long as it does not reduce the text to a case history, this approach may be of help in the feminist effort to integrate an interest in the creative process (the work of fiction as fiction) with an interest in the real conditions producing the work. Indeed, the psychobiographic technique of uncovering a "personal obsessive myth" (Charles Mauron's term) in a body of

---

[10]Freud's own work provides the paradigm for all the various practices of psychoanalytic criticism today. A prototype of reader response theory, "Creative Writers and Daydreaming" deals with the reader's identification with the text, and with the author's desire. The prototype for character analysis is Freud's essay on Jensen's *Gradiva*, which reveals the neurosis of the hero. An early example of psychoanalytic thematics is found in Freud's essay on the motif of the three caskets in Shakespeare's *King Lear*. Freud pioneered genre analysis in "Creative Writers and Daydreaming," which raises tantalizing questions about fiction; and his reading of *Oedipus Rex* tells us a great deal about the appeal of tragedy. Similarly, Freud pioneered the use of the literary text as model for the psyche itself, in his reading of *Oedipus Rex*, which in turn provides the model for Lacan's readings of *Hamlet* as an emblem of psychosis/foreclusion, and of Poe's "The Purloined Letter" as a psycholinguistic allegory of the circulation of intersubjective desire. Even feminist psychoanalysis often finds its source in Freud, where essays such as the celebrated case history of "Dora" have given rise to debate concerning the role of the female subject in analysis. Finally, *The Interpretation of Dreams and Jokes and Their Relation to the Unconscious* are the models for the structural/functional study of how aesthetic processes work; as such they underlie such present-day critical practice as Jean Bellemin-Noël's *textanalyse* (note 9).

[11]Freud, *Leonardo da Vinci and a Memory of His Childhood* (1910), S.E. 11.

work, by superimposing texts and looking for significant knots of recurring imagery, can be useful not only in understanding the author's personal vision, but also in unveiling the collective myths that the text harbors.

In Lacanian terms, we might say that psychobiography plays with Imaginary constructs (the author's personal myths) deployed in a Symbolic intersubjective exchange (reading), which is subject to Real conditions (the work's social context). For in literature, as in many areas of human endeavor, these registers coexist and interact: they ought not to be understood simply as developmental phases of childhood, but as registers that operate simultaneously in all areas of adult life, including aesthetic processes.[12]

For example, the literary transaction displays many Imaginary characteristics (as a mutual reflection of two alter egos—writer and persona, or reader and writer—in a bond of identification; as well as in the fantasies it both engenders and fulfills). But as a function of language, the literary process simultaneously operates in the Symbolic register, as a tripartite libidinal circuit among writer-character-reader (hence as a relation of ongoing desire, alienated in the other). In its Symbolic aspect, literature creates a triangular circuit that interrupts the Imaginary fulfillment of desire between two poles, diverting desire into a three-way detour or long-circuit. The oedipal nature of this intercession is obvious: an idyll between subject and object is obstructed by the presence of a third—the reading other—who as stand-in for social exigency demands that the fantasy be interesting, proprietous, intelligible, artful, in order to be read. In fact, in "Creative Writers and Daydreaming," Freud expressly points out that the presence of the reader imposes formal limitations on the author's fantasy, since the author-dreamer's "egotistical wishes" must be "softened" by "veils and disguises" in order to be palatable to another person.[13]

In other words, the Imaginary constructs of the author (the "misrecognition" of the subject in her own tale, the fabrication of

---

[12]For an interesting discussion of the coexistence of the first two Lacanian registers in literature, see Fredric Jameson's "Imaginary and Symbolic in Lacan: Marxism, Psychoanalytic Criticism, and the Problem of the Subject," in *Literature and Psychoanalysis: The Question of Reading: Otherwise*, ed. Shoshana Felman (Baltimore and London: Johns Hopkins University Press, 1982), 338–95.

[13]Freud, "Creative Writers and Daydreaming" (1908), *S.E.* 9: 143.

a persona, an alter ego who moves in an extended daydream) are realized through the Symbolic processes of language, in a tripolar literary transaction among reader, character, and author. In this triangle, the dual Imaginary axis between author and character is always deflected by the desire of a third term, the onlooking reader, the other to whom Colette confesses that she is not identical to her narrating persona.

This drama could be understood as a play of obstacles, refracting desire and putting it into circulation. For Freud suggests that in dream or revery, the dreamer more or less directly gratifies desire in private fantasy. But in the literary process, the dual axis of absorption or identification—between dreamer and dream, author and text—is constantly interrupted by the intercession of the (oedipal) other, the reader. Freud insists that this outsider not only makes the dream into a text, a self-conscious process, but actually changes the nature of the original fantasy, which must be artfully presented to be appealing to the onlooker, and which must be made understandable—as coherent narrative—as well. The desire of the dreamer turned author is obstructed and shaped by the demands of intelligibility, as well as by the need to please.

But as Colette's work shows, the role of the obstructive other is not always played by the reader: any one of the three poles of the literary transaction—reader, author, character/persona—may play the role of obstacle in this drama of maintained desire. In Colette's case, we could say that the Imaginary relation between persona and author is interrupted by the reader, whose watchful eye reminds the author of the fictitious nature of her creation, in an act of naming that masks the self ("in [these novels] I called myself Renée Néré, or else, prophetically, I introduced a Léa"). But conversely, the writer poses an obstacle to the too-direct gratification of the *reader's* desire, putting the brakes on a too-complete absorption or identification with the fantasy text ("Does anyone *imagine*, as he is reading me, that I am portraying myself?" *BD* 35). Finally, the character/persona poses an obstacle of sorts to a complete identification between the author's hidden "self" and the reader, since the author's persona/alter ego always obscures this deeper self from the reader's view ("By divulging these [secrets], [the writer] manages to hide other important and obscure secrets which she herself does not understand very well" *BD* 62).

Through psychoanalytic theory, the reading process may be understood as an oedipal circuit where three is a crowd, where an outsider disrupts the Imaginary idyll of absorption or identification between the other two poles of the triangle.[14] I want to suggest that this understanding of the reading process as intersubjective circuit may provide one way to *chercher la femme*, to encounter the uncanny subject of Colette's ghostly tales of love lost.

And while a certain traditional psychobiography may help reveal Colette's Imaginary landscape—giving shape to her ghosts and penetrating the shroud of her "screen memories"—we may call upon a more radical (Lacanian) psychoanalytic theory to help elucidate the Symbolic relation between Colette, her reader, and her characters, the spectral shades of her past. Lacanian theory may also serve to attenuate the excessive psychologism of psychobiography, since for Lacan the act of writing is an enactment of the larger human tragedy of desire, rather than a symptom of a single individual's pathology. Furthermore, Lacanian theory may provide a link between psychoanalysis and linguistic/philosophical theories of narrative or textuality (Derrida, Kristeva, Blanchot) since all of these approaches seek to expose the "self" as fictional construct. For Lacan's emphasis on an Imaginary concept of self has revealed that one's own *history* as told to the analyst, and to oneself, is always a fiction (*histoire*) characterized by self-delusion or "misrecognition" (*méconnaissance*).[15] And if Lacanian theory insists on the fictional nature of autobiography, conventional Freudian psychobiography, conversely, points out the autobiographical nature of all fiction, holding that the text veils the desire of an author, in a vicariously gratified fantasy.[16]

This approach to Colette's work—reading the text through a

[14]I discuss this dynamic at length in *The Purloined Punch Line: Freud's Comic Theory and the Postmodern Text* (Baltimore and London: Johns Hopkins University Press, 1991).

[15]For a discussion of "misrecognition" as an Imaginary construct, see Anthony Wilden's *Speech and Language in Psychoanalysis* (Baltimore: Johns Hopkins University Press, 1981), 159–77. Originally published as *The Language of the Self: The Function of Language in Psychoanalysis* (New York: Dell, 1975).

[16]Freud maintains that the writer bribes the reader into lending attention and credence to the psychic drama of wish fulfillment by veiling fantasy in aesthetic form. This theory of vicarious gratification is elaborated in "Creative Writers and Daydreaming."

combination of psychobiographic technique and Lacanian theoretical perspective—is only suggested here, as a prologue to the reading of Colette's autobiography as a kind of ghost story, and to a pursuit of the fantom subject of her narrative. Of course "Colette hunting" in the works of fiction has long been good sport, made all the more titillating by the thinly veiled clues placed there by the author herself. But as Lacan's seminal reading of another great literary text—Poe's "The Purloined Letter"—has taught us, we must be wary of the clue that is too obvious, since the evidence lying out in the open for all to see may be the most difficult to decipher. Indeed, we have seen that Colette herself cautions her reader not to look for the "real" Colette in this "open book."

Who then is "Colette" and what does this woman want? Let us begin our search by looking more closely at the fascinating text *Break of Day*, as a particularly provocative example of the fictionalized self-profile in which Colette excels. Written in the first person, it seems to be an autobiographical memoir. But this "autobiography" goes through the looking glass, providing an inverted image of Colette's actual experience; the text reflects a double perhaps, but it is an "I" reflected "in an *inclined* mirror" (62), an uncanny image that is also a distortion and a fragmentation. As such *Break of Day* is a paradigm of fictional autobiography: in this hall of mirrors we are at a loss to find "Colette" among a host of ghostly reflections.

Refracted Identity: *Break of Day*

> Raising my head, I look at myself, without laughing,
> in the inclined mirror; then I turn to my writing again.
> —*Break of Day*

In *Break of Day* (*La Naissance du jour*, 1928) there is no mystery concerning the identity of the narrating "I": the narrative is in the first person, and the protagonist, a famous writer who is vacationing in Provence in "La Treille Muscate"—the very house that Colette often visited with her younger lover Maurice Goudeket during the early 1920s—is actually called "Mme Colette." Moreover, she is contemplating an affair with a man much younger than she; and her story is filled with allusions to real people, houseguests and friends, some of whom are called by their actual names. So at first reading this seems to be an autobiographical reflection on the author's own change of life, replete with lyric passages concerning the new possibilities of friendships with men, now that the bitter drama of sexual love is coming to an end. It is a survivor's hymn, reflecting a turning away from love characterized not by bitterness, but rather by self-sufficiency and freedom from the pressures of Eros. The narrator speaks with the worldly-wise voice of the warrior home from the fight, in a lyric tribute to her own age and to her strength, which is a result less of progress than of return to a primal source.

"Mme Colette" even reads to us from her mother's letters, drawing on Sido's wisdom to face the coming of old age. And she often addresses her own reflections to her mother, who appears in her imagination as interlocutor, guide, and companion, a "chaste, serene *ghost*" (7) hovering in a kind of benevolent haunting, both protecting her daughter and judging what she sees. The narrator clearly wants to identify with this ghost, who seems to qualify as a classic Freudian ego ideal: "Now that little by little I am beginning to age, and little by little taking on her likeness in the mirror, I wonder whether, if she were to return, she would recognise me for her daughter, in spite of the resemblance of our features" (6). But as this passage implies, this work is more than a statement of identification; it is also the first of many mirrored transmutations in the writer's identity, recording a *difference* between "Colette" and one of her selves, a difference that belies the surface likeness. Colette goes on to explain why she *fails* to resemble that "chaste, serene ghost" of memory, who always used to greet the dawn "in a blue apron with pockets full of grain for the fowls" (6). For though the daughter, too, is up at daybreak, her mother's ghost surprises her in a compromising situation, "half naked in a fluttering wrap hastily slipped on, standing at my door which had admitted a nightly visitor, my arms trembling with passion and shielding—let me hide myself for shame!—the shadow, the thin shadow of a man" (7). What comes between Colette and the chaste matinal spirit of daybreak is a nocturnal ghost of sorts, the "shadow of a man" who taints the light of the mother's memory, by assuring that Sido's double, her child, is neither chaste *nor* serene. The daughter thus fears her mother's visit, which will reveal the presence of this male shadow.

But the ghost whose judgment is so feared turns out to be compassionate. Far from being shocked by the presence of the man in her daughter's bed, she generously (mis)recognizes the interloper as one of her own lovely flowers, and so reestablishes her identity with her daughter, exonerating her from the guilty sensuality that threatens to disjoin them:

> "Stand aside and let me see," my beloved ghost would say. "Why, isn't what you're embracing my pink cactus, that has survived me? How amazingly it's grown and changed! But now that I look into your face, my child, I recognise it. I recognise it by your agitation, your air of waiting, by the devotion in your outspread hands, by the beating of your heart and your suppressed cry, by the growing daylight all about you, yes, I recognise, I lay claim to all of that." (*BD* 7)

Thus Colette opens this remarkable novel with the first of a series of distorted reflections—a highly erotic response ("the beating of your heart, your suppressed cry") has been transformed into something chaste by the purity of Sido's vision. But it is not clear if this is a transformation, or merely a veiling, a guilty cover-up—like the wrap so hastily slipped on when the half-naked daughter greets her "ghost"—because the scene is both a fantasy (a beloved departed parent returns to forgive the prodigal child) and a classic wish fulfillment, written in the conditional tense ("'Stand aside and let me see,' my ghost *would* say"). The narrator is indeed her mother's daughter, duplicating the maternal image in the mirror, but she is a counterfeit Sido, since she is "unchaste." The ensuing identification is established only thanks to Sido's ability to misrecognize a guilty liaison as something pure. In any case, the daughter's fantasy ends with a maternal benediction: "Stay where you are, don't hide, and may you both be left in peace, you and the man you're embracing, for I see that he is in truth my pink cactus, that has at last consented to flower" (7).

The tale's first statement of identification and difference is a kind of inverted reflection of the drama of Eden: here the onlooking judge blesses the guilty union and insists on the right of her "creation" (as Sido often calls her daughter) to continue to enjoy the earthly paradise. This is a kind of secular parable, akin to a fairy tale; and one might even expect this reconciliation to bring the work to a close (they lived happily ever after . . .), since Sido, like a benevolent fairy, has uttered her blessing, transforming guilt into innocence. This spirit is a guardian angel who, having resolved the story's only conflict, perhaps should be gone—like a Shakespearean fairy who blesses the house at play's end and graciously takes his leave.

But the novel has only begun, and curiously, it does not turn out to be about the narrator's *acceptance* of the carnal love her mother blesses, but about a *refusal* of that love. What little plot this lyric chronicle has revolves around whether or not Mme Colette will fall in love again, having become aware that her young friend Vial has fallen in love with her, or whether she will magnanimously cede her young lover to a woman his own age (who, it seems, has asked for her help). In other words, the question is whether Vial will ever make it into Mme Colette's bed: the very place where, oddly enough, her mother's spirit finds him in the opening passage. The novel thus begins with a false resolution, with all the features of a good dream, from which the narrator subsequently awakens, to relive the conflict. And the outcome of the tale is different from what the overture with Sido's ghost would lead us to expect: the narrator-protagonist finally decides, in consultation with her absent mother's spirit, to forgo this relationship and to enjoy her own newfound strength. Witness this lyric passage, where the aging woman emerges from youth as from a shipwreck:

> Come, Man, my friend, let us simply exist side by side . . . What you see emerging from a confused heap of feminine cast-offs, still weighed down like a drowned woman by seaweed (for even if my head is saved, I cannot be sure that my struggling body will be), is your sister, your comrade: a woman who is escaping from the age when she is a woman. . . Let us remain together; you no longer have any reason for saying good-bye to me for ever. (*BD* 18)

This delivery from love is clearly exhilarating, although it is the opposite of the solution offered by the ghost of the first scene (the alter ego who urges her daughter to enjoy the pleasures of physical love). For in this statement of truce with "man," a stoic asceticism, rather than the license of sensual indulgence, is experienced as an emancipation. In fact, the narrator ponders her emergence from *two* great fetters—sexual love and maternal obligation: "Love, one of the great commonplaces of existence, is slowly leaving mine. The maternal instinct is another great commonplace. Once we've left these behind, we find that all the rest is gay and varied, and that there is plenty of it" (18). The novel is a reflection on two kinds of delivery—the deliverance from the emotional bondage of sexual love, and the "delivery" from the physical and emotional labor of maternity, severing the umbilical tie of mother to child.

The retreat from love is a theme throughout Colette's work, as reflected in the title of one of her works (*La Retraite sentimentale*). No fewer than three heroines have preceded Mme Colette in this noble renunciation, and two of them, significantly, are the "older women" explicitly named as alter egos in *Break of Day*: "In [these novels] I called myself Renée Néré, or else, prophetically, I introduced a Léa" (19). The third prototype for Mme Colette is Annie, in *La Retraite sentimentale* (*Retreat from Love*), the last of the Claudine series, published in 1907. (Although Annie is still relatively young, like Mme Colette she goes off into a kind of "retirement" [*retraite*] to spend time reflecting.) Thus the theme of emergence from love into something more sane, something healthier, is one of Colette's founding fables; indeed this leitmotif has the status of an obsessional myth in Mauron's sense of the term. Might the recurrence of this myth in *Break of Day*, this intertextual resemblance to earlier works of fiction, perhaps be a clue that this "autobiography" is something less than the true story—or something more—part of a phantasmal network?

In any case, this renunciation has taken on a troubling new aspect; here it is a question of retreating not only from sensual love, but from maternal love as well, which is curious indeed in a novel that seems to be dedicated to mother-daughter love. Colette's own daughter Bel-Gazou is the absent player here, implicitly excluded from the new paradise and, significantly, missing from this work altogether. This is a telling absence, indicating Colette's *lack* of identification with her own filial "image" (a child who, Colette tells us elsewhere, looks like her father). This meaningful absence marks another difference between the narrator and her alter ego Sido, the maternal ghost/guardian angel of the first scene, who returns to recognize *her* prodigal daughter, and thus to *reaffirm* her own maternal bond.

The Road Up from the Night

The maternal angel also seems to show up to take her daughter home, suggesting that this *récit* is not only a turning away but also a turning back, a return to the (dead) mother, doubled by the final return to Mother Earth. "Is this house going to be my last?" the narrator wonders (8), and then describes the road home:

> The coast road that leads up from the night, the mist and the sea; then a bath, work and rest. How simple everything could be! Can it be that I have attained here what one never starts a second time? Everything is much as it was in the first years of my life, and little by little I recognise the road back. [. . .] My sense of wonder and a serenity whose breath I can feel from far off—a merciful moisture, a promise of healing rain hanging over my still-stormy life—all these help me to recognise it [. . .] Does there then exist here on earth a kitchen-garden path where I can retrace my own footsteps, a path I thought I should never follow again except on the other side of life? Is that maternal ghost, in the old-fashioned dress of blue sateen, filling the watering cans on the edge of the well? This coolness of spray, this sweet enticement, this provincial spirit, in short this innocence, isn't all this the charm of declining years? (9–10)

In this passage there is no hint of renunciation—the effect is less one of a leaving than of a refinding (recalling Freud's famous dictum "Every finding of the object is a refinding"). This primal scene exudes comfort, familiarity, warmth, healing moisture, suggesting that the road coming up from one dark, moist place ("the coast road that leads up from the night") leads back to another, to *"My Mother's House,"* to the maternal womb/tomb. And this image of a female coming up from a watery netherworld doubles the passage cited earlier where the protagonist emerges from womanhood as from a shipwreck: these reflected passages together evoke the experience of birth (the newborn dragging the "cast-off weeds" with her), of renewed virginity (Venus rising from the

sea), of return to the light (Eurydice emerging from Hades to rejoin Orpheus, Persephone returning to her mother from the underworld), where a renewed chastity refinds infantile innocence.
Above all, the narrator is moved by the *familiarity* of her experience of age, which mirrors her childhood experience.

But if this passage exudes the joy of what Freud calls "the rediscovery of something familiar" (the infantile pleasure to which he
attributes much of the delight in aesthetic processes), it also harbors the slightly eerie impression of something "uncanny" (as described in his celebrated essay of that name).[17] For this evocation
of a familiar road that "leads up from the night" suggests something like the feeling of *déjà vu* that Freud attributes to the return
of the repressed, when one is haunted by forgotten material from
the past, and familiar elements, veiled as ghostly doubles, rise up
out of the landscape, in a reflection of our own unconscious. And
just what is the nature of "Colette's" final rediscovery, this return
of shades of the buried past? It is the maternal *revenant* (ghost;
'one who returns'), the spectral figure who, like a mirror reflection of her daughter at the beginning of the passage, emerges out
of the mist at the end of this same road (and at the end of the
passage, itself a "passage" into the past) to meet the daughter
who resembles her.

Even if this meeting with the friendly ghost has little of the
scariness of a *déjà vu* experience, the entire work may be read as
a séance of sorts, permeated by Sido's spirit, who guides the
daughter's return to the pure sensuality of nature, as a prelude
for death. Indeed Sido's voice opens the work, with the daughter's transcription of her mother's famous letter about the cactus
rose. Sido writes to her son-in-law to decline an invitation to visit
the couple: "You ask me to come and spend a week with you,
which means I would be near my daughter, whom I adore [. . .]
All the same I'm not going to accept your kind invitation [. . .
because] my pink cactus is probably going to flower, and I'm told
that in our climate it only flowers once every four years. Now, I
am already a very old woman, and if I went away when my pink
cactus is about to flower, I am certain I shouldn't see it flower
again" (5).

---

[17]"The 'Uncanny'" (1919), *S.E.* 17: 219.

The celebrated "cactus-flower" letter is followed by the narrator's triumphant proclamation that she "is the daughter of this woman," in a statement of identity that makes clear the degree of the daughter's investment in her mother's image—the daughter's very self-worth depends on a mimetic appropriation of Sido's spunk and sensitivity: "Whenever I feel myself inferior to everything about me, threatened by my own mediocrity [. . .] I can still hold up my head and say to myself: 'I am the daughter of the woman who wrote that letter' [. . . which tells me] that waiting for the possible bursting into bloom of a tropical flower held everything up and silenced even her heart, made for love" (5–6).

This is certainly one of the great literary tributes to the mother-daughter bond, and it has often been cited as evidence of the profound affective tie between Colette and Sido. Nonetheless, there is something odd—something uncanny—about this eulogy, and something peculiar about this identification. For what the daughter most cherishes in Sido's memory is a peculiar *hardening* of heart, a kind of egotism (a quality to which Sido herself lays claim in a later passage) that "silences" everything, leaving her deaf to love. (Certainly this beloved daughter might feel more than a little neglected, more than a bit hurt by the mother's refusal to visit, since she takes second place to a plant; but any such feelings, if they exist, are muffled under the proclamations of admiration.) And Sido did die the next year, after having seen, if we are to believe the narrator, the blossoming of her cactus rose; but presumably without having seen her daughter again. (Significantly, the narrator is silent on this point.) What are we to make of this curious anecdote, set as a kind of blazon over the testament of self-realization that is *Break of Day*? It might seem that Sido's sacrifice of her trip to her daughter's house is already a retreat from love, anticipating her daughter's own difficult choice and foreshadowing another renunciation—that of mother love—which is later mentioned in passing as one fetter from which the aging narrator herself seeks to escape.

The lesson of Sido's letter seems to be that a certain narcissistic sensual pleasure is to be preferred over all external loves, even mother-daughter love. Is this closing off of a "heart made for love" Colette's way of "finding the road home," the retracing of her steps from the choice of an external love object to a more primal narcissistic libidinal state? (Freud differentiates on just these grounds between *anaclitic* object choice—the sexual love at the basis of the oedipal complex—and *narcissistic* love, which seems to be both pre-oedipal and egocentric, infolded, based in autoeroticism.[18]) To be sure, there is a certain narcissistic quality to the cactus rose, which is circular, involuted, vaginal, folded upon itself, reluctant to open to the other's gaze.

And there is another underside to this text, undermining its manifest limpidity and its apparent status as sincere confession. It becomes evident, from a reading of Colette's letters to Marguerite Moreno and others, that she considered *Break of Day*—this extraordinary work featuring herself and her friends—to be a work of fiction. Indeed, in one letter, Colette confesses that she is having a terrible time finding something to say, finding "material" for this "novel."[19] And of course at the time of the novel's composition, the real Colette is seeing a young man who is not named Vial but Maurice Goudeket. The writer could be simply veiling the identity of her real lover with a fictitious name, to keep the most intimate details of her life from public scrutiny. But the third character in the love triangle of the novel is quite clearly an invention. She is Hélène Clément, the young girl who is in love with Vial, and to whom "Mme Colette" all but gives her young lover in an act of self-awareness and renunciation. Judging from Colette's own letters and the testimony of Goudeket, there was never any such rival or any such love triangle at "La Treille Muscate." In fact, Goudeket insists that Vial never existed either, and that he himself is not the model for this passionless lover: "If ever a novel appears to be autobiographical, that one does. Everything is in it, 'La Treille Muscate,' the garden, the vineyard, the terrace, the sea . . . except that *La Naissance du jour* evokes the peace of the senses and a renunciation of love, at the moment when Colette and I were living passionate hours together, elated by the heat, the light and the perfume of Provençal summers."[20]

Since renunciation is ostensibly the subject of this work, this one deviation from the real circumstances is no small matter. We

---

[18]Freud, "On Narcissism: An Introduction" (1914), *S.E.* 14: 69.

[19]*Lettres à Marguerite Moreno* (Paris: Flammarion, 1959).

[20]Maurice Goudeket, *Close to Colette*, trans. Harold Nicolson (New York: Farrar, Straus, and Cudahy, 1957), 45.

might reason that the invented love triangle merely serves as a backdrop for reflections about the age of wisdom. Still, how genuine can such reflections about solitude be, when we know that the real Colette, when faced with precisely the same choice as her narrative persona, opts for a long and happy marriage with *her* "Vial"? Read in the light of biographical fact, the following passage is sheer fable:

> And I haven't taken too long to understand that an age comes for a woman when, instead of clinging to beautiful feet that are impatient to roam the world, expressing herself in soothing words, boring tears and burning, ever-shorter sighs—an age comes when the only thing left for her is to enrich her own self.
> She hoards and reckons up everything, even to blows and scars—a scar being a mark she did not carry at birth, an acquisition. [. . .] Little by little she stows them tranquilly away. But there are so many of them that in time she is forced, as her treasure increases, to stand back a little from it, like a painter from his work. (34)

These are lovely sentiments, which trace the acquisition of wisdom, the hoarding of experience like buried treasure, and the eventual unearthing of these buried experiences in the writer's work, bringing to light the bounty of self-knowledge: "She stands back, and returns, and stands back again, pushing some scandalous details into place, bringing into the light of day a memory drowned in shadow" (34). Indeed, these wise words seem to describe something akin to a successful psychoanalysis, in which the writer is both analyst and patient, "dis-covering" and making sense of a wealth of lived experience. But even while "Mme Colette" is finding the peace of old age, immersing herself in her autobiographical work, taking inventory of each and every cherished scar—the real Colette is living it up with her young lover in Provence. We are drawn hypnotically into a web of confidences, seduced by the loveliness of the prose—only to be abruptly awakened by the final line of this passage, when we are caught off-guard by a sudden intervention that both undercuts and doubles the voice of the persona, as it repeats the epigraph to the work: "Is anyone imagining, as he reads me, that I'm portraying myself? Have patience: this is merely my model" (35).

We readers are left holding the empty treasure bag, wondering what is real and what is mirage in this hall of mirrors. We have followed Ariadne's thread only to find ourselves deeper within the labyrinth; for this is a puzzling outcome, cutting us short at the moment of greatest satisfaction (in a move that might be compared to the frustration of the short session in Lacanian analysis, which ends abruptly just when it is "getting good"). The caveat at the end of this passage is a rude reminder that we have "transferred" our belief ("open sesame") and cathected our sympathies to a specter, mistaking "Mme Colette" for the writer herself.

This game of hide-and-seek is even more puzzling given the use of Sido's letters in the novel, since these transcriptions of real correspondence seem to provide compelling evidence for an autobiographical reading of the novel. Indeed the narrator claims that she has reproduced Sido's epistles exactly, even telling us how they look on the page ("She wrote the letter that I have just copied with a hand that was still free. Her pointed nibs scratched the paper" 140). Colette scholars have verified that these letters do indeed exist, and that Colette has transcribed them almost verbatim.[21]

Almost verbatim. It has been shown that Colette acted as a ghostwriter of sorts, correcting errors of spelling and punctuation, adding a few minor touches to Sido's style. Are these changes inconsequential, merely cosmetic? Or are they part of a permutation of "Colette" into "Sido" . . . and vice versa? Not only does the narrator never admit to these cosmetic changes and corrections, but she actually tries to pass Sido off as the *superior* writer of the two (she asks her reader to judge: "Between us two, which is the better writer, she or I? Does it not resound to high heaven that she is?" 141). This rhetorical question lends a new twist to the identification of daughter with mother: for if, as we have seen, the daughter's very self-image depends on her being like the mother, it is nonetheless a fictionalized mother to whom she lays claim—her mirrored textual other mirrors a textualized (m)other, in a series of cross-reflections. Who has formed whom in this complex intersubjective modeling, where mother, child,

[21]For a selection of Sido's letters, including the cactus rose letter, see Robert Phelps, ed., *Letters from Colette* (New York: Farrar, Straus, and Giroux, 1980).

writer, and persona all interact in a series of proliferated mimetic moves?[22]

If we follow Freud's lead, lending our attention to what gets left out or altered in the imaginary portrait of Sido, we find a significant modification in the famous "cactus rose" letter, which serves as the overture to the novel. Whereas the Sido of the novel writes that she must stay to see her cactus rose bloom, even if it means missing a chance to see her daughter, the real mother wrote to *accept* her son-in-law's invitation. This is a slight modification, the matter of a few words. Yet it casts a shadow of doubt across the radiant self-discovery that follows: in light of the real letter, this entire lesson of withdrawal from the world has become Imaginary in every sense of the word, including the Lacanian sense. (The fact is that the real Sido would much rather visit her daughter than perform an act of self-absorbed contemplation.) Indeed, the foundation for the eulogy that follows ("When I feel myself inferior, threatened by my own mediocrity . . . I can still hold up my head and say to myself: 'I am the daughter of of the woman who wrote that letter'" 5) vanishes like the mist that surrounds the hallowed Sido of fictionalized memory.

All of these complications confirm that *Break of Day* is a *fictional* autobiography, where luminous themes and images (the bringing of self-knowledge, the sharing of discoveries with the reader, the recalling of the angelic mother) are shadowed by sinister doubles, inverted mirror phenomena (the veiling of the truth, the luring of the reader, the draping of the dead mother with the veil of fiction). When we lift the fictional shroud that encircles Sido, we find that it cloaks the troubling or unflattering details of bare truth (spelling errors and lapses of grammar; and the choice of gratification over noble renunciation). This naked reality has been veiled by the text-work, the weaving of an Imaginary bond—between an Imaginary self, distorted in an "inclined mirror," and an Imaginary other, reflected larger than life in memory. For the doubling of the real mother by the saintly Sido can only reflect favorably upon the daughter who aspires to be her mirror image.

[22]Lacanians have insisted that this kind of mirroring is essential to the construction of the ego. See the entries under "narcissism" and "identification" in J. Laplanche and J.-B. Pontalis, *Vocabulaire de la psychanalyse* (Paris: Presses Universitaires de France, 1967).

Thus *Break of Day* poses a number of questions that are at the heart of Colette's "ghostwritten" autobiography. First of all, there are questions about the relation of the writing subject to her textual tale. How much does Colette herself believe? Why fashion something so close to life, without telling the true story? Why does the real Colette default on the very challenge upon which the text centers, turning her back on the "birth" of new wisdom (*la naissance du jour*)? Moreover, if *Break of Day* simply enacts a wish fulfillment—as Freud might have suggested—making the Imaginary "Mme Colette" and the Imaginary "Sido" more noble than the real people whom they double, it is nonetheless a curious wish fulfillment that portrays a painful renunciation of desire instead of its gratification, obfuscating the real-life happy ending between Colette and Goudeket.

Second, we may wonder about Colette's relation to the reader. Is she eliciting an identification from her reader, or playing a game of hide-and-seek? If Colette wishes to pass on wisdom about aging, how reliable is a wisdom based on falsified experience? Like the bewildered and disappointed Vial, the puzzled reader is left to ask, "Madame, what do you want of me?" (97). Like Freud, we are left to wonder just what this woman wants; like Lacan, we have to ask just where she is to be found.

And there is another troubling twist to the reader's relation to "Colette" as object of analysis. Why should we believe Colette's statement that she is *not* telling the truth, *not* being completely candid? If this ghostwriter can hedge when apparently telling all, she can certainly deceive the reader about having told all. In fact, given the unreliability of Colette's own testimony concerning her place in the novel, it might be tempting to read Colette's protestations of difference from her "model" as a classic instance of Freudian denial (*Verneinung*) whereby what the patient most emphatically denies is that which is most true at an unconscious level.[23] Or we might look at this same phenomenon from a Lacanian perspective, considering Colette's protestation as an all-too-evident clue (like Poe's "Purloined Letter") that allows her to hide out in the open, precisely where she is most exposed. Could the author be parading herself in the text, leaving her desires in full view,

---

[23]Freud, "Negation" (1925), *S.E.* 19: 235.

even while insisting that "Mme Colette" is a fiction? (Or while the real Colette "lives happily ever after," does she perhaps unconsciously wish to forsake her younger lover, as her alter ego does?) If so, "Colette" may have more in common with her model than she admits, or than she herself knows.

For this is the central point about *Verneinung* as Freud understands the term: the patient's sincerity is not an issue. Freud's patient *believes* that he is telling the truth when he disowns his fantasy ("The person in the dream is *not* my mother!"). But of course the onlooking analyst reads this statement against itself, taking the vehemence of the denial as evidence of the truth of the statement. (Shakespeare understood this phenomenon long before Freud, when he observed that a lady may "protest too much.") Read in the same light, Colette's disowning of "Mme Colette" ("she is *not* myself, for I am only the model") takes on new complications. If Colette's alter ego, a model of her own image of self, reveals something truer about herself than what she herself knows, just what is a model? Indeed, the word "model" itself relays this ambiguity, since it may connote either the original or its copy.

In Gestalt psychology, of course, a model is that other who is necessary to the formation of one's self-image (and Lacanian analysis has adopted this idea, stressing "the narcissistic constitution of the ego," the internalization of the other's image, during the mirror stage of development, as prototype for one's own ego).[24] According to this concept, even the most faithfully rendered self-portrait is still only an imitation of the reflected other, whose likeness has itself been modeled after a series of alter egos, "others" internalized in an infinite chain. Thus even if we take Colette at her word, that her real self is merely the model for the textual person, we must suspect that even this "real self" is an image, a ghost of the subject that is inaccessible even to Colette herself. Accordingly, the notion of psychobiography itself must be revised: the object of the search for the subject of autobiography is a fantom, a fictional construct modeled after other fictional selves. Psychobiography thus revisited becomes the telling of a ghost

---

[24]See Laplanche and Pontalis, *Vocabulaire de la psychanalyse*, and Wilden *Speech and Language in Psychoanalysis*, 113ff.

story, in search of a textual specter modeled after other phantasmal selves. What is the final self-portrait but the image of a self-image, a fictionalized fiction, the reflections of a reflection, the ghostly double of a double, fashioned after a fragmentary perception of the self in the mirror?

This question leads to a third axis. What is Colette's relation to her various role models—the shades of the past who frequent her text—including her own narrating persona? Why do Colette's autobiographical texts dwell on those who are departed, and what is the role of all these ghostly "models"? How does writing help effect the transformation from her mother's child into Colette . . . and back again? ("Did it take only thirty years of my life to reach that point, or rather to get back to it?" *BD* 19). For even when "Colette" finds herself, she refinds a ghost of her past.

All of this suggests that it may be helpful to read Colette's autofiction as a dream of sorts, in the Freudian sense: a scene fashioned from what Freud calls "daily residue," where primary process (condensation, displacement, regression) exploits the license to play with the real material from which it draws, which it reflects in a distorted fashion, through the looking glass (Colette: "I look at myself in the inclined mirror . . . and then I turn to my writing again" 62). But even while violating the rules of chronology, logic, clarity, Colette's text-work, like Freud's dream-work, still obeys its own internal rules, displaying an internal metaphoric coherence, an internal oneiric "sense" that has nothing to do with verisimilitude but plays by its own duplicitous rules, engendering multiple meanings.

Reading Colette, sifting through layers of time and overdetermined meaning, is like reading a good detective story, or a ghost story, or one of Freud's case histories or dream narratives. For in Colette's text, as in a dream or ghost story, layers of experience coexist, synchronically, just as layers of meaning adhere to a single referent. (An example: the central image of the cactus rose is a classic instance of Freudian overdetermination or "condensation," metaphorically evoking multiple themes, characters, and images: sexual love, mother love, self-sufficient narcissism, the mother herself, the cherished daughter, the daughter's lover, dawn, purity, sensuality, and so forth; and these images are layered in the text, like the petals of the rose itself. Indeed, the entire novel mirrors the form of the rose, since it is circular, layered, and arranged around a center—the ghost of Sido.) Hence Colette's fictionalized autobiography is perhaps less a return to the sources of the writer's life and art than it is an experience of beginnings as contemporaneous with endings, undoing linear chronology and recasting the Aristotelian notion of beginning, development, and end.

In order to begin to fathom the strata of Colette's text, I want to look at several issues central to her opus and to her life (all of which are reflected in *Break of Day*): the mother-daughter relation, shadowed by the important but often overlooked relation with the father; the problematic sexuality that ghostwrites all of Colette's works; the ironic-comic double vision that distances the writer from her own ghostly double in the text; writing as a kind of mourning-work that both unearths her ghosts and puts them to rest. Indeed, Colette's writing itself veils the primal conflicts spawned in Sido's nest: for as the complications of Colette's earthly paradise suggest, when considered in oedipal terms the childhood Eden is a *ménage à trois*, an arena of competition and struggle for recognition. But these primal conflicts also induce and sustain Colette's creative labor, her birth as a writer, the passage out of her mother's house and into the Symbolic order.

Perhaps by revisiting the fictional autobiographies we may respond to the challenge of Colette's ghostwriting, retracing her own odyssey among the shades who have shaped her life, asking the Lacanian question of this text (*qui parle?*), and rising to the writer's challenge to find the fantom of the opus, "Colette" herself.

2

"Sido": Imaginary Elegy
as Symbolic Play

The kind of things that we shall love in later life are
fixed in that moment when the child's strong gaze
selects and molds the figures of fantasy
that for it are going to last.
—*Looking Backwards*

Probably we still stand under the magic spell of our
childhood, which a not unbiased memory
presents to us as a time of unalloyed bliss.
—Freud, *Moses and Monotheism*

In the opening chapter of *My Mother's House* (*La Maison de Claudine*, 1922) Colette evokes the memory of her mother, emerging from the kitchen elbow-deep in flour to stand in the midst of her glorious garden, calling out anxiously for her missing brood—who, as children are wont to do, refuse obstinately to respond. The closing passage of this same vignette makes it clear that Colette's mother is deceased at the moment of the writer's recollection, consigned to "a place of waiting after this life," where she continues her vigil:

"Where are the children?"
Two are at rest. The others grow older day by day. If there be a place of waiting after this life, then surely she who has so often waited for us has not ceased to tremble for those two who are yet alive [. . .]
I know for the two who remain she seeks and wanders still, invisible, tormented by her inability to watch over them enough.
'Where, oh where, are the children?'[1]

In the preface to the same work, Colette tells us that this maternal ghost continues to make her watchful presence felt through-

---

[1]Colette, *My Mother's House*, in *My Mother's House and Sido*, trans. Una Vicenzo Troubridge and Enid McLeod (New York: Farrar, Straus, and Giroux, 1978) 10. Hereafter *MMH*.

out her daughter's later years: "I always remained in touch with the personage who, little by little, has dominated all the rest of my work: the personage of my mother. It haunts me still." Long after her mother's death, the daughter continues to sense "the presence of her who, instead of receding far from me through the gates of death, has revealed herself more vividly to me as I grow older" (preface, *MMH*). Indeed the companion works *My Mother's House* and *Sido* (which are often published in tandem) constitute an elegy of sorts for the spirit who increasingly "dominates" the writer's words and images.[2] For these two works form a diptych: in *My Mother's House* (1922), Sido is remembered as she was in Gabrielle's childhood; in *Sido* (1929), she appears as a timeless, mythical figure, standing in her garden, coexisting in past, present, and future ("And there I am sure she still is, with her head thrown back and her inspired look" *Sido* 174).

Thus these two works are more than portraits or tributes: they are acts of communion with the departed. Recalling the keen pleasure her mother took in reading ghost stories ("I can't imagine anything lovelier than the description of the ghost wandering by the moonlight in the churchyard" *MMH* 36) and the lighthearted wish she once voiced to become a ghost herself someday ("If I could become a ghost after my death, I certainly should, to please you and myself too" *MMH* 36), Colette sets out to resummon that prevailing presence in order to share "all that Sido has bequeathed" to her (preface, *MMH*).

In this elegiac spirit, the mother's house is recalled as "a garden and a circle of animals," a tactile paradise of "fleeces and leaves, warm feathers and the exciting dewiness of flowers" (*MMH* 49); a peaceable realm where "beasts and men lived their lives tranquilly together" (*Sido* 154); a garden "where the children never fought" (154); a blissful circle "where for the space of thirty years a husband and wife dwelt with never a harsh word between them" (154). The mother's presence lends the enchanted aura to this arbor, where time itself is circular, nestlike, rather than linear. For without Sido, this Eden seems desolate ("Both house and garden are living still, I know, but what of that, if the magic has

---

[2]All quotes in this essay are from the joint edition of these two works (note 1), which is paginated continuously, beginning with *My Mother's House*.

deserted them?" *MMH* 6). Thus the maternal home is a *lost* paradise, described in images that are not merely charming but haunting; this evocation of bygone days has an incantatory, slightly eerie resonance that has as much in common with the ghost story as with the *Bildungsroman*. The spell wrought by this evocation of lost time surpasses the picturesque; it has an impact more reminiscent of the finest pages of Proust than of the conventional memoir. But the extraordinary appeal of Colette's text cannot reside in the thematic content alone, since the evocation of childhood paradise is, after all, something of a literary commonplace. Just what is the source of this power?

In these enchanting tales of childhood, Colette seems to exercise what Freud calls "the poet's secret," the ability to captivate readers by some ineffable trick of identification.[3] In Freud's view, the writer is a conjurer, who has access to the stores of the unconscious: the poet's psyche is porous, allowing an interchange between conscious art and unconscious source. Thus the writer acts as a medium of sorts, recalling "ghosts" from her own unconscious "beyond."

Freud's theory suggests that the writer is more than a contact with the unconscious: he or she is a medium in a negotiational sense as well, a go-between who has the ability to effect an unconscious transaction between reader, writer, and text. For Freud suggests that reader and writer participate in a process of vicarious and largely unconscious wish fulfillment (*Wünscherfüllung*), a term perhaps better rendered by the French *accomplissement du désir*, which emphasizes the *act* of writing itself as a fulfillment of desire regardless of the content of the story. In addition, Freud has commented at some length on the similarities between the pleasure of child's play and the gratification of the writer's imaginative activity.[4]

Colette herself understands her craft as "a *game*, a challenge," a sport giving chase to fantom words and images: "The pursued object leads me unfeelingly on, it is as elusive as game already

[3] Freud discusses the "poet's secret" in "Creative Writers and Daydreaming."

[4] This aesthetic transaction is discussed in "Creative Writers and Daydreaming," 139–57. See also chapter 4 of *Jokes and Their Relation to the Unconscious* (1905), *S.E.* 8.

stalked a dozen times."[5] Following Colette's lead, I want to look at her tales of childhood both as a game of hide-and-seek and as a kind of ghost story, making use of Freudian aesthetics to trace the effect of the absent ghostly (m)other as playmate. This reading follows three strands of intertwined imagery that both haunt and shape Colette's playful elegy: images of luminous circularity; images of cadenced departure and return; and images of the feminine textile crafts. Each of these thematic knots is a nodal point of the text, providing clues that may help us to unravel the poet's secret, giving chase to the fantom "I" herself.

Sido's Circle

Of the themes that prevail throughout *My Mother's House* and *Sido*—themes suggesting the cyclical giving and preservation of life—none is more insistent than circularity itself. This theme is most evident in the many images of the circle of light, as a luminous pool or aureole surrounding Sido, the soul of the nest where she nurtures her brood. The maternal home is infused with that lustrous central presence, of mythic proportion: "My childish pride and imagination," Colette recalls, "saw our house as the central point of a Mariner's Chart of gardens, winds and rays of light no section of which lay quite beyond my mother's influence" (*Sido* 157–58). In this poet's memory, all roads lead to Sido.

As the gravitational center of her family's orbit, the mother presides over a charmed sphere where nature itself obeys unnatural rules: "We had long considered it natural," Colette writes (*MMH* 50), "that a cat should select for her lair the top of a cage wherein trustful green canaries sing happily." Sido's watchful eye casts this peaceful spell: conjuring up the beloved maternal voice speaking "words that always had the same meaning" (53), the writer recalls her mother's litany of inquiry about all creatures in need, within her seemingly boundless jurisdiction: "That child must have proper care. Can't we save that woman? Have those people got enough to eat? We can hardly kill the creature" (*MMH* 53). This solicitude, echoed in the refrain of the opening chapter ("Where, oh where are the children?"), exerts a kind of gravita-

---

[5]*Evening Star*, in *Recollections*, trans. David Le Vay (New York: Macmillan, 1986), 160. Hereafter *ES*.

tional pull that recalls the vagabond brood at day's end, to the "circle of light spreading beneath a lamp" (25) where Sido sits sewing, binding her family to her.

But when the child Gabrielle (Colette's given name) discovers that this circle of warmth and light may be transcended, that these filial bonds may be broken, the realization is a source of extreme anxiety. Gabrielle thus mirrors the separation anxiety felt so keenly by the solicitous mother, described in the first vignette as "*tormented* by her inability to watch over [her children] enough" (*MMH* 10). A key passage of *My Mother's House* ("The Little One") exquisitely describes this mirrored anxiety: after a day of roaming with playmates, and after having boasted to her friends that she plans to leave the village and "go round the world"—far beyond Sido's sphere—Gabrielle suddenly becomes aware of the fall of evening, cold and damp. "It is the hour of lamps. Leaves rustle together with a sound like the plash of running water and the door of the hayloft flaps against the wall as it does in a winter gale. The garden, grown suddenly hostile, menaces a now sobered little girl with the cold leaves of its laurels, the raised sabres of its yuccas, and the barbed caterpillars of its monkey-puzzle tree. A roar like the ocean comes from the direction of Moutiers" (24–25).

Against the terrors of the now hostile garden, Sido's image, framed by the window, is illuminated by the lamp's glow as she sits sewing:

> The Little One, sitting on the grass, keeps her eyes fixed on the lamp, veiled for a moment by a brief eclipse. A hand has passed in front of the flame, a hand wearing a shining thimble. At the mere sight of this hand the Little One starts to her feet, pale, gentle now, trembling slightly as a child must who for the first time ceases to be the happy little vampire that unconsciously drains the maternal heart; trembling slightly at the conscious realization that this hand and this flame, and the bent anxious head beside the lamp, are the centre and the secret birthplace whence radiate in ripples ever less perceptible, in circles ever more and more remote from the essential light and its vibrations, the warm sitting room with its flora of cut branches and its fauna of peaceful creatures; the echoing house, dry, warm, and crack-

ling as a newly-baked loaf; the garden, the village. . . . Beyond
these all is danger, all is loneliness. (25)

Her eyes "glued to the shining thimble, to the hand that passes to
and fro before the flame" (25), Gabrielle realizes, in a wave of
contrition, that she is a child of her mother's house, encircled by
love and by care, "one of those whose universe is bounded by the
limits of a field, by the entrance of a shop, by the circle of light
spreading beneath a lamp and crossed at intervals by a well-loved
hand drawing a thread and wearing a silver thimble" (25).

Here the adult narrator seems to have reentered the domain of
a child's imagination, a self-contained cosmos with a maternal
sun at its center. The reader is as captivated as is the child Gabrielle by this hypnotic image, and by the inviting radiance of
Sido's hearth, as well as by the sense of cherished belonging with
which this mother illuminates her precious child, her "Jewel-of-
Pure-Gold" (*Sido* 156). Yet in this most lyrical of passages, Colette
does not use the pronoun "I," referring to herself instead as "the
child" or "the Little One," giving us the impression that she is
peering back into this circle, over the years, much as the little girl
peers through the window into Sido's circle of lamplight. The narrator's exile from Sido is infinitely more poignant, however, than
is Gabrielle's separation, since the bereaved adult looks back into
an irretrievable Eden. For Sido's circle is a garden of the imagination.

The Imaginary Sphere

Indeed, one could hardly find a more apt example of the realm
of the Imaginary in the Lacanian sense of the term; this is the
spatial construct of an infantile fantasy, a regression to a domain
consisting simply of an inside and an outside (the house and garden, and the forests beyond the walls that the child scales to gain
her freedom), both of which however are part of a single sphere
of influence where the mother presides ("she held sway there and
watched over it all" 158).[6] Lacan's Imaginary register is characterized by just this kind of contained axiality (good-bad; inside-

---

[6]On the spatial construct of the Imaginary (inside-outside) see Fredric Jameson,
"Imaginary and Symbolic."

outside), as yet unmediated by the Symbolic other, the Law that stands for all the complicated restraints and negotiations of adult social interaction "beyond" the Imaginary sphere. For Colette as well, the truly alien "beyond" is *outside* the mother's sphere, outside the concentric circles that start with Sido's skirts and radiate out to the pool of light, the room, the house, the garden, the village, the forest . . . finally confronting a realm where "all is danger, all is loneliness," where the child will escape the mother's gravitational tug, where the force of the desire to return will no longer be sufficient for the child to reenter the benevolent sphere.[7]

So this passage is not simply an Imaginary fantasy, for the narrator's voice is doubled, reflecting two realms of experience (Imaginary and Symbolic): one hypnotic voice spins a vision, a dreamlike reentry into the Imaginary plenitude of home; but that other exiled voice is the ominous ghost of the future, a voice in which the adult narrator addresses the child in the garden, from the Symbolic beyond. It is almost as though the sudden fall of night, the chill of the garden, the feeling of separation from the lighted window, are effects of the coexistence of Colette's two selves in time—the adult narrator looks in at her childhood self, warning Gabrielle of the tragic separation to come, a separation that *she* is now living, because of the impossibility of reentering Sido's circle. Indeed, this warning reverberates throughout these tales ("Too late! too late! That is always the cry of children, of the negligent and the ungrateful" *Sido* 181). There is a sense of imminent danger here: the child in the garden seems to be on the verge of some kind of guilty knowledge, perilously close to banishment from Eden, having just caught the first glimpse of herself as a serpent, as the "happy little vampire that unconsciously drains the maternal heart." Yet the child ignores this looming danger, manifesting a "tremendous determination not to know, that quiet strength of avoidance and rejection" (34).

It would be difficult to find a better expression of what Lacan calls misrecognition (*méconnaissance*) and what Freud calls resis-

---

[7]This kind of circularity or concentricity has been discussed by feminist critics such as Alice Jardine and Jane Gallop, as a characteristic of feminine writing. See Alice Jardine, *Gynesis* (Ithaca: Cornell University Press, 1986), and Jane Gallop, *The Daughter's Seduction* (Ithaca: Cornell University Press, 1982).

tance: the expression of the Imaginary mode in analysis, where the analysand (the patient) expends energy elaborating an "empty discourse" (*parole vide*), spinning an Imaginary version of things, a fairy tale, avoiding the painful truth by enchanting the listening analyst, as well as the storyteller herself. In psychoanalysis, the realm of the Imaginary is an illusory plenitude, which constructs a fragile identity that must expend energy on not knowing, on refusing to recognize the Symbolic external threat (the "paternal" Law associated with privation).

Nor is the only trouble in paradise the external menace (of knowledge, of oedipal sexuality, of dismemberment or violation, of the father's decree of separation). For as Anthony Wilden has pointed out in *Speech and Language in Psychoanalysis*, the Imaginary relation is among other things "a perceptual relationship to another of the same species," a phase that is "necessary in the normal maturing process" (160); but it is also a relationship of "love and aggressivity between two egos" (165), a battle of mutual objectification between fellow creatures (165) who each strive to be the agent of the relation, consigning the other to the passive role of object. In the Lacanian Imaginary, the self and the other are alter egos of sorts, mirrors who define each other, reflected halves of one consciousness, within a single sphere. As Wilden and other Lacanians understand the Imaginary relation, it is a domain of *illusory* harmony and plenitude, which veils a mutual hostility bred in part by the threat of stultification; the Imaginary relation requires the mediation of a third term in order to escape from mutual fascination, seductive and suffocating (Wilden: "Its very symmetry makes it a closed system from which the subject could never escape without the mediation of the third term" 164).[8]

Thus a certain tension exists within this register, as the doubles strive to overcome their reciprocal and paralyzing magnetism. Indeed, Sido and her child may be likened to the moth and the flame, one of the text's recurring images, two poles whose attrac-

[8]The aggressive rivalry of two *"frères ennemis"*—rival alter egos locked in a mirror reflection—is discussed as an Imaginary construct by Jameson in "Imaginary and Symbolic," 355–57; it is also the theme of René Girard's *Violence and the Sacred*, trans. Patrick Gregory (Baltimore and London: Johns Hopkins University Press, 1977). Girard receives a feminist critique in Sarah Kofman's *L'Enigme de la femme: La Femme dans les textes de Freud* (Paris: Galilée, 1980).

tion poses a mutual threat (for the moth "singes its wing in the flame of a lamp and almost puts it out" *MMH* 68). Feminist theorists, of course, have discussed the complex and ambivalent aspects of the mother-daughter relation in similar terms: as a bond between reflected alter egos implying a certain tension and aggressivity as well as a blissful connectedness.[9]

The Sido-Gabrielle dyad, as the reflective sphere of the child's universe, could be read as an instance of just this sort of Imaginary plenitude, a domain that—even as it provides gratification and security—is fraught with tension or aggressivity, stemming from the unconscious desire to elude the gravitational orbit of the alter ego. The mother, in this Imaginary sphere, is both the mirror and the formative Gestalt, the child's model ("I used to imitate her way of talking, and I still do" *Sido* 167). Moreover the mother's formative gaze endows her daughter with an image that is highly narcissistic in character. Colette recalls: "'Beauty' my mother would call me, and 'Jewel-of-pure-gold'; then she would let me go, watching her creation—her masterpiece, as she said—grow smaller as I ran down the slope" (*Sido* 156). Significantly, the point of view in this passage is Sido's, taken on by the daughter in an act of narrative identification, as she sees herself through her mother's eyes, growing smaller as she runs down the hill.

Sido herself repeatedly emphasizes that she and her daughter are like creatures, with similar roles and similar destinies that are at once a bond and a source of rivalry (Sido once says to Ga-

[9]Among the classic works on this topic are Adrienne Rich's *Of Woman Born* (New York: W. W. Norton, 1976) and Simone de Beauvoir's "The Mother" in *The Second Sex*, trans. H. M. Parshley (New York: Knopf, 1953). More recently, Kim Chernin's work on anorexia, *The Hungry Self: Women, Eating, and Identity* (New York: Harper and Row, 1985), and Janine Chasseguet-Smirgel's psychoanalytic work *Feminine Sexuality* (Ann Arbor: University of Michigan Press, 1984), as well as the work of Nancy Chodorow (*The Reproduction of Mothering* [Berkeley: University of California Press, 1978]) have expanded on the notion of the mother-daughter bond as a mirror relation of competing alter egos, a relation that reproduces itself from generation to generation. Indeed, in the work of some psychoanalytic feminist theorists—who associate the Lacanian Imaginary with the child's pre-oedipal stage—the maternal figure almost appears to be an effect of the Imaginary: Luce Irigaray, for example, emphasizes the seductive and engulfing quality of the mother-child bond, while, on a more affirmative note, theorists such as Naomi Schor and Sarah Kofman have focused on reappropriating the Imaginary (or pre-oedipal) register, stressing the positive aspects of connectedness between the mother and the female child.

brielle, "It won't be so bad for you, after all, you've left me and built a nest for yourself far from me [. . .] Yes, yes, of course you love me, but you're a girl, a female of my own species, my rival" *MMH* 125). There is ample evidence in the narrative that both Sido and her daughter, while they cherish their special bond, continue to long for independence: the child dreams of adventures beyond her mother's influence, while Sido herself feels "an urge to escape from everyone and everything, to soar to a high place" in a kind of apotheosis or ascendancy to a realm "where only her own writ [runs]" (*Sido* 166). Yet like her children, who always return from their escapades, Sido is always recalled into the family solar system, of which she is the center: "But there, under the cherry-tree, she returned to earth once more among us, weighed down with anxieties, and love, and a husband and children who clung to her" (166). The family acts like a ballast, mooring the ethereal mother who threatens to vanish into the heavens in a madonna-like transfiguration. (Indeed the "angelic" nature of the returning mother is evoked in the depiction of her return "with a fluttering of wings," surrounded by a fragrant saintly aura, "chaste and feminine" *Sido* 149.)

Thus the Imaginary tie between mother and child, an invisible umbilical cord that continually recalls the alter egos to each other, is remembered as a bond of security; but this closed sphere is fraught with internal friction. The Imaginary aggressivity or longing to escape from the other's axial pull is still played out, however, in the two-dimensional realm of the mirror: it is the rivalry of the reflected image, not the external aggressivity represented by the Symbolic other, the menacing oedipal third beyond the maternal sphere. Still we shall see that the Imaginary dyad *is* threatened from this Symbolic external "beyond" as well as from within, in a text where both registers interact. The longing to escape from the mutual fascination might even be considered an intimation of the Symbolic order beyond the dual radial axis tethering center and satellite.

"The Abduction": The Lure of the Symbolic Beyond

The Symbolic order, in Lacanian theory, is the domain where the emerging subject encounters the constraint of Law (repre-

sented by the oedipal father) and the attendant threat of "castration." But it is by this encounter that the subject enters the human
community of law and communication; in the Symbolic, one
learns to speak as the subject of one's own discourse, using the
pronoun "I" to order experience.[10] Of course as Lacan himself
suggests, the Imaginary and the Symbolic orders are never totally
distinct stages, but are interacting registers of experience.

One charming vignette in *My Mother's House* will serve as an
illustration of this overlapping of the Imaginary and the Symbolic
registers in Colette's work, thanks to a web or counterpoint of
images. In "The Abduction" Sido's all-encompassing solicitude
(an Imaginary construct) is played against Gabrielle's burgeoning
sexuality (a desire for the external other characteristic of the Symbolic order), as the young girl first experiences the temptations of
the anonymous male "ravisher" who looms beyond her mother's
house. In "The Abduction," the narrator recalls her mother's exaggerated fears of separation: when Gabrielle first moves to her
own room in the rambling house, Sido complains bitterly that her
youngest daughter is in danger of being kidnapped, carried off by
some man. One night, the little girl does indeed feel herself being
stolen away in her sleep, but she is "encircled by two arms so
gentle, so careful to hold [her] close enough to protect [her] dan-
gling feet at every doorway," that she fails to cry out. She has of
course been "abducted" by Sido, who carries her back to her lair
"like a mother cat who secretly changes the hiding place of her
little one" (*MMH* 29).

In this scene, the ever-present circular imagery works in two
registers, evoking much more than the Imaginary sphere of the
maternal embrace, the sheltering arms, the nest. For at the same
time that the girl is being carried away, she is having an erotic
dream of abduction by a real ravisher, in a scene inspired by a
painting that has long fascinated her:

A small old-fashioned engraving, hanging in a dark passage,
suddenly interested me. It represented a post-chaise, harnessed
to two queer horses with necks like fabulous beasts'. In front of

[10]For the role of the pronoun "shifters" in the Symbolic, an idea borrowed from
Jakobson's structuralist linguistics, see Wilden, *Speech and Language in Psychoanalysis*, 179–80.

the gaping coach door a young man, dressed in taffeta, was carrying on one arm with the greatest of ease a fainting young woman. Her little mouth forming an O, and the ruffled petticoats framing her charming legs, strove to express extreme terror. *"The Abduction!"* My imagination was pleasantly stirred by the word and the picture. (*MMH* 28)

Gabrielle's dream makes use of this scene to stage her own fantasy elopement: "In such wise was I departing for the land where a post-chaise, amid the jangling of bells, stops before a church to deposit a young man dressed in taffeta and a young woman whose ruffled skirts suggest the rifled petals of a rose" (29). In this romantic fantasy of allegorical "defloration"—in which the abducted girl is pictured in a complicit swoon, "her little mouth forming an O" (28)—Gabrielle's own sexuality is set against the child's unity with the mother. Thus the conflict between the infantile and the adult, the Imaginary and the Symbolic circles—the mother's arms, and the "rifled rose"—is the occasion for acute feelings of guilt, which the narrator passes off onto her unconscious: "Only a dream could thus turn a loving child into the ungrateful creature she will become tomorrow, the crafty accomplice of a stranger, the forgetful one who will leave her mother's house without a backward glance" (29). These prophetic words take on particular poignancy since the ungrateful creature to whom the narrator alludes here, the ingrate whom Gabrielle "will become tomorrow," is in fact the selfsame person who is now writing these words, the guilty and forgetful daughter who has left her mother's house to marry, not once, but three times.

Thus in "The Abduction" we find at least two actors (child and adult), two registers (Imaginary and Symbolic), two eras (past and present), two pleasures ("innocent" and sexual), two levels of (un)consciousness (dream and reality). Moreover in this tale we encounter the statement of the recurring theme of luminous circularity, a theme that also constitutes a structure or rhythm of the work, giving it shape and organization. (For this is a circular tale, arranged around Sido.) And this vignette serves to introduce the second major structuring theme in Colette's elegy as well—the theme of rhythmic sally and return—a knot of meaning that gives texture to the narrative.

Sally and Return: The "Imaginary" Rhythm of Play

> They say that everything comes round again.
> —*Evening Star*

The motif of oscillation, of going forth and returning, is not only a structural device in the childhood tales, a rhythm replacing the linear plot line of a traditional novel; it is also a major theme of the work, and a source of imagery (the mother cat retrieves her kitten in "The Abduction"; the silver-thimbled hand comes and goes in the light; the father takes his daughter out on electoral campaigns in the old buggy, only to return home by the road that the horse knows by heart). And in those several vignettes where the solicitous mother anxiously awaits the return of her children, as well as in the passages where this same mother sends her daughter forth to publicize her own creative powers ("Go and show them what I can produce!" 171), the theme of sally and return reinforces the impression of the mother-child bond as a dyadic (Imaginary) axis, with two connected poles.

But it may be understood in another way as well, as a metaphor for creative play. To the reader familiar with the work of Freud, this kind of rhythm—*va et vient*, here-there, now-you-see-it, now-you-don't—will recall the cadence of child's play, as discussed in *Beyond the Pleasure Principle* (1920).[11] In this essay Freud describes the celebrated *fort-da* game (*fort*: there/out; *da*: here/in), which his grandson plays when deprived of the mother's presence. The boy uses a wooden spool attached to a thread, a kind of yo-yo, as a substitute gratification, a replacement for the mother whom he plays at casting away (with the cry *fort!*) and retrieving (*da!*) at will. The child thus recreates the Imaginary dyad, in the absence of the object of desire, in the primal creative act. In the case that Freud observes, of course, it is the child who controls the Imaginary strings that bind him to the mother, while in Colette's text, it appears that it is Sido who calls the shots, exerting the retrieving pull. For Sido's adorers pay little attention to one another, their gaze drawn to their primary love-object ("My attention, my fervent admiration were all for Sido

---

[11]Freud, *Beyond the Pleasure Principle* (1920), S.E. 18: 7.

and only fitfully strayed from her. It was just the same with my father" Sido 175).

Sido's realm is perhaps less a family circle than it is a number of individual radii between Sido and each satellite (the husband and children who all "cling to her skirts"). In fact the concept of circularity is associated with the concept of *va et vient* in Colette's description of the family circle as a kind of solar system with orbiting planets around a stellar center, the "Evening Star" who will call the daughter home at life's end. The theme of sally and return is thus related to the first structuring motif of these works—circularity—through the notion of the orbit: each family member goes out from the maternal home only to be drawn back to the source, recalled to the Imaginary center, the maternal deity, reeled in by the tie that binds. As Sido sits sewing or winding her ball of yarn she recalls female mythic types—Penelope, Ariadne, Dante's luminous Beatrice—who serve as beacons, or who sew and wait for the return of their loved ones. From the ends of the earth, the elements themselves return to Sido, the deity "summoning and gathering to her the sounds and whispers and omens that speed faithfully towards her down the eight paths of the Mariner's Chart" (*Sido* 174).

The outward ventures of Sido's child are of two sorts: the first are jaunts sanctioned and even initiated by Sido, within her sphere of influence: the child is as though tethered as she sets forth on one of those cardinal paths that figure in the Imaginary landscape, the maternal cosmos. Sido, for instance, sends Gabrielle out into the dawn to gather berries, giving her the "reward" of daybreak: "For even then I so loved the dawn that my mother granted it to me as a reward [. . .] off I would go, an empty basket on each arm" (*Sido* 156). In this anticipation of the primary theme of *Break of Day*, dawn itself is a gift from Sido, a second birth. (The title *La Naissance du jour* echoes the French phrase for childbirth—*donner le jour*; the mother "gives the day" to her child.) This first venture is, then, still within Sido's realm, where the wanderer may be recalled ("as soon as I landed back on the gravel of our own garden, illusion and faith returned to me" *Sido* 158). Invariably, at day's end Sido frowns and asks where Gabrielle has been, but she soon forgives the prodigal daughter ("I found myself once more among familiar wonders" *Sido* 158). This is an Eden without sin, where the interrogation from the deity, as to what her creation has been up to, does not lead to exile.

A second sort of adventure figures in these tales, however, when the child risks going too far, venturing into the dangerous beyond associated with death, knowledge, sexuality, male company, intoxication. In the chapter titled "Propaganda," for example, Gabrielle accompanies her father on his political outings, enjoying the forbidden pleasure of men's talk and mulled wine, until Sido discovers the transgression: "One night she discovered in my glance a hilarity unmistakably Burgundian, and in my breath, alas, the secret of my mirth! Next day the victoria set forth without me and returned that evening, to set forth no more" (*MMH* 43). In this instance, Sido's stern intercession ends not only her daughter's outings, but also the campaigns of her husband, who feels chastised and complains that he has been robbed of "his best election agent." Sido's judgment thus puts an end to the budding relationship between father and daughter, and to the forbidden pleasures of the male company of outsiders as well. All strangers are regarded by Sido as potential ravishers, especially those who are potential husbands (Sido warns her daughter: "Your ruin begins from the moment when you consent to become the wife of a knave; your fault lies in hoping that the man who has stolen you away from your own hearth has a hearth of his own to offer you" *Sido* 118). In Sido's realm, all men are interlopers, even her beloved husband ("You aren't even a relation!" she reminds him [*MMH* 28]). For of course Sido intuits that the temptation of the forbidden excursion reflects her child's desire to fly the nest and escape the stifling maternal attentions; we might even speculate that the temptation to evade the mother's house (a female dominion, a henhouse of sorts) reflects the need to identify with the father, fleeing the coop under *his* protective wing (even if this king of the roost is decidedly henpecked).

Yet the sexualized beyond that beckons to the child, luring her from the nest, is not always a male menace. In one episode, for instance, the narrator describes her troubled attraction to her mother's exotic friend, Adrienne, as a yearning for all that is *unlike* Sido: "A lively creature, both alert and dreamy, with beautiful, yellow gipsy eyes beneath frizzy hair, she used to wander about in a sort of rustic rapture, as though daily impelled by some nomadic instinct" (*Sido* 171). The narrator goes on to describe her guilt at the erotic feelings stirred by the knowledge that she had once been nursed at this "nomadic" outsider's breast, the breast of the "gipsy" seductress: "How was I to conceal from that clear gaze of [my mother's], blade-grey and threatening, the image that tormented me, of Adrienne's swarthy breast and its hard, purple knot?" (*Sido* 172). Of course, nothing escapes Sido's jealous eye, the "blade" of her gaze (*gris de lame*), for she reacts promptly and decisively to cut off the relationship, summoning her daughter home abruptly from her visit to Adrienne's. Here again, Sido is pictured at her habitual window vantage point, "as though to give the alarm for fire or burglars": "'All this time at Adrienne's?' That was all she said, but what a tone of voice!" (*Sido* 173).

Another version of this scene is played in "My Mother and the Books" (*MMH*), when Gabrielle transgresses her mother's wishes by reading the forbidden books of Zola. In this scene as in the scene from *Sido*, the girl is punished for her sexual curiosity, fainting when she reads a graphic childbirth scene. In a state of panic and vertigo, she tries to summon up her mother's voice, to recall Sido's gentle version of the miracle of birth. But she is "deafened" by "other words" which "painted the flesh split open, the excrement, the polluted blood"; she finally collapses, like a sacrificial virgin of sorts, "prostrate and limp like one of those little leverets that the poachers bring, fresh killed, into the kitchen" (38).

Sido appears in the nick of time, her loving attention retrieving her child from the swoon, the beyond, and from the terrors of unknown sexuality. Gabrielle awakens to her mother's crooning voice: "There, there now. There's nothing so terrible as all that in the birth of a child, nothing terrible at all. It's much more beautiful in real life. The suffering is so quickly forgotten, you'll see! The proof that all women forget is that it is only men—and what business was it of Zola's, anyway?—who write stories about it" (*MMH* 39). The daughter's return to the fold, after what Sido calls this "smart little rap on the knuckles from Above," is characteristically accompanied by an indictment and rejection of the nosy male outsider. For Sido's role is that of censor as well as comforter, who must recast harsh external reality in order to reestablish the harmony of her Imaginary sphere, after expelling the other.

But Sido's reaction is not a narrow-minded or prudish response to sex, an effort to protect her daughter's virtue; she has her own keen sense of ethics which has nothing to do with conventional morality. In fact, in "My Mother and Morals," she refuses to fire the maid who has gotten pregnant out of wedlock, in spite of the scandal. She makes it clear in this instance that the real transgression is not sexual pleasure but the sin of independence and evasion. Asked how she would respond if her own daughter were in that situation, Sido replies: "I should say to my daughter: Carry your burden, my child, not far from me, but far from that man [. . .] Never allow that man to pass our threshold in the daylight" (*MMH* 118). Similarly, in the case of the forbidden readings, the "sin" is not one of sexual curiosity but of knowledge acquired from outside sources ("what business was it of Zola's, anyway?").

The Pre-oedipal Lawgiver

In this second sort of sally and return—the tasting of forbidden fruit—it is clear that Sido's role is something more than that of the haven, the Imaginary site of a blissful plenitude. In these dalliances with forbidden pleasures outside the mother's sphere, it is Sido—and not the father as in Lacan's or Freud's account—who lays down the law, threatening the transgressor not with castration, as in the male model (although there is a kind of "cutting short" of experience), but with the "cutting off" from the maternal home. (Thus when Adrienne's forbidden breast is imagined as a "hard, purple knot," it threatens to replace the umbilical "knot" that binds mother and daughter.) So Sido's role as lawgiver may perhaps not be considered a Symbolic function in Lacan's sense, associated with the paternal commandment of "castration" and death: the maternal figure here apparently lays down the Law in order to keep the *Imaginary* relation intact, to strengthen the *pre-oedipal* bond, to *protect* her daughter from the dangers of the outside, the beyond, and to forestall the Symbolic estrangement. This is Sido the pre-oedipal lawgiver, a maternal function about which psychoanalysis has little to say.[12]

Even in her more traditional oedipal role as maternal object of desire, for whom husband and children compete, Sido is no pas-

---

[12]Freud does concede that the pre-oedipal stage is of primary importance for the little girl, in *New Introductory Lectures on Psychoanalysis*, *S.E.* 22: 105–7. And of course Freud's notions on feminine sexuality have been the subject of feminist critique and revision, in the work of Julia Kristeva, Jane Gallop, Jacqueline Rose, Juliet Mitchell, and many others.

sive object, no simple victim of fate; she is a fierce female who jealously defends her territory. (Indeed this latent ferocity of the female is a theme of Colette's work, as demonstrated by the vignette "Toutouque," in which the sweet family pet is transformed into a savage beast when another dog encroaches upon her territory.) Colette's maternal figure is an *active* oedipal mother: this feisty female cannot be reduced to the classic psychoanalytic role of silent object of contention or exchange. She is neither the passive tribal female of Freud's *Totem and Taboo*, the object who solidifies the social bond when she is given over in marriage by the males of her tribe to those of another tribe; nor is she the silent feminine "place-holder" of Lacan's linguistic version of intersubjective social exchange, reduced to a linguistic category (negativity), or exalted as a mystical absence, a void. Nor may Sido be called a "phallic mother"—another construct of traditional psychoanalysis—for hers is a thoroughly feminine power, without reference to a masculine standard. Indeed, Colette's work seems to require a reevaluation of both the Freudian oedipal schema and Lacan's Symbolic version of it, since here the female category is an active one, where the love-object defends her status, fending off the claims of the outside. In Colette's scenario, unlike the androcentric paradigms of psychoanalysis, the "object" has desires of her own—actively desiring to remain the desire of the other.[13]

These instances of what I have called the pre-oedipal lawgiver occur on the brink, as it were, between the Imaginary and the Symbolic registers, where the mother retains some pre-oedipal characteristics (as the child's alter ego), even while displaying traits of the classic oedipal mother (as the contested object of desire in a love triangle). And there is a further complication: we shall see that Sido's function of lawgiver has a "paternal"/Symbolic aspect as well.

In other words, Sido's role in her daughter's psychic scene is overdetermined: as Imaginary object/deity she offers nurture, quiescence, gratification, a narcissistic love between mother and "like creature"; as pre-oedipal lawgiver she defends her Imaginary

[13]Maternal desire is the focus of much recent feminist theory, including the essays in *The (M)other Tongue: Essays in Psychoanalytic Interpretation*, ed. Shirley Nelson Garner, Claire Kahane, and Madelon Sprengnether (Ithaca: Cornell University Press, 1985).

realm; as Symbolic figure she is a superego and judge, who censures her child's dangerous pleasures. It is perhaps this last side of Sido, in its connection to privation and the Law, that is the most problematic, suggesting that Colette's Imaginary "play" of writing may be doubled by a Symbolic game, involving an interfering, obstructing, or judgmental third term—who is perhaps none other than Sido herself. In any case, this encounter with the other (Symbolic) Sido suggests that the Imaginary and Symbolic functions need not be assigned by gender, and also that mother love may have complexities scarcely divined by traditional psychoanalysis.

The Symbolic Mother

Colette's mother figure, however feminine she may be, displays some of the classic characteristics of the Symbolic father as well (Freud's oedipal father), insofar as she poses a *threat* to her child, or exercises a curtailing ("castrating") function, acting as the harbinger of death or separation. The vignette "Propaganda" presents the most obvious case of Sido's obstructive or "paternal" role (I use the term advisedly, since one's role is less a matter of gender in Lacan's account than of one's place in the desiring circuit). In "Propaganda," there is a switch of the traditional oedipal casting: Sido plays the obstacle between Gabrielle and her father, who, in his turn, plays the "feminine" role of forbidden love-object. Here *Sido* is the oedipal lawgiver and rival, who forbids the "incestuous" pleasures between child and opposite-sex parent. Accordingly we see here an intransigent other side to Sido, a frowning Symbolic face opposed to the Imaginary angelic visage. (Colette herself alludes to two faces of Sido—one stern and reproving, the other a "radiant garden-face" MMH 158).[14]

Just how may we understand this Symbolic role of the mother in Colette's fictional autobiography? In what ways does she serve as obstacle to her daughter's desire, rather than as its object? How may this loving nurturer be associated with initiation into death, separation, and privation (the "castrating" function of the Symbolic father in Lacan's scheme)?

---

[14]In *Sido* (162), Colette speaks of the double visage of the mother, where one expression "veils" another: "As she spoke her face, alight with faith and an all-embracing curiosity, was hidden by another, older face, resigned and gentle."

Intimations of an other side to the loving and angelic Sido occur in at least two vignettes in addition to "Propaganda." Sido shows an underside of brutality in "My Father's Daughter," confessing to Gabrielle that she once tapered or modeled the fingers of her own baby sister in order to perfect her: "Then and there I proceeded, with the cruelty of childhood, to remodel those tender little fingers that seemed to melt between my own. [. . .] Now you realize what a wicked mother you've got. Such a lovely newborn baby. How she screamed!" (*MMH* 60).[15] Here the young sculptor who remodels her creation (in an act of dismemberment of sorts) anticipates the adult Sido who "models" her daughter, in her castigating Symbolic role.

It is this avenging "castrator" who reappears in the fascinating episode "Epitaphs," which tells of Sido's reaction to her younger son's favorite game, the creation of rows of ornate cardboard tombstones in honor of a village of Imaginary deceased:

> He had retained from his earliest childhood the quiet, self-possessed, aloof attitude to life that protects the very young child from fear of death or blood. At thirteen he seemed scarcely to distinguish between the dead and the living. While my games evoked before my eyes imaginary persons, transparent and visible, whom I greeted and of whom I asked news of their relations, my brother, inventing his imaginary dead, treated them with the utmost friendliness and adorned them to the best of his ability. He would surmount one with an ornate cross, another he would lay beneath a Gothic arch and yet a third would rest peacefully covered only by the epitaph that extolled his early life. (*MMH* 57)

It seems that conversations with ghosts—undifferentiated from the living, and untainted by "the fear of death or of blood"—form part of the Imaginary landscape of more than one of Sido's offspring. But of course one aspect of the passage from the Imaginary to the Symbolic realm is precisely an acquisition of fear (as "castration anxiety"), the very "fear of death or of blood" that Leo lacks, as well as the ability to distinguish the dead from the living,

---

[15]Symptomatically, perhaps, Gabrielle refuses to pay attention to the rest of this startling story ("the sequel of her narrative is missing from my memory. The blank is as complete as though I had at that moment been smitten with deafness . . ." 61).

fantasy from reality, even (in the biblical version of Symbolic knowledge) right from wrong.

In Sido's Eden as in the primal garden, the passage from innocence to knowledge (distinguishing child's play from "criminality") is effected by a breaking of the rules, whereby the fledgling subject incurs the wrath of the irate parental deity. For Leo's "Imaginary" cemetery is discovered: "A week later my mother passed that way, paused in amazement, and stared with all her eyes—her lorgnette, her pince-nez and finally her long-distance glasses—and exclaimed in horror, stamping right and left among the graves" (*MMH* 57). Like the enraged Moses down from the mount, Sido sweeps away the "sacrilegious" tombstones that she finds in her garden:

> "This is delirium, sadism, vampirism, sacrilege, it is . . . I really don't know what it is!"
>
> Across the abyss that separates a child from a grown-up person, she gazed at the culprit and with an angry rake swept away tombstones, wreaths and mutilated memorial columns. My brother endured without protest the holding up of his work to obloquy. Left in contemplation of the empty lawn, and of the freshly raked earth shaded by the hedge of thuryas, he called me to witness, with a poet's melancholy:
>
> "Don't you think it looks sad, a garden without graves?" (*MMH* 57–58)

In this scene *the mother* is the interloper into the Imaginary realm, introducing the heretofore unknown "fear of death and blood" (invoking the specters of "sadism" and "vampirism") in a "castrating" act that levels her son's creations. As the Symbolic enforcer, she quashes a kind of morbid pleasure, forbidding the (incestuous) enjoyment of the mother's gardens, ending the indulgence in a kind of play that could be read as a death-wish, as a yearning to return to Mother Earth. ("My brother desired to honour his white tombs with soft, rich-smelling earth, real grass, cypresses and ivy" 57).

For of course the Symbolic other is not simply a villain in the oedipal drama, but is also a hero of sorts, forcing the child out of the deadly stultification of the womb/tomb/garden and initiating the subject into the larger realm of social interaction, the life beyond. But as many of Colette's tales suggest, this guiding function is not primarily paternal in Colette's scheme, since this role is more often than not fulfilled by Sido, as censor/educator, preparing her children for the eventual departure from the nest.

So Sido is the Symbolic mother in two dimensions: both as castigator/villain and as guide/heroine. And Sido's Symbolic function has a third dimension: in addition to her obstructive role and her initiating function, she plays a linguistic role, introducing the rules of the Symbolic order of language. In the episode titled "The Priest on the Wall," for instance, the mother—as teacher of language—sets out the linguistic rules that are to be obeyed, insisting that Gabrielle "call things by their proper names" instead of indulging in the delights of baby talk. She thus curtails the Imaginary inventiveness of verbal child's play, which Freud considers one of the great infantile pleasures.[16] *This* Sido is not the site of infantile pleasure, but is rather the agent for its denial, its rechanneling into the adult functions of communication governed by Law.

Significantly, Gabrielle's response to this curtailment of her pleasure is to create a new game, with her own rules: when she learns that "presbytery" does not mean a "snail's shell" as she has imagined, she reshapes this unpleasant revelation and makes it the source of a new game: "Throwing away the fragments of the little broken snail shell, I picked up the enchanting word and, climbing on to my narrow terrace, shaded by the old lilac trees and adorned with polished pebbles and scraps of coloured glass like a thieving magpie's nest, I christened it the Presbytery and inducted myself the priest on the wall" (32).

Freud suggests that this kind of game is the primal infantile response to adult meddling: the child takes the Symbolic constraint and makes it the occasion of a creative activity, making use of stowed-away scraps of reality to adorn her realm, "like a thieving magpie's nest."[17] And it is perhaps this primal gesture of play

---

[16]In *Jokes and Their Relation to the Unconscious*, Freud argues that the pleasure in infantile babble is a pleasure adults attempt to recreate in the wordplay of nonsense jokes.

[17]Here the child acts like the dreamer, who draws upon what Freud calls "daily residue," scraps of actual lived experience, to fashion the dream.

that the adult writer reconstitutes, in her fictional autobiography, where she alone decides what is "real" and what rules hold sway.

Gabrielle's Game: The Symbolic Rhythm of Play

> Does the rage to die exceed the rage to be born?
> —*Evening Star*

In "Creative Writers and Daydreaming," Freud suggests that the writer's work is the heir of play in children, but in *Beyond the Pleasure Principle* he gives an even larger cast to this notion, by suggesting that one way in which *all* human beings accommodate themselves to their encounter with reality is to learn to play. This argument might be read, among other things, as a recasting of the terms of the oedipal complex, where the child's obstructed desire is deflected onto new objects and directed into substitutive channels. But in *Beyond the Pleasure Principle*, this drama is no longer told simply in developmental terms; here it is described as the rhythm of *all* life, and especially of human life. For in this essay Freud argues that the "end" of all life, the ultimate pleasure in a sense, is the complete discharge of energy, the voiding of all energy in death.[18] The role of the life instincts then is to postpone this pleasure as long as possible, by putting obstacles in the way of a too-hasty satisfaction, the short-circuit in a complete discharge of energy (death), threatening life itself. The obstruction of immediate pleasure is the postponement of the living organism's urge to return to quiescence (the death-drive). Thus paradoxically, the death instinct, the will to "return to a former state," to be quiet, is the energy that moves all life-activity, but it is channeled outward, so that every organism may die in its own good time, after expending energy productively, in an outward-directed detour or long-circuit.

Indeed Freud writes that the human "instinct towards perfection" is an effect of the repetition compulsion, a result of the rechanneled death-drive:

[18]*Beyond the Pleasure Principle* (1920) (New York: W. W. Norton, 1961), section V. Page numbers refer to the Norton paper edition of the Strachey translation. (*BPP* appears in vol. 18 of the *Standard Edition*.) In *Beyond the Pleasure Principle* Freud writes that "death is the only aim of life" (35).

No sublimations will suffice to remove the repressed instinct's persisting tension; and it is the difference in amount between the pleasure of satisfaction which is *demanded* and that which is actually *achieved* that provides the driving factor which will permit of no halting at any position attained, but, in the poet's words, 'Presses ever forward unsubdued.' The backward path that leads to complete satisfaction is as a rule obstructed by the resistances which maintain the repressions. (*BPP* 36)

Freud is attributing all human development to the blocking of the death instinct, which nonetheless persists as the motor for an always unassuaged desire: "So there is no alternative but to advance in the direction in which growth is still free—though with no prospect of being able to bring the process to a conclusion or of being able to reach the goal" (*BPP* 36). What strikes us here is above all a cadence, the rhythm of life, where the "binding" of desire by the life instincts alternates with the emptying of desire by the death instinct.

I have already alluded to *Beyond the Pleasure Principle* as a kind of paradigm for the Imaginary bond linking mother and child, subject and alter ego, in the spatial dyad of sally and return: this pulse of being there (*fort!*) and returning to here (*da!*) is the very rhythm that characterizes Freud's grandchild's game with the spool, "cast" as the maternal love-object. But Lacanian theorists have also emphasized the *Symbolic* nature of play as depicted in Freud's celebrated scenario. In this reading, the child—who is just learning to speak (the moment of entry into the Symbolic order) when he begins the *fort-da* play—uses the toy as a symbol, compensating for the painful absence of the maternal love-object by replaying the scene to his liking.

Freud observes that this creative act is an enormous cultural achievement on the part of the child, who is just beginning his encounter with oedipal law (of enforced separation, of non-gratification of desire) and who has made use of his privation to invent a source of linguistic pleasure. The mediating "third" outside term here may be understood as the oedipal father, who requires the mother's absence from her child. Thus in Lacanian terms, that which lies "beyond" the pleasure principle could be called the Symbolic order, the source of all outward-directed acts of creativity, which says "no" to the shortest distance between two points, the deadly end of incestuous, imploded gratification. In this role, the Symbolic other would be the agent of life, who humanizes the infant by insisting on the long-circuiting of desire, directing the child-initiate outward, into life. In more abstract terms, this outsider may be considered to be society itself, which demands that the human infant learn to defer gratification, differentiating itself from the maternal corpus, taking on the separate identity of the "I" who "calls the shots." For in this first verbal play, the dyadic opposition *fort-da* goes beyond Imaginary mirroring and constitutes a self, which is now the subject of desire, rather than its passive victim.

In other words, we might say that the Imaginary and the Symbolic registers coexist in the play situation, as they do throughout human life. For the *fort-da* has Imaginary, pre-verbal, mirror stage characteristics (where the self is narcissistically bound to its phantasmal alter ego). But the *fort-da* is also a primal differentiation of the self from that Imaginary other, in a playful response to external exigencies (the father's meddling). In Lacan's terms, we could say that this is a passage from the indistinct sense of self, confused or *brouillé* (the self that Lacan wittily terms the *hommelette*, "scrambled" with the image of the other), to the distinct position of subject, the differentiated "I," whose desire for the object is opposed by the Law of the external other.

Thus for Lacan as for Freud, this scaffolding of the Symbolic relation—reared at the child's entry into language—represents a coming to terms with the Law. But for Lacan in particular, this playful confrontation is no laughing matter: it is the first manifestation of the human tragedy of desire—as he argues in his essay on *Hamlet*[19]—whereby the bereaved subject moves from the position of passivity to the role of agency, thanks to his loss. And Lacan's choice of *Hamlet* to illustrate this move is a telling one that is germane to our reading of Colette as guilty child as well; for it suggests that creative agency is motivated not only by privation, but by guilt, a sense of responsibility for the death of the loved parent.

Lacan reads *Hamlet* as a tragedy at the juncture between

---

[19]Jacques Lacan, "Desire and the Interpretation of Desire in *Hamlet*," in Felman, *Literature and Psychoanalysis*, 11–52.

Freud's two great myths concerning murderous children: that of Oedipus, and that of *Totem and Taboo* (1912), the myth of the origin of the incest taboo, wherein the sons slay the tribal father in a dispute over the women of the clan.[20] In each case the Symbolic debt incurred is an effect of filial guilt over the slaying of the father; in acquiescing to the Law/taboo, the human child assumes responsibility for the crime against the father (incestuous desire)—a guilt transmitted from generation to generation—and agrees not to repeat this crime, thus taking a place in the social chain.[21]

When Colette's elegiac play is read in this light, Sido plays two roles to her guilty child, her "Hamlet": she is in some measure like the paternal fantom, the ghost of King Hamlet, a slain parent who returns to inspire haunting guilt—casting the thoughtless Gabrielle, in retrospect, as "the happy little vampire that unconsciously drains the maternal heart." Like Hamlet, this child is driven into action by a parental ghost who gives her no rest, urging the child to compensate for oversights during the parent's life, her unwitting sins of omission and neglect, by taking an action of Symbolic restitution (in Hamlet's case avenging the paternal murder, in Colette's case writing a maternal elegy).

But we might say that Sido also plays the role of Gertrude, the maternal object of "Hamlet's" incestuous desire, the pre-oedipal paradise from which her child has been exiled. Accordingly, the Gabrielle-Sido relation seems to be governed by two kinds of law, one an Imaginary law of gravity, the pull of the reflected alter ego, which refuses to let the child go "beyond" the mother's dominion ("Beyond these all is danger, all is loneliness" *MMH* 25), the other a Symbolic Law, which expels the guilty child into the beyond and which demands action, blocking the road back to a paradise that may never be completely regained, no matter how many times the adult tries to write herself back in.

---

[20]Freud, *Totem and Taboo* (1912), *S.E.* 13.

[21]In this drama, the Symbolic father plays a paradoxical role: on the one hand he forbids a certain quiescence or death; on the other hand, he declares the inevitability of death (as the Law of separation, and the yawning gap or wound of desire). In other words, he symbolizes "endings" and "truncations" of a certain "infinite" Imaginary pleasure, by instigating the Symbolic order of repetition or iteration, and revealing the illusory nature of the dream of plenitude or origins. (Hence the appeal of a certain "French Freud" for poststructuralist thought.)

Thus Colette's text may be read as a rehearsal of the demonic message of *Beyond the Pleasure Principle*—what lies beyond Imaginary pleasure is the repetition compulsion (the motor of the Symbolic order); but this frightening beyond (death, separation, "castration" or violation, sexual difference) is nonetheless that which humanizes us, compelling us to be in contact with a network of others, initiating the repeated striving of our Symbolic acts of communication.

For while Colette's tales of childhood present an image of peace, of circular harmony, of womb-like security, all these images are moments viewed from beyond, in memory, by an exile feeling the boundless loneliness of one who looks in at the family hearth from without, from the garden grown hostile, a darkened Eden that is the adult world of strife and pain. Even in the key image of *My Mother's House*, the circle of light where the mother sits sewing, there is an intermittent moment of darkness or eclipse, which almost seems to function as premonition of separation: "The Little One, sitting on the grass, keeps her eyes fixed on the lamp, veiled for a moment by a brief eclipse. A hand has passed in front of the flame, a hand wearing a shining thimble" (25). The rhythm of *fort* and of *da* is already marked in this phrase, which sets the cadence for the entire work. The hypnotic quality of this image, in which the beloved hand functions both as a source of light ("a hand wearing a shining thimble") and a periodic obstruction of that light ("veiled for a moment by a brief eclipse"), stems perhaps from its resonance in the Imaginary register of infantile memory. But it is an image shadowed by the adult experience of the Symbolic Law which has handed down a decree of separation (since Sido is now gone forever), and which thus serves as the motivation for Colette's "play"—a replay of life in which she may retrieve, refashion, recast the mother at will.

In the rhythm that scans Colette's text—the compulsive and repetitive pulse of Sido's sewing hand—we find an oscillation between two realms of human experience, between work and rest, life and death—the compulsion that drives us "beyond" pleasure. Colette likens this cadence to "the work of the pen or the needle," or the labor of two horses pulling now together, now apart, headed toward home (death), but waylaid in a detour of creativity: "Along an echoing road, beating in time at first, then out of time, then coming together again, can be heard the trotting hoofs of two horses in double harness. Controlled by the same hand, the pen and the needle, the habit of work and the wise desire to put an end to it make friends with one another, part, and then are reconciled. . . Oh, my slow coursers, try to pull together: I can see the end of the road from here."[22]

In Freud's account of the pulse of human progress, we make something of ourselves thanks to the ability to reconcile the impulses of life and death, in the profoundly human rhythm of play. In just this way Colette shapes her own layered and multiple identity as her hand moves to and fro across the page, fashioning her text in an excessive repetition: "It is not for me to say whether my cross-stitch work involves the expenditure of some similar superfluity in me. I pierce my canvas, then pierce it again. My sand eel—my needle—glitters up between two threads, towing its tail of wool behind it. My memoirs are inscribed in greenery that is blue, lilacs that are pink" (*EP* 504).[23] The writer at work is also at play, as she stitches up the wound she has suffered, as she cuts the threads of memory that bind her, embroidering her past anew, even as her pen compulsively repeats the coming and going of Sido's thimbled hand.

The Sempstress: Sewing as Mourning-Work

> I have now begun writing with colored threads on
> canvas . . . What form of art has ever required so
> many hearts and turtle-doves, so many
> forget-me-nots? On a tombstone . . .
> —*Earthly Paradise*

Colette/Sido sits in her circle of light and sews . . . and in this most evocative of images, combining the two structuring thematic knots of circular light and of sally and return, the sempstress is overdetermined by a whole chain of mythological associations

---

[22]Cited from Robert Phelps, ed., *Earthly Paradise: Colette's Autobiography, Drawn from the Writings of Her Lifetime* (New York: Farrar, Straus, and Giroux, 1966), 505. Hereafter *EP*. (This is his translation of the final passage of *Evening Star*.)

[23]Quoted from *Evening Star*, Phelps's translation.

concerning female needlework: she is like Penelope who weaves and unweaves, awaiting her family's return, and like Ariadne whose ball of thread guides her beloved through the darkness. And in her there is also something of the sempstress Fate—who measures and cuts off the thread of life—as she awaits her children's return to her in death.[24] Like the two networks of images we have already examined (circularity and sally and return) this third fabric of female images, concerning the craft of needlework, is not only a nodal point of fantasy, but also a paradigmatic textual structure: the text—both circular and cadenced—is also knitted, woven, spun, embroidered. And this third imagistic network—concerning needlework as metaphor for writing, for memory, and for the intergenerational network of female knowledge—casts first Sido, then Colette (the "spinster" of this tale), and finally Colette's daughter in the role of sempstress.

Chain-Stitching

In the final vignette of *My Mother's House*, Gabrielle has grown up and now watches her own little girl—the beloved "Bel-Gazou" conceived shortly after Sido's death—as *she* sits sewing, like Sido herself years before. Thus the work itself is united by a kind of chain-stitching of related images, where female generations are connected in a repeated pattern. This kind of generational linkage also occurs explicitly in an earlier image, where "Minet-Chéri" ("dear little kitty," Sido's pet name for Gabrielle) watches the family cat nursing her kittens, in a feline chain: "I set to work happily to disentangle the mass of nurses and well-licked nurslings . . . and I discovered that Bijou, four times a mother in three years,

[24]This image of the sewing mother is also part of an extensive literary network, linking the images of countless knitting women (*Heart of Darkness, A Tale of Two Cities*) associated with death, darkness, separation, dismemberment, as well as with healing, connection, life. In Freud's account, interestingly, needlework and weaving are themselves essentially female activities, because they "cover up" female "castration." In the *New Introductory Lectures on Psychoanalysis* (1933), *S.E* 22, chapter 32, Freud writes: "It seems that women have made few contributions to the discoveries and inventions of civilization; there is, however, one technique they may have invented—that of plaiting and weaving. If that is so, we should be tempted to guess the unconscious motive for that achievement. Nature herself would seem to have given the model which this achievement imitates by causing the growth at maturity of the pubic hair that conceals the genitals" (117).

from whose teats hung a chapelet of newborn offspring, was herself engaged in noisily sucking the milk of the aged Nonoche, who lay inert with comfort, one paw across her eyes" (*MMH* 49–50). This image suggests that maternity is an intergenerational affair, where mother and daughter are interlaced—even entangled—with past and future generations.

Perhaps the most poignant and powerful statement of this chain motif occurs in the vignette "Maternity," where it is a question of a lateral tie between mother and daughter—a sort of umbilical connection that cannot be sundered—as well as of Sido's link to the next generation. Here Sido has been estranged from her eldest child, Juliette, who has married someone of whom the family does not approve; although they are neighbors, the two families do not speak. But at the moment when Juliette gives birth, Sido—though forbidden by her son-in-law to attend her daughter's childbed—goes through a sympathetic labor, doubling the act of birth:

> Then a shadowy form in a white dressing gown—my mother—crossed the road and entered the garden opposite. I saw her raise her head and consider the party wall as though she had hopes of climbing it. [. . .] A thin cry, long, drawn-out, and muffled by distance and the intervening walls, reached us at the same moment, and she clasped her hands convulsively to her breast. [. . .] Then I saw my mother grip her own loins with desperate hands, spin round and stamp on the ground as she began to assist and to share, by her low groans, by the rocking of her tormented body, by the clasping of her unwanted arms, and by all her maternal anguish and strength, the anguish and strength of the ungrateful daughter who, so near to her and yet so far away, was bringing a child into the world. (*MMH* 78–79)

Once again Sido is described as a ghostly figure, clad in white and gliding through the night; and as she "gives birth" to her daughter's child, she performs a kind of ghost labor as well. Here the identification between generations and among females is more than a link; it is a *mingling* of identities, stronger than any obstacle. (Gabrielle herself seems to share this labor, since she too is moved by her sister's cries, which reach her and Sido "at the same moment.")

Thus maternity is an intertwining of generations and identities, a tissue or text doubled by the writer's activity; for the book itself is sewn up by the repeated intergenerational image of the sempstress. Indeed, the writer likens her own travail repeatedly to a kind of patchwork, a labor in which she gives birth to her text by stitching together the scraps of images into a completed tapestry.

In "The Sempstress," for instance—where Colette watches her own daughter sewing, in one of the final images of *My Mother's House*—there is a double identification that extends into the past and into the future, where Colette is the intermittent stitch linking Sido with Bel-Gazou. As Colette watches *her* little girl, she muses sadly about the passage of her daughter's childhood, her imminent departure from the garden from which she herself is now excluded. Next year "she may well fail to find again her childish subtlety and the keenness of her senses that can taste a scent, feel a colour, and see—'thin as a hair, thin as a blade of grass'—the cadence of an imaginary song" (141). This wistful evocation of childhood as the "cadence of an imaginary song," woven from threads "thin as a hair," might serve as a metaphor for Colette's own writing, woven from sensual strands of experience, and scanned with the cadence of sally and return.

Since Bel-Gazou's emerging sexuality also implies the aging and eventual death of *her* mother, the novel closes as it opens, with an oblique reference to Colette's own mortality. (In the first passage, Sido waits for her daughter's death; in the closing passage, Bel-Gazou's approaching maturity is a portent of her mother's aging and eventual death.) The circle of the novel is closed by the linkage of maternities in the final passage: the gap left by Sido's absence is darned by Colette's writing hand. But this return to the life-source is also an eloquent death-wish, a longing for final peace in the maternal bosom: "I can see the end of the road from here" (*EP* 505). In any case, it is only through a weaving of Imaginary and Symbolic registers that the writer is able to refashion a version of her lost Eden, embroidering upon its wonders.

Thus the daughter's elegy to that spirit who continues to inspire her—and whose existence is continued in the person of the little sempstress, her own daughter—is on one level an Imaginary exercise, a reconstitution of that first dyadic relation of narcissistic identification between mother and daughter. But insofar as the elegy is also an adult form of play, it is a function of the Symbolic as well as the Imaginary register. The Imaginary persona (Gabrielle) and the Symbolic one (Colette) coexist in this intergenerational tangle of overdetermined personae: for this autofiction is a tapestry across time, which fashions a layered identity after the pattern of Sido.

The Writer at Play

Until now, we have considered the child Gabrielle's play as a structuring theme or image in these childhood tales.[25] But Freud's view of play allows us to read the story of another of the narrator's selves—the author "Colette." Indeed if all autobiography is fiction, as psychoanalysis suggests, then the very ability to write "I" and to tell "my" story is tied to the ability to narrate, to tell a story of the world. The writer, then, in shaping her own story, replays a role we have all played, creating her self through language.

In "Creative Writers and Daydreaming" (1908), Freud makes an explicit connection between the activity of the writer and the activity of child's play, suggesting that both activities require the creation of a narrative scenario in which desire is fulfilled vicariously.[26] But the similarities between the two activities are more than analogical, for in both play and writing there is a move from the passive position (of object or victim, suffering the whims of fate) to the role of agent, who restages reality according to his or her own scenario.[27] Moreover, in child's play, as in the adult form of play that is writing, there is a certain "veiling" of the original object of desire, a cover-up of what is really at stake (the child's toy "veils" the mother whom it represents; similarly, the author,

[25]We ought not to lose sight of the fact that these memories are screen memories, and that a *textual* relation is being analyzed: we can only guess, reading the text as a kind of narrative case history in the manner of psychobiography, what the relation of the real Colette to the real mother might have been. But no analyst has more to go on than the version of his or her "analysand."

[26]In vol. 9 of the *Standard Edition*, 143.

[27]This move is evident in the *fort-da* game, but it is even clearer in a second play-scene discussed by Freud in *Beyond the Pleasure Principle*, where the child, after having suffered a doctor's exam, plays "doctor" on a younger sibling, taking over the active role (*BPP* 11).

in Freud's account, hides the egotistical nature of the imagined scenes in order to lure the reader into the fantasy).[28]

I have suggested that in the case of Colette's fictional autobiography the veiled wish might be expiation for the crime of having "murdered" the parent (as the "happy little vampire that unconsciously drains the maternal heart" *MMH* 25). And since this is a kind of ghost story, this writer's play may also be seen as mourning-work, which seeks to master the writer's ghosts even while it makes them accessible to her. For Freud writes that the mourning-work is an untying of emotional bonds, a *retreat* from love: "It is the task of mourning to carry out this retreat from the object in all the situations in which the object was the recipient of an intense cathexis" (chapter 11, *The Problem of Anxiety*).[29] We have seen—in our reading of *Break of Day* in the previous chapter—that such a *retraite sentimentale* is a fundamental impulse in Colette's work. Indeed, the writer stages a game with two contradictory wishes (the *fort* and the *da* of play): the wish to resummon the beloved ghosts, and the wish to bury them, to free herself from the haunting grief.

Indeed, Colette's writing may be understood as an effort to use her writer's "medium" to make contact with the lost shades of her past, and to put them to rest. For, like the act of child's play, these tales are haunted by an infantile trauma of separation that falls like a chilling shadow on the narrative (Gabrielle wonders, noting the ineffaceable lines in her mother's face: "Is it possible . . . that my mother is nearly fifty-four? I never think about it. I should like to forget it" *MMH* 18). And of course these writings are created even as the bereaved writer is serving the dread sentence of exile from Sido.

In *Sido*, Colette even describes her visit to a séance, where she seeks to make contact with her dead mother, in order not only to be with her again, but also to understand her better, as adult to adult. In a sense, all of her fictional autobiographies seek to per-

---

[28]Freud: "Laws of poetic economy necessitate this way of presenting the situation, for the author's deeper motivation could not be explicitly enunciated. It must remain concealed, kept from the easy perception of the spectator or reader" (*S.E.* 14: 329).

[29]*The Problem of Anxiety, S.E.* 20. Freud discusses this process further in "Mourning and Melancholia" (1917), *S.E.* 14: 239.

form the same rite of understanding and recognition: "After death, [our loved ones] take on a firmer outline and then cease to change. 'So that's the real you? Now I see, I'd never understood you'" (*Sido* 186). Her mourning-work thus wants to fix her memories in their proper place, erecting a monument at their final resting place.

So Colette writes an elegy that brings Sido back to life (*da!*) reinstating the Imaginary relation, at the same time that it performs a Symbolic rite that endeavors to put Sido to rest in her "real" shape, paying the Symbolic debt to the past. But of course this cannot be a finished act, however much the writer might wish to sew up her past and exorcise her ghosts; "I am not at all sure that I have put the finishing touches to these portraits of her" (preface, *MMH*). For the writer's play is always a repeat performance, where the always unfinished desire of the writer, the inability to put the "finishing touches" on her portrait, is mimed and reenacted by each new reader.

Still, like her whimsical brother, who treats his imaginary dead "with the utmost friendliness" (57), Colette makes peace with her ghosts, glorifying their exploits and giving flesh to their ghostly outline, seen so much more clearly because of their absence. Having passed out of the "profound silence" of her childhood ("Our uncanny turbulence was never accompanied by any sound" 8), the writer performs a kind of penance for her obstinate childhood refusal to respond to Sido's call—evoked in that eerie opening scene of *My Mother's House*, where the children lie hidden in the garden like so many silent fantoms, witnessing and even enjoying their mother's tormented concern.[30] Through her vocation, Colette "undertakes" the task of rewriting her life-sentence of exile from Sido. In so doing, she reinscribes the maternal garden—just as her brother has done, re-erecting the ornamented tombstones that Sido has swept away in her uncomprehending rage, "across the abyss that separates a child from a grown-up person" (58). Colette

---

[30]The image of the guiltily unresponsive child is repeated in *My Apprenticeships*, trans. Helen Beauclerk (New York: Farrar, Straus, and Giroux, 1957), 4: "I also knew a little girl of eight years old who let her mother call her for a long while . . . she already knew too much of the various terrible ways of giving oneself pleasure." This formulation links the child's guilt with the erotic "sins" of the onanist or voyeur.

endeavors to cross this abyss, rewriting the family epitaphs and making use of her family "plot" as the page of invention. She thus both retrieves Sido from "the abyss" and puts her to rest—*fort* and *da*—in an elegy that mourns her loss and deploys it as the occasion for play, renewed with the inscription of each new reader into her intersubjective tapestry.

3

Colette and the Captain: Daughter as Ghostwriter

My new work sings . . . "When I was in my father's
house—little freckled girl . . ."
—*Earthly Paradise*

The pledge was given to honour his life, that is not to
repeat the act through which the father had perished.
—Freud, *Totem and Taboo*

The Paternal Intertext

We have seen that Colette's accounts of childhood are infused
with a luminous central presence, the maternal figure who assumes mythic proportions in her daughter's memory: it is impossible to know the daughter without encountering the extraordinary mother who has shaped and accompanied her.

But there is a corollary absence—or rather, a displacement. Colette's father, hardly a father-figure, is a mere *figurant* in the tales
of childhood; he is relegated to the sidelines, glimpsed only in
fleeting asides to the mother-daughter love story. When he is
mentioned, it is as an outsider, an exile from the family circle
("We felt vaguely vexed with him for not being sufficiently like
the rest of us" *Sido* 183). Indeed, we have seen that the mother is
the titular figure of an entire work (*Sido*) and the dominant interest of another (*My Mother's House*), in which she is claimed with
the possessive, as "my mother," in no fewer than six chapter
headings. Yet the father merits only a section of *Sido*, in which he
is dubbed "the Captain," rather than "my father"; and he appears
only once in the chapter headings of *My Mother's House* (in "Fa-

A shorter version of this essay ("Colette and the Captain: Daughter as Ghostwriter") first appeared in *Refiguring the Father: New Feminist Readings of Patriarchy*, ed.
Patricia Yaeger and Beth Kowaleski-Wallace (Carbondale: Southern Illinois University Press, 1989).

ther and Madame Bruneau," a title that links him to an outsider). "Sido" is thus literally and figuratively her daughter's text; "the Captain" is simply intertext.

Or perhaps not so simply: psychoanalysis has shown us the importance of the marginal, the in-between, the forgotten, the trivialized. Certainly, after Freud, things have ceased to be simply what they seem, especially in family history. Reading the paternal intertext in Colette's writing, then, requires a close attention to the complications of her earthly paradise. Yet encountering the fantom father is not an easy task: reading between the lines requires a displaced attention, and calls for the art of collage, of patching and pasting.

Colette's own narrative persona seems to elicit this effort on the part of her reader, by the wistfulness of her evocations of the Captain: "It seems strange to me now, that I knew him so little" (*Sido* 175); "Were we not worthy, he and I, of a mutual effort to know each other better?" (182). One poignant anecdote in *Sido* is particularly revealing, indicating the crucial, if elided, importance of the Captain in the emergence of his daughter's vocation. For it turns out that Sido is not the only beloved ghost to haunt the writer.

The Fantom Father

Significantly, the father's most memorable appearance in the autobiographical writings is as an apparition who visits his daughter long after his death. In "The Captain" (the chapter in *Sido* devoted to the father), there is an account of a séance "chez Mme B . . ." (the tantalizing initial itself lending an air of mystery to the scene). At this séance, attended casually, "at the suggestion of a friend" (193), Colette characteristically asks for news of her mother, and is "vaguely jealous" to learn that Sido's ghost is occupied with her brother Leo. Mme B reports, however, that the *paternal* ghost is present:

> "Behind you the 'spirit' of an old man is sitting . . . He has a spreading, untrimmed beard, nearly white, and rather long, grey hair, brushed back. His eyebrows—my word, what eyebrows, extraordinarily bushy—and as for the eyes under them!

They're small, but so brilliant one can hardly endure their gaze. Have you any idea who it might be?"

"Yes, indeed I have." (194)

Mme B goes on to assert that this spirit is "very much taken up with" his daughter, and when Colette expresses her skepticism, the medium explains: "He is very much taken up with you *at present* . . . Because you represent what he would have so much liked to be when he was on earth. You are exactly what he longed to be. But he himself was never able" (194).

The narrator then describes the rest of the afternoon, before returning to the question of her father, almost as an afterthought: "As for my father . . . 'You are exactly what he longed to be, and in his lifetime was never able'" (195). This second quote from Mme B represents a slight but significant variation from the first ("he himself was never able" has become "in his *lifetime* [*de son vivant*] was never able"). This modification, barely perceptible, nonetheless suggests that a profound identification is taking place; for the Captain apparently has new capacities *after* his death, thanks to his daughter's work. And this impression of identification is reinforced by Colette's admission that *she* has somehow summoned the paternal ghost ("But doubtless she was seeing him, through the transparent veil of my subconscious, as I had seen him" 195). Leaving this observation in its marginal place, Colette goes on to another anecdote, one of the most disturbing and powerful moments in her work.

She begins by revealing that the Captain spent a good part of his retirement locked away in his library, writing his memoirs (an amputee, he had ended his military career; and his political career had been a failure):

I can still see, on one of the highest shelves of the library, a row of volumes, bound in boards, with black linen spines. The firmness of the boards, so smoothly covered in marbled paper, bore witness to my father's manual dexterity. But the titles, handwritten in Gothic lettering, never tempted me, more especially since the black-rimmed labels bore no author's name. I quote from memory: *My Campaigns, The Lessons of '70, The Geodesy of Geodesies, Elegant Algebra, Marshall MacMahon seen by a Fellow-Soldier,*

From Village to Parliament, Zouave Songs (in verse) . . . I forget the
rest. (195–96)

These volumes remain unopened, in full view but neglected, until
one day after the Captain's death, when his library is being con-
verted to a bedroom. It is only at this moment that the family
discovers that all of these volumes, systematically arranged and
titled, are composed of blank pages. "The dozen volumes bound
in boards revealed to us their secret, a secret so long disdained by
us, accessible though it was. Two hundred, three hundred, one
hundred and fifty pages to a volume; beautiful, cream-laid paper,
or thick 'foolscap' carefully trimmed, hundreds and hundreds of
blank pages. Imaginary works, the mirage of a writer's career"
(196).

The only writing in all these "virgin volumes" is a poignant and
chilling dedication to the Captain's one love, that same "Sido"
who is the primary love-object for her child, the focal point in the
primal triangle. "The single page lovingly completed and signed
[was] the page that bore the dedication: To MY DEAR SOUL, HER
FAITHFUL HUSBAND: JULES-JOSEPH COLETTE" (197). Sido herself,
"out of piercing regret and the painful desire to blot out this proof
of incapacity" (196)—this testimony of impotence and creative
sterility dedicated to her alone—tries to use up these "cream-laid
notebooks, his invisible works" in a "fever of destruction" (196),
but to no avail: the white pages prove inexhaustible ("we never
saw the end of them . . . there were so many of these virgin pages
[that] we never exhausted his invisible 'works'" 196).

In later years, Colette continues to be haunted by this "mirage
of a writer's career," the image of all these blank pages of mute
adoration, dedicated to the beloved matriarch: "At the time when
I was beginning to write, I too drew on this spiritual legacy. Was
that where I got my extravagant taste for writing on smooth
sheets of fine paper, without the least regard for economy? I
dared to cover with my large handwriting the invisible cursive
script, perceptible to only one person in the world" (197). The
agonizing discovery of the ungrateful child who understands "too
late" the unbearably painful secret of her father's incapacity turns
out to be an invisible resource, which guides her "like a shining
tracery" (197).

Colette was to marry another creatively sterile paternal figure who "suffered from nervous horror before the white page" (*My Apprenticeships* 76) and who, in his turn, enjoined her to do what he was unable to do, to fill the blank page with writing he could sign. And as ghostwriter for Willy, as well as for the paternal figure who continues to haunt her, Colette abandons her childhood name (Gabrielle) and is christened by Willy, her new "father," with a doubly patriarchal name, comprised of the "pen names" of father and husband. But Colette Willy, ghostwriter, of course subsequently became—and remains—"Colette." In Lacanian terms, one could say that Colette's identity as a writer, in spite of detours and transformations, is by way of the Name of the Father.

But it is the detours and transformations that make this ghost story so intriguing and cause us to wonder just how the maimed, sterile patriarch, figure of great pathos, has contributed to his daughter's vocation, and what this contribution might suggest about the role of the father-daughter relation in the formation of the woman artist. How can that paternal ghost, known too little and too late, provide access to the shadowy subtext of Colette's subjectivity? Might this encounter with Colette as father's daughter in turn encourage a rereading of psychoanalytic theory, shedding light on the question that continues to "haunt" psychoanalysis? What *does* woman want?

Screen Memories

Smoke Screens . . .

All of Colette's portraits of her father bear some family resemblance to that ghostly apparition encountered at the séance in *Sido*: for these intermittent and fleeting remembrances are veiled by mystery, shrouded in guilt, shaded with nostalgia. When the Captain makes a rare appearance in *Sido* or in *My Mother's House*, the *récit* more often than not veers into the minor mode, even when the anecdote recounted is burlesque or caricatural. For in this comic portrait of the Captain, an undertone of sadness persists: the one-legged officer, confined to his home and forever barred from the exercise of his military career by his infirmity, has

become a farcical conqueror, his exploits reduced to ribald pleas-
antry (as when he "pursues" the neighbor woman Mme Bruneau,
offering to initiate her sexually for the price of a packet of tobacco). Even the Captain's effusiveness is underwritten by melancholy: "It is true," his daughter recalls, "that melody bubbled out
of him; but did I ever see him gay?" (*Sido* 179). The Captain's very
creativity, his gift of captivating an audience, is characterized as a
kind of protective coloration, a smoke screen: "Wherever he went,
his song preceded and protected him" (179).

Colette's father is a paradox and an enigma: sad and gay, silent
and sociable, hot-blooded and distant ("in our midst a man
brooded bitterly" 186). It is the Captain's sadness that constitutes
his mystery, especially puzzling since his relationship with Sido is
characterized as one of great mutual love and joy. For the Captain's false gaiety is a decoy for something ineffable: "Who could
have believed that this baritone, still nimble with the aid of a
crutch and a stick, is projecting his song like a smoke screen in
front of him, so as to detract attention from himself?" (180). Even
his gaze, the color of smoke, is shrouded in mystery, "that extraordinary, challenging grey-blue gaze of his, which revealed its
secrets to no one, though sometimes admitting that such secrets
exist" (188). Like his "smoke screen" song, this gaze is impenetrable; and yet, like a cipher, it hints at secrets, inviting interpretation. Like the empty volumes in his library, like the ghost at the
séance, the Captain's secret is tantalizingly present and yet intangible, an open book that asks to be read, and that remains invisible. Of course for psychoanalysis, it is just this sort of sign that is
the most elusive—like the purloined letter of Lacan's essay, a clue
in full view but invisible—obscured by the screen of unconscious
desire and motivated forgetting ("a secret so long disdained by
us, accessible though it was" 195). It is these ciphers that the Captain's daughter tries now to read, in order to peer behind the
screen and to clear the air.

Colette herself draws attention to the fogginess of her recollections: "I can only see my father's face vaguely and intermittently"
as a "wandering, floating figure, full of gaps, obscured by clouds
and only visible in patches" (177). The paternal portrait is at once
angelic ("obscured by clouds") and ghostly, errant, floating. When
Colette does succeed in fixing her father's memory, the experi-

ence is equally eerie, for the Captain appears frozen in time, corpse-like, silent as the sphinx: "He is clear enough sitting in the big, rep-covered armchair. The two oval mirrors of his open pince-nez gleam on his chest, and the red line of his peculiar lower lip, like a rolled rim, protrudes a little beneath the moustache which joins his beard. In that position he is fixed forever" (177).

Colette often seems to attribute the patchy nature of her recollections to faulty memory, the result of childhood indifference, of "Gabrielle's" failure to look behind the clouds. Yet there is surely more to this patchy recollection than lack of information, since these memories are such a source of torment for the adult daughter ("But now the thought of my father tortures me" 179). We are reminded of an important concept in psychoanalytic theory—that of "screen memories," those fragmentary and apparently innocent childhood recollections that Freud reads as ciphers of repressed experience.[1] Colette's remembrances often have many of the earmarks of classic psychoanalytic screen memories, in which the apparently insignificant content becomes troubling because of the haunting quality of the images. The sense of filial culpability in these passages is striking indeed, evinced by the melancholic, uncanny nature of those fragments of memory that persist, where the child's indifference toward her father is shadowed by the adult's tormented curiosity.

According to Colette, the fogginess of childhood recollections of her father derives from the deliberate air of mystery with which the Captain screened himself, as well as her own indifference at the time. In a classic Freudian screen memory, however, the uncanniness and incompleteness of the recollection result from the "screen" of repression, the motivated forgetting of the patient, rather than from any external barriers. Whatever the source of the screen that obscures the memory of the Captain, his daughter now sets herself the task of piercing the shield, dispersing the smoke screen, piecing the fragments into a whole portrait ("It takes time for the dead to assume their true shape in our thoughts" 186). Even more than the composition of Sido's portrait, the labor

---

[1]Freud, "A Childhood Recollection on *Dichtung und Wahrheit*" (1917), *S.E.* 17: 147.

of the father's re-membrance is a work of reconstruction, because of the daughter's faulty memory. It is even a kind of detective work, in which the writer functions first as archaeologist and then as sempstress, assembling clues that have long lain unexamined, stitching them into their "true shape." But this process is also a kind of séance or auto-analysis, a work of mourning that reanimates the shades of the past in order to put them to rest.

Smoke Gets in Your Eyes

The patchwork portrait is slow to emerge, hindered by the obstruction of time, the screens of the Captain's enigmatic personality, and the mutual blindness of father and daughter during their time together. Colette attributes this mutual blindness to an all-consuming love for Sido: "My attention, my fervent admiration were all for Sido. It was just the same with my father. His eyes dwelt on Sido" (*Sido* 175). Father and child are invisible in the glare of their shared adoration, unable to see each other in the dazzling presence of the maternal star.

In a telling passage, Colette relates an incident in which Sido reproaches her mate for a ribald anecdote, because of the presence of the child. The Captain retorts, "Oh the child, it doesn't matter about her" (188), and having thus summarily dismissed and excluded his daughter, proceeds to envelop himself and Sido in the smoldering and impenetrable circle of his smoke-colored gaze, which annuls the presence of all outsiders ("And he would fasten on his chosen one that extraordinary, challenging grey-blue gaze of his" 188). Colette goes on to describe her father's blindness as an actual physical debility; or rather, she analogizes the Captain's physical defect with his emotional tunnel vision, first perceived, interestingly, when the daughter is an adolescent, the age of a certain enhanced erotic perception: "I was not more than thirteen when I noticed that my father was ceasing to see, in the physical sense of the word, his Sido herself. 'Another new dress?' he would exclaim with surprise. 'Bless my soul, Madam!'" (189). Sido protests that the dress is three years old, but the Captain has already ceased to see and to hear her, retreating to the hazy reverie of days gone by: "But he was no longer listening to her. He had already jealously rejoined her in some favourite spot, where she wore a chignon with Victorian side-curls" (189). In this light, the Captain's blindness is almost a hysterical symptom, an emotional state with a physical result, a visual castration of sorts; his loss of "the gift of observation and the power of comparison" (189) reflects the loss of limb and parallels that other paralysis, before the glare of the white page.

In this perspective, Captain Colette's love for Sido has become the *cause* for his emotional and artistic truncation, a curtailment of creative powers for which his physical amputation seems almost emblematic. Indeed, as Colette relates in another passage, his creative powers do decline, absorbed by the white heat of his love: at first anxious to shine before his love, "as his love increased, he came to abandon even his desire to *dazzle* Sido" (177, my emphasis). His own dazzle, his own heat, seems to be reduced progressively to the sphere of his smoldering gaze, which not only excludes outsiders but also finally limits his own vision, even while it provides an encircling and even stifling atmosphere for the beloved object of his attention. Under the Captain's gaze, Sido's "grey eyes glanced rapidly in all directions," Colette recalls. "This confusion and the vain attempt of those eyes to escape from a man's gaze, blue-grey as new-cut lead, was all that was revealed to me of the passion which bound Sido and the Captain throughout their lives" (192).

The Captain's passion is thus both a bond and an oppression—as piercing and inescapable as dense smoke—which at once binds and blinds both parties it engulfs. For Sido is not the only one to be oppressed by this stifling love; the Captain himself is "reduced now to his village and his family, his whole love being absorbed by the great love that [binds] his horizon" (181). Beneath the surface of perfect conjugal harmony, "a garden where for the space of thirty years a husband and wife dwelt together with never a harsh word between them" (154), within this circle of perfect love, there simmers an atmosphere as restive and ardent as a Racinian tragedy, within a horizon bound not only by mutual love, but by mutual evasiveness and incomprehension. For the Captain is not the only one to suffer from the blindness of love: if he is increasingly incapable of seeing his family, and even his Sido herself, his mate is equally blind to the truth of the man she has married: "She thought he was gay because he sang" (179).

Ciphers/Smoke Signals

If Sido is blinded by these smoke screens of song and narrative, her daughter is less easily fooled, at least in retrospect. For her, the father's melancholic song and enigmatic gaze are signs that not only hide but also bear witness, "admitting that secrets exist," "revealing unspoken passion." Now, as an adult, the Captain's daughter attempts to decipher these signs, yielding to her avowed passion to eavesdrop, to lay bare. But this posthumous detective work is no simple case of curiosity; it is part of the writer's oedipal quest (as the revealer of the riddle of the sphinx) to see, to understand, and to tell all. Treasure-hunter or grave-robber, the writer "undertakes" her task of unearthing the father's secret.

Her first hypotheses concerning the Captain's mysterious sadness focus on material, tangible circumstances: the Captain's impending financial failure ("he sings in the hope that perhaps today SHE will forget to ask him if he has been able to borrow 100 louis on the security of his disabled officer's pension" 180) and the retired officer's frustration at no longer being able to exercise his military vocation ("Sido and his love for her were all that he had been able to keep" 187). But always, underlying these explanations of the Captain's sadness, there is the ominous suggestion that the father's all-consuming love, rather than being a compensation for his infirmity, his bound horizon and diminishing view, is actually a source of that diminution. Perhaps more important than his visible wound, his amputation, is his hidden wound, the wound of love. In any case, the Captain's diversionary tactics seem to work on Sido, who listens to his song spellbound, "in spite of herself, unable to interrupt" (179).

But the adult daughter knows better, because she has come to identify profoundly with her father's secret sadness, his hidden hurt: "But I who whistle whenever I am sad, and turn the pulsations of fever, or the syllables of a name that tortures me, into endless variations on a theme, could wish that she had understood that pity is the supreme insult. My father and I have no use for pity: our nature rejects it" (179). This remarkable passage is at once a reproach to the mother and an expression of identification with the father, who is resurrected here, spoken about in the present tense ("My father and I have no use for pity"); and it reveals as much about the Captain's daughter as it does about the Captain himself.[2] For this passage suggests that the Captain's mysterious sadness has less to do with financial failure, curtailed career, or under-requited love than it does with the difficulties of his other, secret vocation, shared with his daughter: the calling of writer. Here language is described as an obsession, a feverish repetition of variations on a theme—not unlike Freud's demonic repetition compulsion—recalling Colette's comparison of writing to a chase of maddeningly elusive "ghost-words": "The pursued object leads me unfeelingly on . . . To catch up with it I find myself singing to its veiled homonyms, to its vaguely glimpsed rhythm" (*Evening Star* 160).

The passage from *Sido* concerning the torment of language concludes with yet another haunting revelation: "And now the thought of my father tortures me, because I know he possessed a virtue more precious than any facile charms: that of knowing full well why he was sad, and never revealing it" (*Sido* 179). The Captain is above all a *silent* poet, Orpheus dismembered, torn limb from limb, a singer without tongue, a writer without pen, paralyzed before the page; and yet his silence—"more precious than facile charms"—is also a strength. Orpheus's greatest virtue, prized and shared by his daughter, is the gift of simultaneous self-knowledge and self-dissimulation.

Re-membering Orpheus

It is Sido who suggests that the Captain is a kind of Orpheus (*"le roi des maître-chanteurs"*); and Colette's account of this remark suggests that Sido's ironic quip has as much to do with her mate's stifling possessiveness and relentless passion as with his songful nature. For it is Orpheus, the ultimate lovesick poet, who descends into Hades to retrieve Eurydice after death, but who cannot keep his pledge not to look at her, thus losing her forever.

---

[2]This almost seems to be an instance of Freudian *Nachträglichkeit*—whereby childhood events only take on their full psychic traumatic significance with the coming of adulthood. For a discussion of *Nachträglichkeit*, see J. Laplanche and J.-B. Pontalis, *Vocabulaire de la psychanalyse*, under the entry *après-coup* or *Nachträglichkeit*. The work has been translated as *The Language of Psycho-Analysis*, trans. Donald Nicholson-Smith (New York: W. W. Norton, 1973). See the entry "deferred action."

Like Orpheus, the Captain cannot bear to think of his mate as mortal: "Don't you dare not to recover," he scolds her when she is ill (*Sido* 191); exasperated by this "masculine attitude," Sido banishes her husband from her sickroom, where at any rate, she insists, a man has no place. But like Orpheus, the Captain continues his vigil, singing beneath the window of his beloved: "I think of thee, I see thee, I adore thee, at every moment, everywhere." It is at this moment that the aggravated "Eurydice" exclaims to her daughter—who has *not* been exiled from her bedside—"Would you like to know what your father is? I'll tell you. Your father is the modern Orpheus" (192).

Of course the narrator of this tale would like nothing better than to "know what her father is"—and this anecdote occurs, interestingly, in the chapter that sets out to solve the Captain's riddle. And it is the daughter's role as sleuth—seeking to fathom the paternal mystery—that suggests a parallel with a second poetic myth: the tragedy of Oedipus. The myth of Oedipus (the uncoverer of secrets and the paternal assassin, "castrated" for his crime by blindness) doubles the myth of Orpheus (the underworld discoverer and the conjugal assassin, "castrated" for his obsessive love by dismemberment). Of course the myth of the unhappy Orphic poet is suggested by Colette's text, while the myth of the unhappy oedipal riddle-solver merely shadows the text, a latent subtext of desire. But both convey the tragic consequences of desire, whose symptom is an obsession with "dis-covery."

Orphic Desire

> To me the important thing is to lay bare and to bring
> to light something that no human eye before mine has
> gazed upon.
> —*Sido*

Orpheus, the tragic lover, the emblem of unsatisfied longing, is a curious reverse ghost, a living man who goes to the underworld to haunt the dead (not unlike Colette herself, who seeks to use *her* poetic powers to bring back the shades of her past). But Orpheus loves too well; unable to resist the temptation to look at Eurydice when he leads her into the light, he violates the conditions of her release and causes her to be lost, to vanish forever. Thus Orpheus's tragic flaw is the insatiable desire visually to possess his object. Just so, Colette's father, the modern Orpheus, is a voyeur of sorts ("I see thee always, at every moment, everywhere"); the Captain's stifling gaze is the very image of Orphic desire, which causes him to be banished from Sido, driven from her bedside, where "a man has no place," losing his beloved from view at the moment when he most desperately needs to be reassured of her presence.

Significantly, the Captain is remembered as a hot-blooded and jealous lover, who even carries a weapon (as a kind of compensation for his missing limb, an extra "arm"?): "My father always carried in his pocket a dagger whose horn handle concealed a spring" (*Sido* 178). But this concealed arm remains unused, an emblem of impotence, like the harmless "sham southern rages" ignored by his family ("he would give vent to growls and high-sounding oaths to which we paid not the slightest attention" 178). This is no classic oedipal father, whose ire weighs upon a cowering family circle; even his rage is perceived as an impotent threat, disregarded by the daughter, ridiculed by the mother: "'Italian! Knife-man!' were the names my mother used to call him, when she was displeased with him" (178). An interloper into female territory, this "knife-man" has no cutting power, wields no "castrating" authority. Like the mythic Orpheus—who meets the maddened maenads engaged in a revel where "a man has no place," and who suffers dismemberment at their hands—the Captain "has no place" in *My Mother's House*, and his chastisement (the withering ridicule of his familiars) seems to leave this poet dismembered, the author of empty volumes.

But Orpheus is more than a hapless lover, for his voice haunts us ("always, everywhere") as the voice of the eternal poet, a songster whose lyre accompanies his outpourings of unsatisfied longing. Likewise the modern Orpheus—remembered by his daughter as "a born writer," an orator "born to please," yet doomed to dismemberment and silence—is immortalized, remembered in the daughter's song, as she takes up the pen in his name (as "Colette"). But just how does this identification come about, between a father and child who are little better than hostile strangers (like Oedipus and Laius)? Just what is the nature of the father's wound, which the daughter will assume and overcome?

The Clue in Full View

"When I am alone, I try to imitate that look of my father's. Sometimes I succeed fairly well, especially when I use it to face up to some hidden hurt, which proves how efficacious insult can be against something which has you in its power, and how great is the pleasure of standing up to a tyrant" (*Sido* 188–89). Here Colette hints that this silent Orpheus has suffered a psychological wound more significant than the physical one, and insists on her resemblance to her father: daughter and father alike mount a stubborn and united defiance of "the hidden hurt inflicted by some tyrant" (189), a nameless enemy who seeks to leave them without a voice, dismembered. Not only is the enemy invisible, but the wound itself is unseen, rendered invisible by its very familiarity ("We were hardly aware that one of his legs was missing, amputated just below the hip" 187). And the daughter insists that she most admires the Captain's ability to hide his wound, to suffer in *silence*, "knowing full well why he was sad, and never revealing it" (179).

But the invisibility of the Captain's wound is additional evidence of the blindness that obscures Colette's family members from one another ("dismembering" the family), causing them to miss the obvious. For the daughter remembers the "glaringly obvious" nature of her parents' love, but also suggests that the "obvious" character of this passion (175) blinds the family to Captain Colette's secret suffering, as well as to his hidden affection for his children: "I knew also that, outwardly at least, he took little interest in his children" (175). Only death has revealed the true love of the Captain for his daughter, as she reads the only written texts left behind as eloquent testimony: "Now, twenty years after his death, I find that his letters are full of my name, and of his 'little one's' illness" (181).

Interestingly, the father's silence—concerning the love for the daughter, of which he almost seems ashamed—is associated with another silence. In the same passage, Colette says that the Captain never speaks of his military career, abandoned because of his war wound; and above all, he is silent about the ordeal of his wounding ("that hour when he hoped to die, in the midst of the tumult and surrounded by the love of his men" 180). The thematic juxtaposition of these two silences is telling: the wound of guilty love (the love for his children, hidden, Colette says, out of timidity) and the wound that has put an end to his military career are both repressed, covered up. Both, perhaps, are blows to his masculinity; but on a deeper level, there seems to be a psychic association between (hidden, guilty) love and his own dismemberment.

For the deepest of the Captain's secrets, Colette tells us, is not this hidden affection, but something that has always been out in the open, in plain sight. The daughter/detective now claims to dig up the secret that was always there in full view, too obvious to be noticed: Captain Colette suffers from "the sadness" of his physical wound. With what confidence she proclaims her discovery: "Now I have *fathomed* what my youth formerly hid from me: my brilliant, cheerful father harbored the profound sadness of those who have lost a limb" (186–87, my emphasis). Still, this discovery does not lay bare the deeper wound, the hidden familial tragedy: the Captain's failure as a writer, his *poetic* dismemberment. Just who is the nameless tyrant who steals Orpheus's poetic voice, robbing the poet of his potency? Colette declines to say, limiting herself to a description of the symptom. Looking back, she can now see that her father was sad because he was maimed. But she seems to overlook a more troubling possibility: perhaps the Orphic father was maimed because he was sad.

For although she claims to have fathomed the Captain's secret (the "sadness of one who has lost a limb"), this daughter is perhaps like Oedipus: rashly claiming to solve the most profound riddle while remaining blind to the essential mystery before her, and to her own possible culpability. Like Oedipus in search of the culprit at Thebes, she searches for answers that are perhaps all too close to home. And like Oedipus/Orpheus, she is unable *not* to look.

Oedipal Curiosity

Thus this Orphic scopophilia (the desire to *have* by looking) suggests an intertwining with a second myth of discovery, the oedipal subtext of this mystery. Colette likens the pleasure of writing to the thrill of the treasure hunt: "A treasure is not merely something hidden under the earth, or under the rocks, or the sea. To me the important thing is to lay bare and bring to light something that no human eye before mine has gazed upon" (*Sido* 163). But interestingly, Colette describes her fascination with buried secrets as a trait inherited from her *mother*, who also has "a flair for hidden treasure" (*BD* 136).

For example, in one of the most evocative passages of *Sido*, the mother is worriedly scrutinizing a mound of earth, unable to remember if she has planted crocus bulbs there, or the "chrysalis of a emperor moth" (a "shroud," or a cocoon). She enjoins her daughter not to look in either case—for the light would kill the moth, while the cold would kill the shoot: "As she spoke her face, alight with faith and an all-embracing curiosity, was hidden by another, older face, resigned and gentle. She knew that I should not be able to resist, any more than she could, the desire to know, and that like herself I should ferret in the earth of that flower pot until it had given up its secret" (162–63).

Curiously, Colette attributes her own murderous desire to her mother, from whom she claims to have inherited this thirst to know: "She knew I was her own daughter and that, child though I was, I was already seeking for that sense of shock, the quickened heart-beat, and the sudden stoppage of breath—symptoms of the private ecstasy of the treasure-seeker" (163). These are the confessions of a thrill seeker, a voyeur, whose Orphic gaze destroys what it lays bare, whose Oedipal need to see will raise ghosts better left buried. Thus the Captain is not the only member of this family plagued with the tragic flaw of Orphic desire—the desire to see what should be left covered, doubled by the Oedipal desire to know, whatever the consequences. In this same passage, in fact, Gabrielle is characterized as a *murderess* whose guilty curiosity—satisfied "on the sly"—will cause her withering gaze to destroy the object of her desire: "She knew then that I was going to scratch on the sly in her trial-ground until I came upon the sturdy sprout urged out of its sheath by the spring. I thwarted the blind purpose of the bilious-looking, black-brown chrysalis, and hurled it from its temporary death into a final nothingness" (163). Here mother and daughter are both grave-robbers, determined to reveal the most vulnerable of shrouded secrets—as well as castrators of sorts, who uncover the phallic bud "urged out of its sheath," only to destroy it.

Colette shows a similar pitiless curiosity concerning her father, at least after his death; having shown little interest during his life, she now refuses to let him "lie" in peace and is determined to expose his cover-up. Her parents' daughter, she suffers from a fatal desire: she loves the forbidden objects too well (Sido/Eurydice/Jocasta; the shrouded emperor moth; the slain father), refusing to let them rest. But exposure is an enemy to Orpheus/Oedipus, whom light robs of what it reveals. What is at risk in these unhappy revelations?

In terms of the Oedipus myth: were the mother revealed as an accomplice in the patricide, a Jocasta whose unseemly love for her child dethrones her mate, it might mean the disappearance of the illusion of a chaste angelic mother, unsullied by sexual conflict or desire. Or perhaps the answer is even closer to home, all too evident, a clue that the sleuth must fail to see because such sight would be too painful. Accordingly even the posthumous revelation of her father's sadness, however triumphantly proclaimed, seems off the track: if Colette declines to shed light on this greatest of mysteries, it is perhaps because she never sees so little as when she sees too much.

For the Captain's daughter, like her father before her, seems to reenact the parallel myths of Oedipus and of Orpheus, incurring the same blindness, a family characteristic in a house obscured by "smoke screens" and bathed in the white glare of familial passion. (Indeed the daughter speaks of her own need to dazzle Sido [177], a repetition of the father's need, all the while admitting that Sido outshines them both, making them invisible to each other, like planets in the same orbit.) Thus the father seems mysterious or shadowy only in retrospect, away from Sido's resplendence: during the Captain's life, his secrets are, like the empty volumes in his library, there for all to see and none to read. Re-membering Orpheus, then, means recalling him to view, reopening his case, taking a second look, to play out an unfinished relation of love.

Indeed, this daughter cannot resist the compulsion to throw light on the most fragile of mysteries, whatever the cost: she confesses that she has never been able to keep from touching the vulnerable butterfly's wing, or from digging up the butterfly's buried cocoon. And as she digs for the moth, Gabrielle recalls yet another too-curious mythic figure: she is also Pandora, dead set on reopening the casket that contains so many secret ills (as well as a hidden treasure, the "butterfly" Hope). But does this Orpheus/Oedipus/Pandora, this guilty child-analyst, ever fathom the cause of her father's mystery, that "hidden hurt" invisible to the naked eye, the secret of the silenced paternal poet? If so, is this feminine explorer, like Pandora, compensated as well as chastised for her curiosity?

Oedipus Revisited: The Stolen Object

Like Oedipus, this child must sound the mystery of the paternal assassin, determining just who is the unseen tyrant who has stolen the Captain's pen/voice. Who is the slayer of Laius, the dismemberer of Orpheus, the castrating maenad? The posthumous detective work is complicated by the guilt of the ungrateful child, who suffers from pangs of remorse at not having tried hard enough to know the lost father; her remorse even appears to be in some measure the fallout from a classic oedipal hostility toward the father, which she has only now—"too late!"—begun to understand. For the text suggests that the heat of Sido's astral presence (her "star quality") is intensified by yet another glare— the hot heat of competition between rivals for the object of their affection.

Even as an adult, the daughter continues to judge her father's passion for Sido as inappropriate, embarrassing, ludicrous: "How can it be otherwise in families where the father, though almost past the age for passion, remains in love with his mate?" (177). Yet this comment reveals a subtle shift in the classic oedipal configuration: here, it is the father who is cast in the role of the inappropriate suitor, rather than the child; and it is the child who passes judgment on the offender, even "castrating" him in her appraisal of him as someone "past the age for passion." And this judgment seems to be seconded by the mother herself, who pronounces the sentence of exile ("this is no place for a man"), emphasizing the paternal alienation from her family, and hence casting doubts on any natural paternal rights, marital or otherwise

("And after all you, what have you to do with me? You aren't even a relation!" *MMH* 28). If in Freud's oedipal scenario it is the father who thunders the "thou shalt not" of incest, in Colette's replay of this scene it is the mother who denies herself to the father, and the child who triumphantly affirms the decision. Thus the first theft in this drama is that of the love-object herself: the affection of Jocasta, the father's mate, is usurped by his child.

This reading suggests that the guilt in this feminized Oedipal/ Orphic tale perhaps lies with the females of the family, the mother and daughter in league, united against this interloper at their feminine bacchanal, the domestic rites of "my mother's house." So the daughter's Oedipal attempt to seek out the culprit in the patricide (who killed the stranger at the crossroads?) is a risky business, since it may reveal maternal and filial culpability, separately or in league. For the father's dismemberment is perhaps the result of a guilty forgetting, the neglecting of the daughterly responsibility of mourning/burial, which leaves the fragmented father forgotten by the crossroads, a paternal corpus riddled by gaps of memory, victim of hostility and negligence. And there are hints that the daughter's accomplice, the beloved to whom volumes of silence are dedicated, is also a guilty party. For Sido acts penitent when the empty volumes are found; driven by "piercing regret and painful desire," she tries to use up the too-white sheets of her husband's invisible work, to destroy the evidence of impotence. But try as she may, those *"virgin* pages, *spared* through timidity or listlessness" (196), those unsullied sheets, continue to haunt her, like defiantly pristine ghosts, untouched by the sabreless warrior's impotent pen.

This haunting image of the blank page suggests that the first theft—of the beloved object of affection, who is cast as a virginal madonna rather than a passionate lover—is doubled by the theft of a second object. For these snowy white pages suggest that the Captain has been the victim of the theft of a second precious object, the writer's tool. And the daughter's guilt in this theft of the pen is perhaps even more explicit than in the theft of the object of affection. In another of her memoirs, Colette recalls her envy of the father's writing materials: "From the age of ten I had never stopped coveting those material goods, invented for the glory and convenience of a mental power" (*EP* 49). Moreover, she has lifted her pen name, her writer's identity, from Captain Colette: like the rebel Prometheus, she has stolen the father's fire.

But insofar as she identifies with her father ("when I am alone I try to imitate that look") Colette must assume the wound that she herself has inflicted, the self-wound borne by every guilty child who discovers "too late" that she has caused anguish to a parent. When the hidden wound is revealed in the silent volumes dedicated to Sido, she picks up the stolen pen and begins her labor of remembrance, urged on by her father's ghost.

Oedipus Recast: Antigone as Alter Ego

Thus in spite of the classic oedipal overtones of Colette's relation to her father, the Captain is far from the frightening lawgiver of psychoanalytic tradition. In fact, more often than not, the Captain is not even a paternal figure in Colette's memory: in this caricature, he is often depicted as too aged to be a sexual threat; or he is belittled as an overgrown child, one of a band of children clinging to Sido's skirts ("Far from being a support to her, my Father was one of the cluster that clung round and hung on her arms" *Sido* 191). In this configuration, Colette and the Captain are *fraternal* rivals for a mother's affection—they are Oedipus and Antigone, siblings as well as father and daughter, both cathected to the maternal object. Their relation often seems to be more Imaginary than Symbolic, for they often appear as sibling rivals who both identify with one another and fiercely compete on the same level, rather than as traditional players in the triangular oedipal drama, where the father holds all the power. In this feminized scenario, even the Name of the Father, rather than being the possessive stigma of patriarchy handed *down* to a subject, is shared with, or even stolen from, the father—as "Colette's" personal *nom de plume*, a feather in her cap.

This theft suggests that the shared passion for the written word is as important a source of primal rivalry and identification as is the shared passion for Sido. Colette describes this fraternal collaboration between writers, recalling how as a child she pitilessly condemned her father's overblown oratory: "I was still quite small when he began to appeal to my critical sense [. . .] I well remember how severe a judge I was at ten years: 'Too many adjectives, as usual'[. . .] At that moment we glared at each other as equals, already on a *fraternal* footing" (176, my emphasis). Even far from Sido's radiance there is another kind of glare between these sibling rivals, "equals" on "fraternal footing": the mirror glare of the narcissistic Imaginary relation, reflecting identification *and* aggressivity.[3]

Significantly, this sibling recollection is doubled by another remembrance. In the same passage, Colette goes on to recall how her husband Willy would turn precisely the same criticism on *her* writing that she had once leveled at her paternal alter ego—the sarcastic denunciation of too much lyricism: "It was [my father] who inspired my first fumbling attempts to write, *and earned for me that most biting, and assuredly most useful praise from my husband. Can it be that I've married the last of the lyric poets?*" (176, my emphasis). The cycle of identification is complete, with Colette now playing the Captain's role, and Willy in Gabrielle's place, the critical sibling rival. In fact, Willy is the double of both father and daughter: like the Captain, he is impotent, unable to produce without his legion of ghostwriters; and, in forcing his young wife to work, he repeats the role of the father who inspires Colette's "first fumbling attempts to write." But like Gabrielle, he is a sibling of sorts, an alter ego on "a fraternal footing" with his ghostwriter (as indicated by her curious dual pen name of the time: "Colette Willy"). In both scenarios, the "siblings" are rival-colleagues.

Thus Colette's relation to her father (repeated with Willy) has all the earmarks of an Imaginary relation of narcissistic alter egos. Nonetheless, there are some overtones of the classic Symbolic father-child relation here as well, especially at those moments when the Captain is depicted as a *superior* rival endowed with the accoutrements of creation: the pen, the paper, the mother. Colette recalls, as a child, "prowling, hungrily, around all these treasures

---

[3]Fredric Jameson ("Imaginary and Symbolic") comments on this Imaginary sibling rivalry as a mirror relation of "struggle, violence, and antagonism, in which the child can occupy either term indifferently, or indeed, as in transitivism, both at once." He goes on to quote St. Augustine on the primordial nature of this rivalry: "I have myself seen jealousy in a baby and know what it means. He was not old enough to speak, but, whenever his foster-brother was at the breast, would glare at him pale with envy" (Jameson 356).

of stationery" (*EP* 48), and on one occasion, going so far as to steal two implements from the Captain's worktable. This transgression does not go unpunished: "I received full in my face the glare of a small, blazing, grey eye . . . so fierce that I did not risk it a third time" (48). As an adult, Colette still feels the heat of that paternal eye, from beyond the grave, at the séance where she meets the paternal ghost, with eyes "so brilliant one can hardly endure their gaze." And this Symbolic father lives on in Willy as well—in his stern role as warden and judge meting out "harsh but useful" criticism, laying down the laws of writing, curtailing the pleasure of invention with a cutting remark ("too many adjectives, as usual").

Still this doubling of Colette's memories of the Captain with her memory of Willy reveals a *feminized* version of the Symbolic tragedy, where the daughter is both Oedipus (the triumphant rival of an impotent/dead father) and Antigone (Oedipus's sister/daughter who makes restitution for her father's shortcomings, as companion-guide after his blinding). This contrast suggests that somewhere between Gabrielle's sibling rivalry and Colette's daughterly grief a shift from the Imaginary to the Symbolic has taken place, moving the daughter from the Imaginary position of mirror rival to the oedipal position of assassin, and on to a post-oedipal resolution, where Antigone pays her Symbolic debt to the dismembered brother-patriarch.

Of course none of these profoundly overdetermined feelings toward the father would come as a surprise to Freud, for whom every child is her parent's assassin. In fact, in *Totem and Taboo* (1912), Freud claims that the incest taboo, excluding the mother as object of sexual interest, results from a residual psychogenetic guilt—a collective unconscious memory of the trauma of having once killed the tribal father. (In Lacan's account this repressed memory takes on full Symbolic weight as the paternal metaphor, the Name of the Father: the father, although dead and buried, nonetheless lives on, Symbolized in his name, emblem of the social order to which every child accedes.[4]) In Freud's classic resolution of this residual guilt, each new generation renounces the con-

---

[4]The paternal metaphor, which both represents and buries the dead father, is the paradigm for all metaphoric expression that alludes to the repressed term of the comparison, even while it "buries" or hides it.

flict with the father, by renouncing the incestuous love and looking for an exogamous love object; a woman *like* the mother, but *beyond* the family fold. Thus the successful resolution of the Oedipus complex insures against the repetition of the primal patricide, for the child agrees to be *like* the father, to take his role without taking his place.[5] In Colette's case, this final filial identification is clear: the daughter seeks not to replace the father, but to complete his work.

With the writer's successful realization of her father's desire, has this complicated story reached a happy end? If Gabrielle were Gabriel, the Captain's son, this might be the case. But between Colette and Captain Colette there is a difference, the sexual difference signified by the term "Captain": this intricate intergenerational drama is further complicated by Gabrielle's gender. This child is not only Oedipus (nor even Antigone); she is also Electra, a daughter who must deal with a second tragic conflict, the murderous feelings evoked by the other beloved rival, her like creature, the mother.

Electra's Story

As both Freud and Lacan tried to demonstrate, the question of female subjectivity and sexuality presents another twist in the drama of Oedipus. For the daughter seems to have two oedipal stages: the first is as the father's rival for the mother (like the male child), but it is reversed in a second stage, a "feminine" love for the male object and rivalry with the mother. (In Freud's view the girl-child resents her mother for creating her ill-equipped, and turns away from her to the father, desiring to have a child by him, to compensate for her anatomical deficiency.[6]) Freud once called this stage the Electra complex, although he later abandoned the term. But like the Electra myth, this developmental stage does entail a turning from the mother as object to the confrontation with mother as rival, a step that psychoanalysis sees as crucial in the formation of femininity. Of course one might question

---

[5]See Freud's "The Dissolution of the Oedipus Complex" (1924), *S.E.* 19: 173.

[6]Freud discusses the permutations of the long and complex relation between little girls and their mothers in *New Introductory Lectures on Psychoanalysis* (1933), *S.E.* 22: 105–6.

whether this passage to "true femininity" (i.e., a desire for the father and repudiation of the mother) happens at all in Colette. For she is a celebrated mother's daughter, who appears to have but one enduring love.

The inadequacies of Freud's account have been debated at length by feminist theorists, who have pointed to Freud's lack of consideration of the mother's own desire, and who have criticized the bias inherent in the notion of penis envy. To be fair, it should be noted that Freudian psychoanalysis never pretends to give an unequivocal answer to feminine sexuality; Freud admits, albeit in yet another unfortunate metaphor, that this is the "dark continent" of psychoanalytic theory (female sexuality is presumably calling out to be explored and colonized).

In any case, in Freud as in Lacan, the riddle of the sphinx, answered in the Oedipus myth (what is man?) is haunted and transformed by an unanswered question (what does woman want?). Certainly *Totem and Taboo* sheds little light here, since it says nothing about the rivalry of the females of the clan. And nowhere in traditional psychoanalysis is there a suggestion that the "passing of the Oedipus complex" in the little girl should result in a post-oedipal identification with the rival mother. In other words, the problem with Freud's female oedipal scenario is that he fails to posit a passing of the Oedipus complex for girls, as for boys: whereas the male child gets over his competition with the father because of castration anxiety, accepting the interdiction of the forbidden love-object, there is no parallel resolution for the girl-child.[7] In fact, by extension of Freud's logic, presumably the girl-child, immune to the threat of castration as a penalty for incest, would choose her father as mate if she were not handed over in marriage to the outsider beyond the family fold.

Colette's opus paints a strikingly different picture: the girl's passage through a second oedipal phase *does* seem to take place, and to get resolved, suggesting that the absence of a castration

---

[7]Freud even suggests that the female's immunity to the threat of castration (because, of course, she is already "castrated") means she has no way of getting out of the rivalry with the opposite sex parent, of submitting to the Law, and of becoming a full, moral human being. Freud writes, in the *New Introductory Lectures* (114): "In the absence of fear of castration the chief motive is lacking which leads boys to surmount the Oedipus complex [. . .] In these circumstances, the formation of the super-ego must suffer [. . .] and feminists are not pleased when we point out to them the effects of this factor upon the average feminine character."

complex is perhaps not as crucial to human development as the fathers of psychoanalysis would have us believe. For Colette of course does experience a resolution with Sido, who returns as the friendly ghost of *Break of Day*, to counsel her daughter. In fact, in several of Colette's works, female rivals come to an understanding and establish a bond beyond their initial jealousy.[8] In Colette's mythology, mother and daughter are reconciled just as father and son are in Freud's founding myth.

But in order for this reconciliation to take place, there must first have been a conflict between mother and daughter. Gabrielle's beloved Eurydice/Jocasta can also be cast as Clytemnestra, the deadly rival who is both assassin to her husband and victim of her daughter. In this familial drama the father, Agamemnon, must be avenged by Electra, the ultimate father's daughter. If the riddle of man is solved by the son, Oedipus, the riddle of woman is posed by the daughter, Electra.

Rewriting the Tragedy

In Colette's autofiction, Gabrielle's position as "father's daughter" is not nearly as explicit as is her connection to Sido; nevertheless, a hint of yearning for the paternal love-object may be divined in the portrayal of the Captain as a negligent father who refuses to acknowledge his daughter's importance: "'Oh the child, it doesn't matter about her' . . . Well that was frank enough, and what a challenge to his one and only love!" (*Sido* 189). One senses an underlying bitterness at this kind of dismissal (Gabrielle is, after all, the Captain's only girl-child and the baby of the family), a hint that the daughter feels excluded from her father's vision, a gaze monopolized by his "one and only love." This longing to be seen by the father makes itself felt, for instance, in this remark: "All the same, he liked me for certain characteristics, in which— had he seen me more clearly—he might have recognized himself" (189). Here again the child's indifference is doubled by the bereaved adult's retrospective search for connections: Electra remembers the lost father with longing.

In this version of the familial triangle, father and daughter are

[8]This is the theme, for instance, of *La Seconde* (Paris: J. Ferenczi et Fils, 1929), trans. Elizabeth Tait and Roger Senhouse, *The Other One* (New York: Farrar, Straus, and Giroux, 1979).

libidinally bonded. Witness, for instance, the lyrical memory of Gabrielle's "intoxicating" campaign excursions with her father ("Propaganda," *MMH* 42–43):

> I would fall asleep, completely tipsy, my head on the table, lulled by the friendly tumult. Finally, labourers' brawny arms would pick me up and deposit me tenderly at the bottom of the carriage, well swaddled in the red tartan shawl that smelt of orris root and of my mother.
>
> Ten miles, sometimes fifteen, a real expedition under the breathless stars of a winter sky, to the trot of the mare gorged on oats. Are there really people who remain unmoved and never feel their throats tighten with a childish sob when they hear the sound of a trotting horse upon a frozen road, the bark of a hunting fox or the hoot of an owl struck by the light of the passing carriage-lamps?

Interestingly, this evocative passage echoes two other passages we have encountered: first, it evokes the imagery of "The Abduction," where the sleepy little girl is borne away by sheltering arms, with a rocking motion that lulls her to sleep: "Two arms, singularly adept at lifting a sleeping form, encircled my waist and my neck, at the same time gathering the blankets and the sheet about me. My cheek felt the colder air of the stairs, a muffled step descended slowly, rocking me at each pace with a gentle motion" ("The Abduction," *MMH* 29). But of course in "Propaganda," the encircling arms are no longer those of the mother, but those of the male "ravisher" (the "labourers' brawny arms" 42) so feared by Sido and so desired by the daughter. In fact, the little girl's guilty erotic dream in "The Abduction" (*"L'Enlèvement"*)—"in such wise was I departing for the land where a post-chaise [. . .] stops before a church to deposit a young man dressed in taffeta and a young woman whose ruffled skirts suggest the rifled petals of a rose" (*MMH* 29)—seems to come true in "Propaganda," when the sleeping girl is "carried away" (*enlevé*) to a waiting carriage, by "brawny arms."

This same passage in "Progaganda"—recounting the return home with the father along a lonely road in a carriage—also anticipates the final image of *Evening Star*, the image of writing as sewing, the pen/needle drawn by a team of horses that pull sometimes together, sometimes apart: "Along an echoing road, beating in time at first, then out of time, then coming together again, can be heard the trotting of hoof of two horses in double harness. Controlled by the same hand, the pen and the needle, the habit of work and the wise desire to put an end to it" (*EP* 505). This imagistic doubling suggests that the libidinal tie with the father is perhaps unconsciously intertwined with the notion of the writer's work as embroidery, and with the impulse to finish the father's work and "come home" in death, at long last winding up the sempstress's labor of love.

To be sure, the vignette "Propaganda" recalls the lost intimacy between father and daughter with intense longing and regret. For the final line of this passage—following Sido's discovery of the child's tipsiness—cuts short the idyll: "Next day the victoria set forth without me and returned that evening, to set forth no more" (43). This abrupt ending hints at the most frightening aspect of Sido, as the vengeful queen (Clytemnestra) who desires and commits the dethroning and murder of her mate, and who acts as obstacle to the daughter Electra's desire. Is the angel mother then the mysterious and murderous "tyrant" who inflicts a "hidden hurt" on father and daughter alike, in her pronouncement of separation which curtails their forbidden relation?

A second more subtle intercession between father and daughter occurs in "My Father's Daughter," where the title leads us to expect that Colette will discuss her relationship with her father. But this title turns out to be a quote from Sido, referring to *her* father—and to *her* illegitimate baby sister ("my father's daughter"). (Interestingly, Colette never refers to herself as "her father's daughter," perhaps because, as the only child of her mother's second marriage, she is reluctant to confirm the sexual tie between her parents, evinced by her birth.) In any case, "My Father's Daughter" reveals Sido as someone capable of ferocious jealousy and cruelty, a dismemberer who secretly "remodels" the fingertips of her father's baby girl. Might this not be another indication that the beloved Sido herself may be the mysterious tyrant who is capable of inflicting secret wounds on father and daughter alike? In this shifting oedipal drama—where the father is often the "feminine" dismembered object—not the least of the blows inflicted may be that which severs the *father* from his child, wounding both victims and requiring an act of mourning to help heal the loss.

We have seen that this mourning includes a posthumous act of filial recognition, imitating the defiant gaze of the father ("which proves how great is the pleasure of standing up to a tyrant: 'You may cause my death in the end, but I shall take as long as possible about it, never fear'" 189). And what "look" is being imitated in this face-off with death and torture? The Captain's impenetrable blue-grey gaze, the "smoke screen" thrown up in defense of the wounding acts of some unnamed foe. Here the child is no longer an oedipal rival of the father: like Electra, she clearly identifies with her father's cause against the enemy who hurts them both. In Electra's myth, the mother is no longer the innocent victim of fate, a Jocasta whose excessive love for her child unwittingly undoes her mate, but a deadly Clytemnestra, opponent of daughter and husband alike, a ferocious mother who even has something of the maddened Medea, whose passion causes her children to be wounded by her own hand. Might this be true on some level of the gentle Sido? Is the beloved of the modern Orpheus a castrating maenad in disguise, stilling the poet's voice, his "propaganda"? What is the meaning of the Captain's dedication of *silence* to Sido ("To my dear soul, her faithful husband" 197)? To lay these questions to rest, we need to return to Orpheus's missing grave, to reopen those blank pages of the Captain's works, reading his silent testament.

Decrypting the Captain

Colette's own vocation is certainly, among other things, Electra's vocation of remembrance, restitution, giving voice to the silenced father. Still she reveals that the quality she considers her father's "most precious gift" is not the gift of speech or song, but that of silence—of torment "nobly and silently borne." This is a virtue the daughter now claims for herself, in an act of mimetic tribute, "imitating that look" of her father's under "torture" (*Sido* 188). In other words, if what the daughter admires most, paradoxically, is her father's mystery, his impenetrable gaze, his capacity for *veiling* a hidden hurt in song, it is perhaps because this quality is tied to the artist's gift of embroidery and dissimulation, the ability to veil the bare facts with poetic overlay. The labor of the artist becomes paradoxically both a laying-bare/capture (stalking the "vaguely glimpsed rhythms" of an elusive word [*ES* 160]) and a draping/setting free (transforming the "syllables of a name" into "endless variations on a theme" *Sido* 179).

Such a vision of the writer's work, of course, is in many ways like the psychoanalytic vision of therapy. In Lacanian theory in particular, analysis is a kind of mourning-work, a coming to terms with one's ghosts through the transference, an encounter with one's own wound as yawning gap or *béance*, one's own inexhaustible desire, one's own loss and separation from those who are loved.[9] This wound is the Symbolic debt transmitted from parent to child, in a human linkage; and the therapeutic task of the children left behind is to remember, to dig and to fathom, to lay bare the repressed "signified" that subtends the paternal metaphor, to remember the dead (father) by lifting the shroud of forgetfulness, by assuming the "hidden hurt" (of his death, of dismemberment) and by using the hidden hurt to create, to play a role in the human order. But the Symbolic debt is also, paradoxically, the requirement of the burial of the dead—in language, in metaphor—which entails putting the father to rest with due mourning: making sense from loss, metaphorizing the tragedy of human desire.

For Freud, both of these functions—of bringing to light, and of burial or veiling—are seen as components of the artist's labor, the poet's secret: the poet brings to light buried unconscious material, and also manages to veil that material in artistic form.[10] For the writer Colette, this mourning-work entails the remembering of the dismembered father, the amputee, the reassembly of Orpheus (dis-remembered, forgotten by the guilty child and by the jealous mother-spouse); this process entails first discovering the "hidden hurt" in the unfathomable blue-grey gaze, and then assuming that Symbolic debt as the motor of writing, the desire that engenders the writer's "endless variations on a theme." The double

[9]Lacan's notion of *béance* (a yawning gap) is related to this idea of universal wounding, which requires every human subject to pay the Symbolic debt. For a discussion of *béance*, see Wilden, *Speech and Language in Psychoanalysis*, 67–70.

[10]In addition to "Creative Writers and Daydreaming" (1908), Freud discusses this "veiling" in "Delusion and Dream in Jensen's *Gradiva*" (1906), *S.E.* 9, and *The Psychopathology of Everyday Life* (1901), *S.E.* 6.

labor of the daughter, undertaken in the presence of her father's spirit, is at once a labor of great joy and of endless torment, necessary and painful: almost in spite of herself ("and now the thought of my father tortures me") this daughter returns to her father's blank pages, to reopen her father's "case" (the mystery of the paternal demise).

The Symbolic Ghost-Limb

In Colette's daughterly labor of love, it is the specter of her father's hand—disembodied, severed, like the lost limb—that rises before her: "I can always see his white hands, particularly since I've begun to hold my thumb bent out awkwardly, as he did, and found my hands crumpling and rolling and destroying paper, with explosive rage, just as his hands used to do" (*Sido* 177). Like her father before her, Colette is all thumbs before the challenge of the page. And she is haunted by her father's incapacity, because his hidden hurt precedes, reflects, and signifies her own unhealed wound: the desire for Sido, the desire for the father, but above all the obsessive desire to write, undermined by painful incapacity. Moreover, this ghostly thumb—this extra limb which sticks out awkwardly, like the hidden "arm" in the Captain's pocket, the knife that will not wound—is the sign of excessive passion (the useless member is an importune erection of sorts, signifying a compulsive desire). And all these extra limbs recall the third limb in the riddle of the sphinx, solved by Oedipus: the cane that signifies the impotence of advancing age.

Yet another sounding of this layered motif—of the extra limb, impeding the function of the writer-investigator, who seeks to rectify the father's castration—occurs at the opening of "The Captain," significantly just before the passage relating the daughter's meeting with her father's ghost at Madame B's séance. In this passage, Colette relates that she has been stung by an insect toward which she has shown, as usual, too much curiosity, too great a desire to know: "One of my latest imprudences was concerned with the big hymenoptera of blue steel which abounds in Provence from July to August, when the sunflowers are in bloom. Vexed at not knowing the name of this steel-clad warrior, I kept asking myself: 'Has he or has he not got a sting? Is he merely a magnificent but sabreless samurai?'" (*Sido* 193).

It is significant that this passage should serve as an introduction to the séance where the daughter's curiosity will cause her to meet that other sabreless samurai, the ghost of the impotent "knife-man"; for it echoes the question that drives her entire inquest ("has he or has he not got a sting?")—a question that deals not only with the father's hidden wound of impotence, but also with his ability to wound, to enforce his Law, to "castrate" in his turn. In this passage, her search for the hidden nature of the concealed insect repeats her exhuming of the hidden cocoon in the passage analyzed earlier. But this time, her act of uncovering ends not in the death of the exposed creature, but in the chastisement of the too-curious treasure-seeker: "A funny little disfigurement on the middle joint of one of my fingers is proof that the blue warrior is not only superbly armed, but quick on the draw" (192).

The seeker of truth, the modern Pandora, is punished for her curiosity, but she is also rewarded by knowledge ("It is a great relief to have this uncertainty removed"); just as her visit to the séance will remove another uncertainty, concerning her father's view of her work, allowing her to make peace with the paternal ghost. For just as the "sabreless samurai" has proved his ability to deliver a certain sting—fulfilling the role of warrior-enforcer—the paternal ghost will regain his potency through his daughter's work.

This ghost is like Oedipus's father, whose paternal rights are belatedly enforced, from beyond the grave, thanks to the child's detective labor. Still the inspirational legacy of this paternal ghost is not one of power but of desire: for the Symbolic father passes on his own castration, in a wounding that makes his child part of the human community. Similarly, in Colette's passage concerning the winged insect, the wounding suffered by the investigator, even if it satisfies a quotient of the writer's burning need to know, paradoxically results in an awkward incapacity to write—the rising of an importune ghostly limb ("a funny little disfigurement on my middle finger") in a kind of curious "castration" that *adds* an arm that is also a wound. Like Orpheus, the daughter must look; like Oedipus, she must know; like Pandora, she will be stung by too much knowledge.

For in Lacan's Symbolic scenario the only inherited prerogative is the discovery of the inevitability of the Law proclaiming universal dismemberment, the universal experience of desire unfulfilled. It is nonetheless a curious dismemberment, for it enables the child to speak, to create: it is a *stigma* in every sense of the word (wound, pollination, election), conferring the necessity of social interaction. Like the fire that Prometheus steals from the gods, this gift, passed from generation to generation, brings both pain and enrichment.

Like the red ribbon worn in the Captain's lapel—a military "decoration" that both rewards the loss of limb and serves as a reminder of that diminution (187)—the wound of language is at once a red badge of honor, a sign of humanity passed from parent to child, and a scarlet letter, a branding by the Law that provides every child access to the human community. The child's assumption of the Symbolic debt is the assumption of the torment of language as symptom and source of desire, as a tool of memory that delves into the past, yet enables a coming to terms with that past.

Thus the Captain's daughter is a ghostwriter who gives shape to the dead father's desire, even as she repeats his Symbolic gesture, "rolling and discarding" the white page, writing and rewriting. In reenacting her father's desire, "Colette" repays "Gabrielle's" debt, the adult's sight compensating for the child's blindness ("It is never too late, since now I have fathomed what formerly my youth hid from me" 186).

Like the empty volumes, like Lacan's "clue in full view," like the purloined letter, this secret is at first overlooked by those too close to see the wound of burning love, the helplessness of the "born writer" who cannot write. Indeed, the Captain's chilling dedication of so many "virgin pages" to his Sido suggests that she is not only Eurydice but Medusa, the other who inspires and paralyzes. (For Freud of course the Medusa is the emblem of castration fear, as well as the mythic emblem of fetishism.[11]) But if Sido is Medusa to Captain Colette—the monstrous and beautiful creature who freezes, and dazzles—to the father's daughter she has become Muse.

In other words, the story of the Captain's daughter may be read as an oedipal history—with a pre-oedipal Imaginary preface and a

---

[11]See the 1922 article "Medusa's Head," *S.E.* 18.

post-oedipal Symbolic postscript. For whereas the awful paternal glare encountered in childhood seems to be that of a hostile or judgmental rival, the brilliant ghostly gaze encountered at Madame B's séance is benevolent, enjoining the sister-daughter to sign written pages with the paternal name. If this father-daughter story is an oedipal history, then, it is nonetheless a transformation from the standard patriarchal version of psychoanalysis: here the male subject, Oedipus, is haunted by his mythic female doubles—Antigone (sister-daughter to Oedipus) and Electra (the father's daughter)—while Orpheus, the too-curious male poet, is doubled by the meddlesome female Pandora (whose feminine curiosity is both chastened and rewarded). Of all of these mythic female ghosts, perhaps the figure of Antigone is the most appropriate "double" for Colette, since she retains her love for her mother (Jocasta), even while carrying out her father's mission. (Antigone is also of course the most devoted of mythical mourners, a sister who demands the proper burial of her mutilated brother Polynices, with due attention and remembrance.) She is sister and daughter to Oedipus, her father and brother; a companion who guides her father after his blinding, his debilitation, his Symbolic castration. She thus takes on the consequences of her father's act—or, in this case, his inability to act—lending her father her voice, her eyes, her writing hand.

Thanks to Colette-Antigone, the white page ceases to hold the Captain captive, as she fills the page and signs it with a signature shared with the paternal ghost, "decrypting" his message of love and loss. Her paradoxical task is at once a laying bare of the missing limb, a seeing of the invisible clue in full view, and a clothing and compensating for the awkward excessive limb, the excessive desire that both drives and stymies the human subject ("I've begun to hold my thumb bent out awkwardly, as he did" 177). As she tells the story of the mother beloved by them both, she draws on the "spiritual legacy" that is both a wound and a commission. Her writing is "carried like a shining tracery to that triumphant conclusion" (197), as the ghostwriter covers "with large round handwriting the invisible cursive script" that will henceforth be signed "Colette."

4

The Veiled Face of a Woman: Colette's Discursive Sexuality

> The veiled face of a woman, refined, disillusioned, is a
> suitable preface to this book which will treat sadly of
> sensual pleasure.
> —*The Pure and the Impure*

> The consultations and examinations; the anguish of
> answering questions and the delights of having one's
> words interpreted; all the stories told to oneself and to
> others; [these are] the errant fragments of an erotic art
> that is secretly transmitted by the confession and the
> science of sex.
> —Michel Foucault, *The History of Sexuality*

Discursive Sexuality

In the Introduction to the *History of Sexuality*, Michel Foucault refutes the myth of modern sexuality as the object of a post-Victorian repression, maintaining that we moderns have never *stopped* talking about sex: "What is peculiar to modern societies is not that they have consigned sex to a shadow existence, but that they have dedicated themselves to speaking of it ad infinitum, while exploiting it as *the* secret."[1] Such a statement could serve as an introduction to Colette's most puzzling work, *The Pure and the Impure* (1941; first published as *Ces Plaisirs . . .* in 1932), which consigns sex to a shadow existence, even while promising an exposé of its veiled mysteries.[2]

In this enigmatic text, the riddle of sexuality is a modern construct, at least according to Foucault's definition. For Foucault has brilliantly exposed modern sexuality as an effect of discourse, a

---

[1]Michel Foucault, *The History of Sexuality: Vol. I: An Introduction*, trans. Robert Hurley (New York: Vintage–Random House, 1980), 35.

[2]Colette, *The Pure and the Impure*, trans. Herma Briffault (New York: Farrar, Straus, and Giroux, 1966, 1980), 25. Hereafter *PI*.

corollary of the pleasure of analysis, incited by that most fundamental of passions, the will to know: in our modern *scientia sexualis* (Foucault's term), the pleasure of uncovering and looking is
itself an erotic act. Freud and Foucault might concur, then, that
the thirst for knowledge that characterizes Oedipus, the detective
urge to solve all riddles, is a kind of voyeurism; we might even
say that the contemporary expert sexologist (as media star) is the
modern sphinx, the holder of answers who questions the questioner, as we all look on. Yet discursive sexuality is a paradox that
at once veils and reveals what it discusses, making of sex an open
secret, enveloping sexuality without hiding it.

Discursive sexuality works neither to put questions to rest nor
to liberate repressed concerns; rather, it generates new questions:
in Lacan's terms, *scientia sexualis* might be considered a
metonymic function, where an endless chain of meanings may
only give rise to new questions, in a desiring chain. Indeed,
Foucault points to psychoanalysis itself as a prime example of a
"sexual science" in which desire is actually engendered by the
incitement of discourse. And since Foucault argues that *scientia
sexualis* is always based on a power relation—a function of the
power of the interrogator and the relatively powerless position of
the object—he does not find it surprising that the modern discursive science of psychoanalysis, with its patriarchal bias, should
have chosen the "dark Continent" of female sexuality as a favorite
object for exploration and colonization.[3] From Dora to the objects
of the Hite report, woman continues to be the object of a psychoanalytic discourse that incites erotic pleasure: like a veil, this discourse adheres to biological sex, concealing and enhancing the
facts of life; embroidering upon these facts, it transforms sex into
sexuality.

Of course, Foucault is only one of many proponents of contem-

---

[3]Of course in Foucault's view, all relations are power relations, and discourse
about sexual matters is part of a power dynamic in our society. Indeed, he argues
that in modern society, the power to interrogate, to penetrate the mystery as confessor or analyst—rather than the power to repress or silence discourse about
sex—has become a coveted social prerogative. Thus as Foucault notes, the objects
of this endless sexual interrogation have often been marginal and relatively powerless elements of society (women, children, deviants) who as objects of sexology
have been invested with a kind of hypersexuality by the prurient activity of looking itself.

porary French theory who have examined sexuality as an effect of discourse: the discourse about sex has proliferated into a discourse about this discourse, adding another fold to the veil of discursive sexuality. Perhaps the most interesting wrinkle in all these veiled discourses is provided by Lacan and by the post-Lacanian "French feminists."[4] For Lacan, discursive sexuality is more than a manifestation of the will to know; it is the grounding of knowledge itself, determining the structure of the Symbolic; even the unconscious "is structured like a language," around the gap of sexual difference. Language *is* sexual and sexuality is linguistic, since the access to social intercourse (the entry into the Symbolic order) coincides with the acquisition of language and is enabled by the experience of sexualized difference as desire.

For Lacan as for Freud, woman—the object of desire—remains an object of curiosity and investigation; indeed in Lacan's late seminars woman is a mysterious veiled figure, an absence (Lacan casts woman as the veiled or absent phallus, the ultimate sign of desire, the veiled threat of castration).[5] And as is apparent to anyone who has grappled with Lacan's hermetic prose, the Lacanian text could itself serve as an example of discursive sexuality, a strip-tease that hides as much as it reveals in its undulating folds. In Lacan's erotic text, the Freudian "virile" will to uncover is accompanied by a "feminine" coquetry, which both invites and eludes analysis.[6]

[4]The term is from Elaine Marks and Isabelle de Courtivron, *New French Feminisms* (New York: Schocken Books, 1981).

[5]I am referring of course to Lacan's infamous statement (in Seminar XX, 1972–73, *Encore*) that "woman does not exist" (*"la femme n'existe pas"*), with the word "woman" written under erasure, barred. This itself is a hermetic veiled statement, like so many of Lacan's oracular pronouncements, and has been interpreted either as the height of phallocentrism or as an indictment of the patriarchal ideal of femininity. For a feminist reading of Lacan, see the two introductions by Juliet Mitchell and Jacqueline Rose to their edition of Lacan's writings about feminine sexuality (*Feminine Sexuality: Jacques Lacan and the Ecole freudienne* [New York: W. W. Norton, 1982]). Lacan's own statements about woman as veiled phallus, and about the mythical status of The Woman, are translated as chapters 6 and 7 of *Feminine Sexuality*.

[6]For Freud's treatment of the "masculine" nature of the active urge to look, coupled with the "passive" or even "masochistic" exhibitionism of the female, see his essay "The Economic Problem of Masochism" (1924), *S.E.* 19: 157. Freud briefly alludes to the same question in *Jokes and Their Relation to the Unconscious, S.E.* 8: 98.

Lacanian feminists have been trying for some time to reappropriate the question of *scientia sexualis* (What does woman want?), reclaiming the right to pose the question from the position of subject (What do I want? What is my version of Oedipus?).[7] This French feminist politics of *jouissance* has rejected a simple equation of discourse with sexuality, and of sexuality with masculine sexuality, by rephrasing the central question of *scientia sexualis*; these theorists point out that merely asking what woman (as object of investigation) "wants" is too often a veiled allusion to castration, complicit with the notion that woman *is* wanting, that she *is* lack (as implied by the French *"Qu'est-ce qui* manque *à la femme?"*). In other words, the effort to resexualize discourse in woman's image is an attempt to counter the patriarchal version of *scientia sexualis*, which objectifies woman and denies or defers her pleasure.[8]

Long before Lacan, Foucault, and the French feminists, Colette was grappling with the question of female sexuality and its veiled relation to discourse. Colette's own discourse about sexuality in *The Pure and the Impure*—part journalistic essay, part confessional novel—represents one artist's approach to these veiled mysteries, combining a *scientia sexualis* with an *ars erotica*. And hers is a curi-

[7]This is the emphasis of work by Shoshana Felman, Jane Gallop, Luce Irigaray, Naomi Schor, Barbara Johnson, and others. See, for instance, the essays in *The (M)other Tongue*, ed. Shirley Nelson Garner, Claire Kahane, and Madelon Sprengnether. Moreover many of these "new feminisms" based on the experience of feminine pleasure (termed *jouissance* by the French theorists) have reinvented the relation between sexuality and discourse, by seeking to create a radically "other" non-discursive expression, characteristic of feminine sexuality.

[8]The problem with some of these efforts, however, is that they tend to replace the phallocentric version of pleasure with a regressive ideal of narcissistic pleasure, associated with the maternal body as plenitude. As Julia Kristeva argues, for instance, by sidestepping discourse with all of its patriarchal prejudices one also runs the risk of stepping out of social interaction, agency, history—all effects of the social pact that the Symbolic (as language) signifies, seals, enables. In *About Chinese Women*, Kristeva writes: "Let us know that an ostensibly masculine, paternal identification, because it supports symbol and time, is necessary in order to have a voice in the chapter of politics and history" (quoted from *The Kristeva Reader*, ed. Toril Moi [New York: Columbia University Press, 1986], 156). In the same spirit, more recent French feminist thought—particularly the work of Sarah Kofman, Michèle Montrelay, and Janine Chasseguet-Smirgel—takes a second look at the Symbolic, with an eye to revising the old oedipal scenario, accounting for a specifically female subjectivity/sexuality with reference to a specifically feminine pleasure, without doing away with the notion of the Symbolic altogether.

ously androgynous eye, reflecting the duplicity of the human "I," which as Freud tells us, doubles the urge to secrecy with the urge to expose.

Ars erotica: Colette's Veiled Investigation

> It is the sane eye that changes, is affected, becomes
> fascinated with the mystery it has seen and can never
> cease to question.
> —*The Pure and the Impure*

Written under the sign of the veil ("the veiled face of a woman [. . .] is a suitable preface to this book which will treat sadly of sensual pleasure" 25), *The Pure and the Impure* is an enigma; its very title links two opposites by the ambiguous "and," performing a kind of "now-you-see-it/now-you-don't" dance between the ineffable concepts of "pure" and "impure." And this titular dance is already an allusion, a second version, layered onto the original title, *Ces Plaisirs . . .* , with its provocative ellipsis, a tantalizing come-on, an invitation to open the book, to turn the page, to lift the veil. If we follow Colette's lead into the labyrinth of sexuality, miming her attempt to gaze at the face of woman unveiled, we discover a face that is perhaps the writer's own. For this text may be read as Colette's quest for a certain truth (rather than a search for facts), the "truth" that subtends the pose of her objective reporting. The text casts its author as the *new* Oedipus of *scientia sexualis*, asking the feminized riddle of humanity—not "What is man?" but "What do I, a woman, want?"

In the earlier fictional autobiographies, Colette has already revealed her passionate need to lift the veil, whatever the cost to the object. A similar impulse seems to motivate the loosely connected vignettes of *The Pure and the Impure*, where the author herself recounts her experiences in the sexual underworld of turn-of-the-century Paris, exposing secrets to a public of avid onlookers. This chronicle is ostensibly a true account, backed by the authenticity of the first-person pronoun; indeed, nothing appears more transparent than the narrator's identity in this work, since she is repeatedly called "Mme Colette." Hence this apparently autobiographical account raises expectations of a salacious and candid memoir.

Still this is a curious true story, where the identities of some, including the author-journalist herself, are revealed, while other characters are renamed, ostensibly to protect their identity (in oblique references such as: "let us call her Justine, for that was absolutely not her name" 90). And others are designated by mysterious codes ("Amalia X"; "My friend X, a celebrity") that sometimes contain clues to the real identity of the character, in the manner of a *roman à clef* ("La Chevalière" is the thinly veiled allusion to La Marquise de Belboeuf, Colette's own lesbian lover; the male seducer who is the subject of an entire chapter has been christened "Damien," "a name which recalls his true name, a rather old-fashioned one" 42). Others are identified by first name only ("Charlotte"), or are veiled by pen name ("Renée Vivien"). Even when an identity is no secret, eponyms are deployed as an ornamental overlay, as in the appellation "The Ladies of Llangollen," cited in English in the original, retaining the decorative alliteration. Thanks to the veils in this erotic chronicle, the real or fictional status of its characters is undecidable.

And even if the dominant impression is that of a true account, Colette herself veils this appearance by acceding to the editor's wish to label the work a novel. (Colette wrote to a friend: "*Unfortunately* the publisher will write on the title page 'A Novel.' But it will not be a novel" *EP* xviii.) The fictional veneer may be invoked in the interests of discretion—these murky half-truths are sometimes sordid—but the veil of fiction might also be just another tantalizing device, adding to the air of mystery that surrounds these sexual intrigues. For this is a shadow world.

These tales visit the smoky realm of opium dens, the curtained caves of harem girls turned fortune-tellers, the dark banquets of the alcoholic lesbian poet Renée Vivien (whose decadence recalls the excesses of a Huysmans or a Baudelaire). The writer relates the confessions of transvestites of both sexes, explores the uncanny bond of two jealous women, comments on the art of dissimulation practiced by male homosexuals, shares the confessions of a compulsive seducer, relates the strange tale of two eighteenth-century aristocratic lesbians. In each of these exotic episodes, the narrator herself is Scheherazade, raconteur, voyeur, and guide, a veiled odalisque who lures the reader into a dance of appearance and reality in these murky realms of "impure" sexual practice. Since Colette herself is the storyteller at the center of these episodes, her own veiled face is in a sense the subject of her *"Mille et une nuits"* (the French translation of *Arabian Nights*.) And her primary themes—the veil, the occult, androgynous sexuality—may serve as metaphors for writing itself, as a paradox that cloaks and reveals, costumes and lays bare.

For nothing is what it seems in this hazy *ars erotica*, which opens in the half-light of an opium haunt, where the fragrant smoke creates an atmosphere as indeterminate as it is luxuriant. Colette sets the stage for her *Arabian Nights* with a banquet of images, sumptuous and ghostly:

> I settled down on the mat allotted to me and watched the opium smoke wastefully and sluggishly streaming upward to collide, as if regretfully, with the glass panes of the skylight. Its black, appetizing aroma of fresh truffles or burnt cocoa bestowed upon me patience, optimism, and a vague hunger. I decided I liked the dull red glow of the shaded lights, the almond-shaped white flames of the opium lamps, one of them nearby, the other two flickering like will-o'-the-wisps farther on, in a kind of alcove under the balustraded balcony. (4)

In this environment of half-drawn shades, curtained alcoves, flickering lights, and "vague hunger," the basic facts of identity are obscured: the revelers are floating specters of indeterminate sex: "Someone leaned over that balustrade, a youthful head caught the red ray of the hanging lanterns . . . a loose white sleeve wavered and disappeared before I could make out whether the white silk sleeve and the head of hair slicked down like the hair of a drowned person belonged to a woman or a man" (4).

The lure of this episode consists in great measure in the use of the first-person pronoun, the confession of "Mme Colette's" own association with the shady goings-on. Still this confessional stance veils more than it reveals, as the accoutrement of a persistent coquetry that plays against the writer's objective investigative pose, adopted at the outset ("I shook hands with an acquaintance, like me a novelist and a journalist, and I exchanged nods with my unknown hosts, who, thank God, seemed to be as little inclined as I was for any friendlier exchange" 4).

The cool, "masculine" inquisitioner/journalist is shadowed by her own "feminine" ghost, who speaks in a second style—richly allusive, decorative, flirtatious. An almost coy quality sometimes colors the narrator's observations; there is a certain preciosity in speaking of sex as *ces plaisirs*, obliquely, in the most delicately allusive of terms. Of course such delicacy is more than an effect of modesty or even good taste: it seems to be an artifice, adding a layer of intrigue, calling on the reader to guess and to invent, at precisely the moment when a salacious revelation seems to be forthcoming.

Renée Vivien: The Lure of the Non-dit

This seems to be the case, for instance, in the vignette about the poet Renée Vivien, which relates Colette's shocked reaction to her friend's use of an obscenity to designate a fellow poet (whom she calls a "cunt with a pen" *PI* 87). In the original French the offending term is represented only elliptically, giving a peek at the veiled obscenity (*"Ce B . . . C'est un c . . . à plume"*), calling the reader into the play of hide-and-seek.[9] The textual play replicates Renée's own curious game of now-you-see-me/now-you-don't: this consummate role-player conceals the secret of her alcoholism, even while she compulsively displays her lesbianism. Thus when Colette upbraids the poet for being overly explicit, the subject is the details of her sex life: "And when, beyond the poet who praised the pallor of her Lesbian loves, their sobbing in the desolate dawns, I caught a glimpse of 'Madame How-many-times,' counting on her fingers, mentioning by name things and gestures, I put an end to the indiscretion of those young half-conscious lips, and not very tactfully" (93).

What shocks Mme Colette here is not her friend's lesbianism, but the blatant statement of her sexuality; obscenity resides not in deed but in word, in the too-direct discourse that calls things by their proper names, a sin that, as we have seen, Colette herself is loathe to commit.[10] For she feels that this kind of directness—

[9]*Le Pur et l'impur* (Paris: Hachette, 1979), 70.

[10]This reluctance concerning the use of proper names goes back to the struggle over language as "plaything," described in "The Priest on the Wall" (*My Mother's House*), in which Sido scolds Gabrielle for inventing imaginary definitions of the word "presbytery" and firmly commands her to "call things by their proper names." But Gabrielle simply makes use of the word to fashion a new game.

counting orgasms and calling things by name—is especially
shocking in a poet, whose craft resides in dissimulation and embellishment. It is Scheherazade's poetic task to re-veil what has
been too abruptly revealed, to reendow Renée with seductive
mystery.

And so Colette recreates the uncanny aura of lurid exoticism
surrounding Renée, an ambiance that both attracts and repels
her, in terms reminiscent of the earlier opium-den scene: "Nothing could dispel the uneasiness engendered by the strangeness of
the place, bound to astonish a guest, the semi-darkness, the exotic foods on plates of jade, vermeil, or Chinese porcelain, foods
that had come from countries too far away" (83). An eerie quality
pervades Colette's reminiscences of the doomed poet, an ethereal
being who "abstains totally from food" (83) and whose milieu is
shrouded in mystery:

> Except for some gigantic Buddhas, all the furnishings moved
> mysteriously: after provoking surprise and admiration for a time,
> they had a way of disappearing . . .
>
> Among the unstable marvels, Renée wandered, not so much
> clad as veiled in black or purple, almost invisible in the scented
> darkness of the immense rooms barricaded with leaded win-
> dows, the air heavy with curtains and incense. (81)

Renée herself is as changeable and ineffable as her surroundings;
"veiled" and "invisible," lacking substance, she glides around a
scene worthy of Poe. Her costume is a series of layers to be shed
at will: "She was constantly giving things away: the bracelets on
her arms opened up, the necklace slipped from her martyr's
throat. She was as if deciduous. Her languorous body rejected
anything that would give it a third dimension" (82). In an equally
evocative passage, Colette recalls the toxic quality of Renée's dwelling, which seems menacing, without exit: "[The air], like stagnant
water, slowed down my steps, the odor of incense, of flowers, or
overripe apples [. . .] I was nauseated by the funereal perfumes
and tried to open the window: it was nailed shut" (84).

After steeping the reader in this weird luxury, the narrator
switches positions abruptly, standing back to take a writer's stance,
to observe her work, taking inventory of the opulent images at
her disposal: "What a contribution such a detail is, what a flourish

it adds to a theme already rich! What a quantity of lurid gleams and glints of gold in the semi-darkness, of whispering voices behind the doors, of Chinese masks, of ancient instruments hanging on the walls, mute, only vaguely whimpering at the banging of a door beneath my heavy hand" (85). In this wondrous passage, Colette intertwines all the themes associated with the doomed poet (who was to die of her addiction at the age of thirty): the creaking doors and the obscurity evoke a haunted house, the nailed window suggests the inevitability of the tomb, the lavish surroundings evoke Renée's own lurid sensuality, her masochistic relation with the "ghoul" who is her "master" (the tyrannical but unseen lesbian lover to whom Renée often alludes).

Moreover, Colette's own stance in this passage—which shifts between those of involved actor and of detached artist—evokes a larger issue: the "autobiographical" writer's doubled position as observer and as observed. Here at least Colette suggests that there is no such thing as a disinterested stance; like Oedipus in search of truth, the observer runs the risk of being contaminated by the information that is uncovered, just as the voyeur is always contaminated by the object of "his" gaze: "The wily lunatic is lost if through the narrowest crack he allows a sane eye to peer into his locked universe and thus profane it. Afterwards, it is the sane eye that changes, is affected, becomes fascinated with the mystery it has seen and can never cease to question" (87). Colette even likens this addiction to knowledge to the "habit" of orgasm; both are compulsive flirtations with the abyss:

The habit of obtaining sexual satisfaction is less tyrannical than the tobacco habit, but it gains on one. O voluptuous pleasure, O lascivious ram, cracking your skull against all obstacles, time and again! Perhaps the only misplaced curiosity is that which persists in trying to find out here, on this side of death, what lies beyond the grave . . . Voluptuaries, consumed by their senses, always begin by flinging themselves with a great display of frenzy into an abyss. But they survive, they come to the surface again [. . .] It is possible that this young woman poet, who rejected the laws of ordinary love, led a sensible enough life until her personal abyss at half past eight in the evening. An abyss she imagined? Ghouls are rare. (97)

These remarks, which conclude the chapter on Renée Vivien—
remarks concerning the poet's "abyss," her passion, addiction,
and death—are about fiction, about veiling. For they cast doubt
on Renée's claim of being enslaved by a sadistic mistress (the absent "ghoul" who she claims drives her to a frenzy) and leave
us wondering what is real and what is invented—just as Colette's
autobiographical writing does. Renée is the only one who knows
the truth of her private abyss, and her face remains veiled by the
ultimate mystery of death ("She carried off more than one secret
beneath her purple veil" 97). The search for mysteries beyond this
life, Colette reminds her reader, is one addiction that must remain
unsatisfied: "The only misplaced curiosity is that which persists in
trying to find out here, on this side of death, what lies beyond the
grave" (97). But of course this is the very addiction—the desire to
peer over the edge of the grave, to rouse her veiled specters—to
which the writer herself falls prey.

Diaphanies: Veiled Allusion

Although Colette's text deals with one sordid erotic situation
after another, her writing employs only the most delicately allusive expression, preferring the veil of style to direct appellation.
And in this text, the technique of veiling is perhaps not so much a
question of sensibility as it is a love of elaboration, a taste for the
sheer sumptuousness of language. Colette writes (in *My Mother's
House*) that even the sound of her childhood nickname—"Bel-
Gazou"—is a magical veil of sorts, everyday and exotic, transparent and opaque: "Whence comes the name and why did my father call me by it, long ago?" (30). For this ornament is a name
that "would not disgrace the hero or the heroine of a Persian fairy
tale"; like Aladdin's lamp, the magical sonorities of "Bel-Gazou"
contain a writer's *génie* that waits to be let loose.[11]

In *The Pure and the Impure*, Colette gives full play to this inventiveness, the flair for disguise that Freud calls *Ankleidung*, the
cloak of literary style. Witness, for example, this oblique reference

[11]This is a passion of long standing: we are reminded not only of the child Gabrielle's inventive play with the word "presbytery," but also of the writer's confessed
penchant for lyricism ("too many adjectives, as usual!" *Sido* 176).

to the female genitals and to the sex act, veiled in the superimposed image of a sea cavern and a beating heart: "[Charlotte] also
barred me from the cavern of odors, colors, the secret refuge
where surely frolicked a powerful arabesque of flesh, a cipher of
limbs entwined, symbolic monogram of the Inexorable" (24).

The veiled Charlotte of the opening opium-parlor scene—like
the spooky poet Renée Vivien—is an enigmatic mystery woman,
who hides her secrets from the inquisitive eye of the narrator; but
her person has more of the sea nymph than the night creature;
the web of sea images that surrounds her is like a net in which
the creature of the deep is both veiled and snared. Indeed Colette
tells us that the clouding of Charlotte's aquamarine eyes ("like the
pools the sea leaves at ebb-tide" 13), like the sea-green veil she
pulls over her face, acts as a screen that forbids her interlocutor to
fathom her mystery. In a related image, Colette likens the encounter with the beloved's gaze to a voyage into the sea: "What
more seductive depths could one plunge into than the eyes of a
loved one, and descend in thought and blissfully lose one's life
between the seaweed and the star?" (76). Between the seaweed
and the star, the heavens and the deep, the realm of the mermaid
and of the spirit—this stunning image might serve as an emblem
of femininity throughout Colette's work, from the angelic maternal star, which shines chaste and disembodied, to the explorations of the deep associated with female sexuality. In this *ars erotica*, Charlotte's is the veiled face of the siren, Renée's the veiled
face of the ghost; one belongs to the marine depths, the other to
the ethereal "beyond."

The complexity of this thematic web suggests that the veil is
much more than a technique of Colette's writing: it functions as
the central metaphor of her text, an image that generates an entire
thematic network, unfolding into the components of the text (dissimulation, play-acting, seduction, narcissism, adornment, fetish)
and even serving as backdrop for the narrative itself (the curtained alcoves of the opium den; the salon of Renée Vivien,
where the shades are drawn; the draped fortune-teller's parlor
where Amalia X looks into a clouded crystal ball; the layers of lace
that cloak the male transvestites; the love-nest of the Ladies of
Llangollen, hidden from society's inquisitive gaze). Thus the veil
functions as an allegory of sorts—as de Man and other poststruc-

turalists have defined the term[12]—that is, as an object-metaphor that is also a multilayered structure, enfolding and generating the text, a working model for the unfolding narrative itself.

Even the title of this not-quite-fictional book is a veil, an enigmatic allusion to a concept ("purity") that appears transparent but is anything but crystal clear. In 1935, when the writer renames her work—changing the title *Ces Plaisirs . . .* to *Le Pur et l'impur*—she claims to be clearing things up, to be giving a sharper focus and less ambiguity to the title, citing on the one hand a "certain antipathy for suspension points, bordering an unfinished title" and on the other hand "an intense taste for crystalline sonorities." But what in fact has been "cleared up" by this "crystalline" choice? The new title's "and" even seems to layer on a veil of sorts, separating the pure from the impure, rather than joining them; or perhaps suggesting that these are two communicating concepts, two sides of one curtained recess. In any case, the "crystal sonorities" of the new title deepen the mystery—like the transparent but occult crystal ball of a seer—since the author pointedly declines to qualify any of the actions she describes as either pure or impure, refusing to pass judgment on her characters, even admitting that "the word 'pure' has never revealed an intelligible meaning to me" (175). In choosing a new title, then, perhaps Colette has merely added another drape to this body of essays; indeed her choice of title seems simply to be an instance of what Freud calls forepleasure, sheer ornament, a lure to the reader's attention.[13]

The last passage of the work, a reflection on the word *pur*, makes "clear" the seductive aesthetic function of the veil of language, which enfolds many meanings in its resonances, inciting an optical thirst:

> As that word "pure" fell from her lips, I heard the trembling of the plaintive "u", the icy limpidity of the "r", and the sound aroused nothing in me but the need to hear again its unique

[12]Paul de Man, "The Rhetoric of Temporality," *Blindness and Insight: Essays in the Rhetoric of Contemporary Criticism* (New York and London: Oxford University Press, 1971).

[13]Freud discusses the notion of aesthetic forepleasure in *Jokes and Their Relation to the Unconscious*, 136–37.

resonance, its echo of a drop that trickles out, breaks off, and falls somewhere with a plash. The word "pure" has never revealed an intelligible meaning to me. I can only use the word to quench an optical thirst for purity in the transparencies that evoke it—in bubbles, in a volume of water, and in the imaginary latitudes entrenched, beyond reach, at the very center of a dense crystal. (174–75)

The visual resonances of this final passage "crystallize" an obsession—the desire to *see* what is heard, a desire to follow the siren's call, the impossible desire of Orpheus for Eurydice, which is both visual and auditory. This same desire is expressed earlier in another exotic fable—from the *The Tendrils of the Vine* (1908)— which describes a singing nightingale as the object of intensely erotic visual desire: "He varied his theme, embellishing it with vocalizations, became infatuated with his voice, became that wildly passionate and palpitating songster that one listens to with the unbearable longing to *see* him sing" (*EP* 136). *The Pure and the Impure* is such a song, an "embellishment" on the theme of optical thirst, but one in which the voyeur herself is *also* the "passionate and palpitating songster" who arouses her reader's longing.

Indeed, the deceptively simple query at the heart of the work— what does woman want—makes woman an object of scrutiny, like the word *pur* itself, an enigma at the center "of a very dense crystal," unreachable, indecipherable. Even the most transparent exposure of "Colette" herself is not what it seems; the siren is hidden in the "crystal bubbles" of her limpid work; a *génie* bottled in her own odyssey of a thousand and one nights.

The Female Genius

> When I think of Charlotte, I embark upon a drifting
> souvenir of nights graced neither by sleep
> nor by certitude.
> —*The Pure and the Impure*

Thus *The Pure and the Impure* is an investigation, but it is an inquiry without answers, which performs an almost cubist exploration of its various objects and their relation—sexuality, perversion, femininity—taking them apart (woman, sex, woman as sex, sex as woman) and looking at the fragments from many angles. Like the modernist project, this act of disassembly and analysis does not yield a clear vision, but rather leads the reader into a hall of mirrors: it is an apparently random selection of case studies pieced together by reflection or association, in which one word (such as "veil") is enough to spin off another tale, from this "spinster" who writes without married name. In these stories, Scheherazade herself remains in the shadows, like a good analyst, encouraging others to reveal themselves, drawing from conversations, from diaries, from interviews, from rumor—and in the process effacing her own narrating persona, taking her place among a throng of shadowy figures. And if these tales owe something to the tradition of the *moralistes*, they nonetheless remain modern fables without moral, fables that are *immoralistes* in Gide's sense of the term. The most able of clairvoyants cannot see clearly in Colette's crystalline text, where the meaning of its objects (woman/ sex/purity/impurity) lies obscured.

Still the work begins like a detective novel, its door opening on a drug den, luxuriously "draped with Chinese embroideries." This narrator is a Mata Hari of sorts, working undercover, slipping in and out of the shadowy underworld to see what she can see, a private eye trying to ferret out the secret of Charlotte (as Everywoman), to discover what "makes her sing." In the opening scene, the narrating "I" claims to be visiting the opium den to do research for a book (which in a typically modern *mise-en-abîme* seems to be the one we are reading); in fact, she insists on her professional objectivity ("you're here as a sightseer?" "no, on a professional assignment"). Yet it is the sights that attract her, appealing to her optical thirst ("I decided I liked the dull-red glow of the shaded lamps"). And when the first mysterious, androgynous apparition floats by, draped in white, disappearing before the observer can tell whether "the head of hair slicked down like the hair of a drowned person" belongs "to a woman or a man," the investigator *declines* to investigate. Now you see him/her, now you don't. Colette's professionalism reports all, but decides nothing, encasing her subjects in a "dense crystal," a fishbowl whose transparency is illusory.

Thus in a sense Colette's work is what the French call *une his-*

toire de femmes, and Colette herself is *une femme à histoires* (a busy-body, a meddlesome female) since she is a teller of tales steeped in intrigue. But "Colette's" first encounter in this plot, with "Charlotte"—a woman of her own age and whose name mirrors her own (with the word "harlot" reflected in its depths)—is not merely the encounter of the investigative reporter with a recalcitrant interviewee. This conversation is also an interior monologue, containing more than one clue to something the narrator is hiding about herself: "I had brought with me only a well-concealed grief which gave me no rest and a frightful passivity of the senses" (5). Behind Charlotte's veiled face—the "veiled face of a woman" that haunts these tales—we may catch a glimpse of the inscrutable author herself. Enigmatic as the sphinx she resembles (how often Colette reminds us of her "cat-like face"), Colette/Charlotte is a sibyl who stages an always partial unveiling.

Charlotte: The Nightingale

> She fastened her coat collar unhurriedly and carefully
> at her round throat, the refuge of that deceptive
> warbling [. . .] as she pulled down a fine veil
> over her face.
> —*The Pure and the Impure*

In the suggestive fable of the beautiful Charlotte, we witness a tryst between the *femme fatale* and her much younger lover (and this lad, significantly, turns out to be none other than the spooky white-clad Pierrot of uncertain sex, "with slicked-back hair like a drowned person," who is the first fleeting figure we catch sight of in the opium salon). Charlotte and her lover retire to a curtained alcove, where Charlotte begins to sing, in "a furry, sweet, yet husky voice that had the qualities of a hard and thick-skinned velvety peach" (6), a siren's call that paralyzes its listeners with pleasure ("We were all so charmed that we took care not to applaud or even to murmur our praise" 6). But Charlotte is abruptly silenced by her boy-lover, who reminds her crudely that "she has not come to sing." He goes on to provoke Charlotte into a very vocal orgasm, a rhapsody of sorts, in a display that makes voyeurs of everyone in the salon: "But from the depths of this very silence a sound imperceptibly began in a woman's throat, at first husky, then clear, asserting its firmness and amplitude as it was repeated, becoming clear and firm like the notes the nightingale repeats and accumulates until they pour out in a flood of arpeggios" (9). This is a hypnotic passage, where the notes of the nightingale mimic the crescendo of orgasm, and where Charlotte is the entertainer who lures the narrator into a kind of mimetic participation in the erotic cadence: "Up there in the balcony a woman was trying to delay her pleasure and in doing so was hurrying it toward its climax and destruction, in a rhythm at first so calm and harmonious, so marked that I involuntarily beat time with my head, for its cadence was as perfect as its melody" (9).

This erotic concert ends "with a subdued sob." After this public "destruction," Charlotte falls silent. Later, she shares a ride home with Mme Colette, who wryly teases her about her public display, with a kind of voyeuristic pleasure. Charlotte confides that her young lover—the ghostly "drowned person" of the first passage—is in fact deathly ill, and worries that sensual pleasure may hasten *his* "destruction." But later, when Colette meets Charlotte again in the dark opium haunt, Charlotte confesses—in response to discreet but probing questions—that she has faked her orgasm, *staged* her public pleasure, in order to reward her young lover for following doctor's orders ("But don't you agree that when he's been good for a fortnight, taken his pills, eaten his red meat, slept as he should with his windows wide open, he deserves a recompense now and then?" 13).

Colette presses her about her lack of sexual satisfaction—in a veiled allusion—asking if she has really tried to solve her sexual incompatibility with her young lover: "And the thing you lack . . . ," she asks delicately, "is it really beyond reach?" (23). In yet another surprise revelation, Charlotte confesses that she could attain "what she lacks" with her lover, but abstains because she cannot bear the thought of losing control. In a passage of titillating voyeurism, Colette imagines what Charlotte would look like having an orgasm, and even suggests that her own question has provoked something like this response: "In agitation she turned her head from side to side on the white cushion, her lips parted, like a woman threatened by a paroxysm of pleasure. Two points of red light attached themselves to the back-and-forth movement of her big, glistening gray eyes, and it was not hard to imagine that, were she to stop lying, Charlotte merely risked becoming more beautiful" (24).

In this voyeuristic fantasy, we find a resonance of the optical thirst that spawns these tales, and all of Colette's work. For Charlotte, the "nightingale" who sings so beautifully, inspires the very same desire as the real nightingale in the earlier fable of *The Tendrils of the Vine*, whose passionate vocalizations kindle the "unbearable desire to *see* him sing" (*EP* 136). Indeed the earlier fable describes the nightingale's "passion," perceived by the voyeur when he "did not know he was being spied upon," in terms remarkably like that of Charlotte's fantasized orgasm, suggesting the profoundly erotic nature of the writer's spying, "optical thirst": "He interrupts himself at times, his head inclined, as if listening within himself to the prolongation of a note that has died down . . . Then, swelling his throat, he takes up his song again with all his might, his head thrown back, the picture of amorous despair" (*EP* 136).

The second nightingale, Charlotte, is as resistant to spying as is the first: Charlotte's discomfiture at the writer's suggestion—that she only "risked being more beautiful" by letting herself go—is a sign that the investigation has gone too far, that the prurient will to know has distanced its object. Charlotte falls silent, grows cold, and drawing a sea-green veil over her face, disappears into the night, retaining her mystery ("How many shadows still obscure her . . . it is not for me to dispel them" 25). This episode is a first warning, a sign of the spy's inevitable failure to learn all that she wants to know, because (as with Orpheus) her desire to see destroys what it covets.

Charlotte's tale is a reflection on the poetics of veiling, of mysteries that remain unsolved. It is also a tribute to the art of dissimulation, which Colette calls "female genius," deploying the multiple resonances of the French *génie* (as spirit/genius/inventor/ muse): "This substantial Charlotte was a female genius, indulging in tender subterfuge, consideration, and self-denial" (18). Hers is the "perfect dupery of the woman who thus subtly contrived to give a weak and sensitive boy the very highest concept of himself that a man can have" (18).

Charlotte's artful gift to her dying lover is the mirage of himself as the donor of pleasure. Self-denial is no small portion of this genius; yet as in all masochistic acts, there is a large quotient of sadism, the need to master the master. The narrator suggests that the despotic senses are the sultan that this wily harem girl out-wits, as she refuses to submit: "O intractable, lordly senses, as intractable and ignorant as the princes of bygone days who learned only what was indispensable: to dissimulate, to hate, to command! Yet it is you that Charlotte held in check, couched be-neath the quiet night soothed by opium" (24–25). The female gen-ius plays the human pleasure-game extremely well, and seems unable to lose: her most precious gift is the ability to generate fantasy for all those who witness her faked destruction. These voyeurs, the narrator among them, are held rapt, taken in by the art of the "victim."

What is the effect of this revelation of Charlotte's game on the narrator herself? She *boasts* about having found out Charlotte's secret, even while she herself has succeeded in hiding the inti-mate details of her own life from "this stranger to whom I told nothing, as though I had finished telling her all I had to tell" (18). But the optative mode in this phrase—the wistful "as though"— almost seems to harbor a longing for confession, a need to finish what she has begun, stifled by an imposed silence. (A similar longing to confess is awakened by the sight of the rhapsodic nightingale in the moonlight, in the passage from *The Tendrils of the Vine* that is the double of Charlotte's tale. For no sooner is this yearning to confess aroused than it is stifled: "I want to tell, tell, tell everything I know, all my thoughts, all my surmises, every-thing that enchants or hurts or astounds me; but always, toward the dawn of this resonant night, a wise cool hand is laid across my mouth" *EP* 137.) Thus Mme Colette, the cool master-sleuth, does not escape the evocative power of the female genius on whom she spies. For here it is *Charlotte* who plays the role of the Salome/Scheherazade, spinning tales that arouse the guilty imag-ination of her audience; it is she who turns the tables on her in-quisitor, becoming the analyst who awakens unsuspected ghosts, conjuring up the listener's own past, summoning sirens drowned in the unconscious: "Her presence lured other ephemera from the depths of my memory, phantoms I seem always to be losing and finding again, restless ghosts unrecovered from wounds sustained in the past when they crashed headlong or sidelong against that barrier reef, mysterious and incomprehensible, the human body" (18).

Here Charlotte is medium and therapist, luring those ghosts who inhabit her interlocutor's most secret recesses ("They recognized Charlotte, for they had, like her, not talked except in safety, that is, to strangers, in the presence of strangers" 19).[14] And there are indications that the revelations that surface are not simply the ghosts of an erotic past, but also the traces of a present secret. For the force of Colette's identification with "Charlotte" (how few letters separate this name, real or invented, from Colette's own) seems to point to a shared secret, perhaps concerning frigidity. The two women tiptoe delicately around this subject: "I wonder if you understand what I mean?" Charlotte asks haltingly, and receives the revealing reply: "Very likely, Mme Charlotte, I understand you better than anyone in the world" (22). The appellation "Mme Charlotte" reinforces this identification, since the narrator herself is addressed as "Mme Colette," combining a feminine first name with a formal mode of address. Is this passage then a veiled allusion to the narrator's own frigidity, as that "barrier reef" of sexuality that has wounded her in the past? In any case, Colette's analysis of her "object" turns out to be a kind of séance, calling forth her own ghosts "in the presence of strangers." (Is this a veiled allusion to the ghostly stranger who hovers above the writer's page, the reader?) Moreover, this emergence of long-submerged erotic ghosts seems to bear witness to an earlier repression of sorts—and to the fear of what Colette calls "destruction" in the dispersive force of orgasm—a submersion of the wild sexuality of the *bacchante*, which wounds and "crashes headlong" into the body.

This profound fear is reflected throughout Colette's text, both in her reaction to the "ghoulishness" of Renée Vivien's debauch-

---

[14]This entire episode causes some of the writer's submerged erotic ghosts to surface, for in baring the *questioner's* own voyeuristic tendencies (as she fantasizes about Charlotte's orgasm, not once, but twice), the text provides a hint of the author's own submerged homosexual inclinations. (In a later passage, dealing with the "amorous ménage of two women," the narrator will obliquely confess to this tendency, by asserting that "the time is past in which I could be emotionally affected" 109.)

ery, and in the fear felt by Charlotte, her alter ego, at the thought of losing control. This fear haunts another of the narrator's alter egos as well; a fearful reaction is manifest in the revulsion that certain women inspire in Damien, the Don Juan of Colette's perverse gallery. The professional libertine admits that he is horrified and exhausted by a woman who "goes too far," like a "she-goat at a witches' revel," demanding multiple orgasms, seeming "never to have had quite enough" (49). But this time, the wry voice of the narrator qualifies this characterization of female sexuality ("'They go too far.' They go, to begin with, as far as the man leads them" 49). And the narrator even wonders if Damien himself, the rogue seducer, has not been taken in by more than one clever actress ("And what would he have said had he ever met the woman who, out of sheer generosity, fools the man by simulating ecstasy? But I need not worry on that score: most surely he encountered Charlotte, and perhaps more than once" 58). In the battle of the sexes, Colette seems to rule in favor of the female genius.

But a more reliable character echoes the sentiments of Damien. La Chevalière, the transvestite of noble breeding and impeccable character, admits that she herself has never had an orgasm, and that she too fears the insatiability of her female lovers:

> "I do not know anything about completeness in love," she said, "except the *idea* I have of it. But they, the women, have never allowed me to stop at that point . . ."
>
> [. . .] The expression that appeared on her face recalled for a minute Damien's expression when he had assured me that "women go too far . . ." Like Damien, she seemed to be recalling something rather sad, rather repellent, and she was about to say more, but like him she contained herself. (74)

All these reflections on the insatiability of women reflect a fear of unrestrained sexual desire, the inexorable sex urge, again compared to a creature of the deep, but this time depicted not as a mermaid or sea nymph but as a kind of grasping and devouring sea monster. Colette writes (24): "The senses? Why not *the* sense? [. . .] *The* sense, dominating the five inferior senses, for let them venture far from it and they will be called back with a jerk—like those delicate and stinging ribbons, part weed, part arm, delegated by a deep-sea creature to . . ." (the ellipsis leaves the rest to the imagination). Here again, we get the impression that the narrator is profoundly ambivalent about sexual pleasure—like Charlotte, like La Chevalière, she longs for the pleasure of surrender, but she is also repelled at the prospect of the monster unleashed. (And of course, Scheherazade has good reason to fear the unleashing of the deadly passion of the "sultan," the tyrant sense.) Indeed, in *My Apprenticeships*, the writer hints that her own sexual initiation with the monstrous Willy was a scene of violence and humiliation. So perhaps at least one aspect of the veiled visage— which she endeavors both to lay bare and to cover—is that of the *bacchante*, "the she-goat at a witches' revel," whose unsatisfied lust may underlie the cool visage of the reporter-journalist herself.

White Lies: Cosmetic Veils

Charlotte's case suggests another complication: there are hints that hers is a voluntary frigidity, motivated by a will to control, a director's love of the staged scene, rather than any clinical problem. It is perhaps even a matter of aesthetics, a preference for forepleasure rather than paroxysm, for the deferred and elaborated ornament to sex rather than the "destructive" end of sex itself. Indeed there are indications that Mme Colette's own "frigidity," like that of the "female genius," is also a purely aesthetic choice—motivated by a revulsion for the crudeness of performance-oriented sex—a choice of the oblique or veiled over the direct. The female genius represents the opposite of the mentality of both the male seducer, who compartmentalizes sex with his emphasis on numbers, and the performance-oriented woman, "Madame How-many-times," "counting on her fingers, mentioning by name things and gestures" (93).

It is significant, for example, that Colette contrasts the "indecency" of Renée Vivien's remarks about quantifiable sexual performance to her delicacy in matters of poetry: "Our friendship was in no way literary," Colette writes, "thanks to my respect for literature [. . .] and in Renée Vivien I found the same diffidence and well-bred restraint. She, too, refused to 'talk shop.' Whenever she gave me any of her books, she always hid them under a bouquet of violets or a basket of fruit or a length of Oriental silk"

(81). The female genius envelops and adorns, the antithesis of "Mme-How-many-times," who is playing a man's numbers game. This is precisely the kind of tallying Colette despises in the male seducer Damien, who shows her a cabinet of drawers subdivided inside, filled with lovers' letters filed by category (42). The forte of the *female* genius is not in finishing and classifying, but in deferring and blending, avoiding the too blunt, the too goal-oriented, in an aesthetically prolonged foreplay. In this sense, the writer herself is the exemplary female genius, the "last of the lyric poets" (*Sido* 176) who says *more* than the occasion warrants, even while refusing to "call things by their proper names" (*MMH* 32).

Interestingly, a similar tendency to diversion from goal is what Freud defines as the perverse: perversion is a lingering along the way to sexual satisfaction; or it is a diversion from the primary sexual object to a fetish object (which veils the scandal of the female's castration).[15] And Freud writes that a certain supplementary "forepleasure" also characterizes the aesthetic act, where form and style become ends in themselves, as well as disguises that cloak the writer's desire. Reading Colette through the veil of Freudian theory, then, casts the female genius as the ultimate aesthete, as well as a kind of fetishist, practicing the feminine textile art of weaving/cover-up, in order to defer and amplify pleasure.[16]

In this sense, Colette's *ars erotica* is pervaded with a perverse aesthetic preference for fabrication over the naked truth of numbers and ends. Accordingly Colette expresses her admiration for Charlotte's duplicity, her artful practice of the "deferential lie" (18), in "an unrecognized feat of valor that expects no reward," a kind of art for art's sake. In Colette's artful dance it is the truth (the real orgasm that Charlotte defers and avoids) that risks "going too far," rather than the lie. Thus the whispered confidences among strangers are more interesting as tales than as confessions, for, as Colette writes, "even if they contain some seeds of truth," they are still *fictions* "bobbing about on the surface of a rich deposit of unfermented and unfiltered wine" (19). (This im-

---

[15]Freud elaborates on the notion of perversion in the *Three Essays on the Theory of Sexuality* (1905), *S.E.* 7, and in the later essay "Fetishism" (1927), *S.E.* 21.

[16]In the *New Introductory Lectures on Psychoanalysis* (1933), Freud speculates that weaving is a female activity motivated by the unconscious wish to cover up castration (117). See Chapter 2, note 24.

age could also serve to describe what Lacan calls the "empty speech" [*parole vide*] of the analysand, which lies in spite of itself, afloat on an unfathomable unconscious.)

Here the truth, the excess of female desire, is the abyss, much less "pure" than the lie, the playacting, the artifice. For in this fan dance, the notions of pure and impure change places so often as to lose any intelligible meaning, becoming pure ornament. Pure truth is overlaid with the impurity of the pure, boldfaced lie. Impurity veils purity in the undecidable web of truth and fiction, the erotic recesses of the curtained chamber, where the veiled poet writes in secret. In the writer's seraglio, the subservience of the female genius, the reader's wily concubine, stems from the need to control, veiled by the *"fallacious* vocation of a servant" (60). Lies become cosmetics, which enhance appeal, masking what they seem to display.

Colette's Aesthetic: The Androgynous Writer

Thus Colette's aesthetic seems to imply a repudiation of a certain "masculine" compartmentalizing or enumerating tendency that destroys the poetry of the mystery it examines. And we have seen that Colette describes the sensual female genius as a nymph submerged in a watery cave, a grotto in which the siren may elude the too-inquisitive gaze of the male suitor. But Freud has taught us to be wary of a too-simple equation of the "masculine" with the position of the active-sadist-voyeur and the "feminine" with the position of the passive-masochist-object; for Freud insists that a seemingly masochistic or passive position may often be a strategy that allows the "object" to wield some degree of control.[17] Colette would no doubt concur, for her intriguing victim Charlotte, exposed in all her vulnerability before a crowd of spellbound onlookers, is actually the one who controls the show; con-

---

[17]Freud himself insists on the inadequacy of the equation of active with masculine and passive with feminine, in the *New Introductory Lectures*: "Even in the sphere of human sexual life you soon see how inadequate it is to make masculine behavior coincide with activity and feminine with passivity [. . .] The further you go from the narrow sexual sphere the more obvious will the 'error of superimposition' become. Women can display great activity in various directions, men are not able to live in company with their own kind unless they develop a large amount of passive adaptability" (101–2).

versely, the masterly Damien is at the mercy of his conquests who demand more than he can give.

Similarly, Colette's position as writer is undecidable, never purely "feminine" nor purely "masculine," in the conventional understanding of these terms that she sometimes seems to adopt. For though inspired by "female genius" she also frequently assumes a "male" role of investigator-voyeur. Even during her interview with the rake Damien, Colette occupies the position of voyeur ("I believe he assigned to me the place of spectator" 65), where a degree of sadism is apparent ("I am very fond of seeing him denuded and stewing in a boiling cauldron" 28). In fact, the narrator admits to "goading Damien on" to intimate revelations in a kind of locker-room camaraderie, begun with a neutral collegial exchange ("We begin by talking a little about our work") that leads to juicier topics: "I feel as responsible as he, since, from the minute he first sets his feet in the ignited traces, I follow him and even *goad him on*" (*PI* 37, my emphasis). The "maleness" of this bonding is indicated first by the narrator's willingness to talk shop with her male colleague—which she refuses to do with Renée Vivien; moreover the "male" nature of this bonding with Damien is underscored by her reference to women as "they" in the following passage: "All I can say is, they were drawn straight to him [. . .] and bruised themselves against him as if against a piece of furniture, to such an extent did they not seem to see him" (41).

But at fleeting moments, this facade gives way, exposing the narrator's very female attraction to Damien ("I have tried to persuade myself a hundred times that nothing in him stirred my senses, only to admit a hundred times that this was only a part of the truth" 46) as well as her sense of rejection when Damien denies her femininity ("You a woman? Why try as you will . . ." 58). She confesses to the reader: "I never had the opportunity to admit to him that, oddly enough, I was secretly craving just then to be completely a woman" (59). Even though the narrator pretends to listen to Damien's escapades as a disinterested (sexless) friend, or even as a male accomplice, these confidences make her feel that she is lacking. But this is not because of anatomical deficiency: her problem is not a "castration" complex but a *surfeit* of masculinity, the stigma of her profession, her pen serving as emblem of a certain virility, which gets in the way of her desire for Damien. Nor is her "secret craving" a question of frigidity, at least in this instance: the confessor is incomplete not because she has no desire, but because she fails to inspire desire, because her own veiled femininity remains unperceived.

Of course the narrator herself lays claim to a certain sexual indeterminacy, a certain "hermaphroditism" quite distinct from her theatrical public cross-dressing: "I am not alluding to a former self, a public and legendary figure that I had ostentatiously cultivated and arranged as to costume and external details. I am alluding to a genuine mental hermaphroditism which burdens certain highly complex human beings" (60); even her dear friend Marguerite Moreno points out the "virility" of Colette's work and wit (60). There follows a passage reflecting on "the powerful seduction emanating from persons of uncertain sex," where Colette acknowledges that her "male" side has been drawn to the "female" nature of a certain unnamed man, in this masked ball of androgynous desire. Here she casts herself as sultan and her male lover as recumbent odalisque: "From forehead to mouth he was, behind his closed eyelids, all smiles, with the arch nonchalance of a sultana behind a barred window. And I who would willingly have been completely woman, completely and stupidly female, with what male wistfulness did I gaze at that man who had such a delightful laugh and who could respond to a beautiful poem or landscape" (63). This passage introduces an imbroglio of shifting gender identities: here Colette speaks of being virile under her female disguise and bemoans her incapacity to be "completely, stupidly female"; a few pages later, she asserts that she is hopelessly female under her masculine "disguise" of short hair and smoking jacket ("how feminine I was beneath my disguise of cropped hair" 67). One gender is always layered on the other, so that disguise itself seems to constitute Mme Colette's only essence, for, in spite of her efforts at sincerity, she seems incapable of stripping away all veils and baring one unambiguous identity.

In a final complication of genders, in this same passage, the writer speaks of turning her "male gaze" on her friend Marguerite as she sleeps, observing *her* androgyny, her "strong, sexless features" which look so "masculine" in repose (Marguerite's unconscious virility, repressed by her waking self, comes out in sleep):

"When our breasts and hands and stomachs are hidden, what remains of our feminine exteriors? Sleep brings an incalculable number of women to assume the form they would no doubt have chosen if their waking state did not keep them in ignorance of themselves" (63). Here the narrator is again the onlooker—but this time she gazes on a "male" woman, and with a "woman's eyes." In a single passage, then, the writer has displayed her male gaze looking at a man who looks like a woman, and her female gaze looking at a woman who looks like a man. Finally, at the end of this passage—after an act of feminine, even maternal, tenderness—the writer's male traits are once again emphasized, as she records her observations with a laborer's hands: "Cautiously I reached for a light coverlet and laid it over Chimène and Le Cid, closely united in the sleep of a single body. Then I resumed my post at the side of a worktable, where my woman's eyes followed, on the pale blue bonded paper, the hard and stubby hand of a gardener writing" (64). The "hermaphroditism" of this writing creature is apparent here, where "women's eyes" are joined with the male "gardener's" writing hand (*une courte et dure main de jardin*ier, in the masculine form in French). Writing seems to be an androgynous function as well as a highly erotic one, joining the pleasures of voyeurism with the tactile pleasures of pen and paper.

If it is difficult to keep track of Colette's position in all these shifting gender configurations, it is perhaps because androgyny itself, by Colette's own account, is something ineffable, ghostly and monstrous: "Anxious and veiled, never exposed to the light of day, the androgynous creature wanders, wonders, and implores in a whisper [. . .] It trails irrevocably among us its seraphic suffering, its glimmering tears" (76). This uncanny passage seems to say a great deal about the pain that haunts *The Pure and the Impure* ("this book which will treat sadly of sensual pleasure" 25): like the pathetic fantom creature she evokes, the writer suffers from a stigmatized and veiled sexuality, at once indeterminate (a creature of uncertain sex) and overdetermined (a creature of dissimulated or double sex). Her own sexuality—alluded to obliquely —nonetheless haunts the narrative, "anxious and veiled, never exposed to the light of day." In this ghost story, the shades of one gender always haunt the other, overdetermining the writing persona. Indeed, it is Mme Colette's ghostly quality that permits her to slip unseen into the private sexual lives of others. In *My Apprenticeships*, for example, Colette writes that she makes use of her own invisibility of sorts ("Absent yet present, a translucent witness" 139) to infiltrate clandestine homosexual haunts, just as she will later succeed in infiltrating opium dens as well as secret lesbian societies and even the male company of "Don Juan."

But of course the writer's sexual indeterminacy should not be read as a symptom of a clinical problem. It is rather a pervasive structuring theme of the work, which unveils the androgyny of all sexual beings, each also capable of occupying different positions in the intersubjective drama of desire, each capable of being alternately or simultaneously subject and object. Colette's reflections lead to a virtual aesthetic of androgyny, where female genius or male desire is not the province of one gender only. (She herself asserts that her own "virile" investigative powers are enhanced by her "feminine" powers of divination.) As a writer, Colette excels in the transvestite art of titillation (which sex is veiled, under cover?), which is also the diversionary dance of the fetishist. Androgyny is not just a theme of this text: it is an allegory of writing as courtship, part of Salome's dance of advance and retreat, courting the reader's gaze.

The Veil of Difference: The Impossibility of "Purity"

We have seen that if there is any explicitly condemned "impurity" in this work, it is the masculine numbers game that wants only to look and to triumph. Anticipating the recent feminist critique of the specular nature of male desire, Colette repeatedly condemns the indecency of this kind of appropriative conquest, even if, paradoxically, she herself is driven in some measure by this desire.[18] But in what is perhaps the most puzzling section of the book, there is an equally strong criticism of the corollary notion, that of an inturned female purity, shut away from the world, hidden from the view of the other. This problematic purity is a

---

[18]This critique of the visual or the specular occurs in Luce Irigaray's *Speculum de l'autre femme* (Paris: Editions de Minuit, 1974), trans. Gillian C. Gill, *Speculum of the Other Woman* (Ithaca: Cornell University Press, 1985); a similar critique occurs in Annie Leclerc's *Parole de femme* (Paris: Grasset, 1974).

too-female eroticism, closed off from view, reflecting an impulse to exclude the male onlooker altogether in order to enjoy a protracted bliss, an imploded *jouissance* in which the female body finds narcissistic delight in its own mirror image. The first hint of the dangers of this narcissism is perhaps the description of the occluded world of Renée Vivien and her "ghoulish" mistress (where even the windows are nailed shut): this intoxicating self-enclosed world is the Imaginary idyll turned nightmare. But a more subtle exploration of the dangers of a certain non-differentiation occurs in the curious meditation on the "Ladies of Llangollen," an eighteenth-century lesbian couple who escape from society to find a secluded life of perfect contentment. Long before the theoretical explorations of female narcissism/autoeroticism by the French feminists and others, Colette seems to suggest that the bliss of such relations, mirroring the Imaginary mother-daughter dyad, may be illusory and even dangerous.

The Ladies of Llangollen: The Deep Peace of a Harem

In *En pays connu* (1949; translated as *Places*), Colette describes a tranquil scene from her childhood; sitting at her mother's feet while Sido plaits her hair, Gabrielle watches the female animals taking care of their young: "No half-grown males anywhere. No sign of a man. Mothers. Children still ignorant of their sex. The deep peace of a harem, under the nests of May and the wisteria shot with sunlight. I was no longer linked with the real world except by the purring of the cat, the clear ringing of a nearby anvil, and the hands of my mother at the back of my neck, deftly braiding my hair" (*EP* 35).[19]

Colette's account of the Ladies of Llangollen has a similar dreamy, fairy-tale quality, imbued with its own kind of female purity: "It is this unresolved and undemanding sensuality that finds happiness in an exchange of glances, an arm laid on a shoulder, and is thrilled by the odor of sun-warmed wheat caught in a head of hair. These are the delights of a constant companionship and shared habits that engender and excuse fidelity. How

---

[19]*En pays connu* (Paris: Manuel Bruker, 1949). *Places*, trans. David Le Vay and Margaret Crosland (New York: Bobbs-Merrill, 1971). The passage cited is from Robert Phelps's translation in *Earthly Paradise*, 35.

marvelously compact, the repetition of days, repeated like the reflections of a lamp in a perspective of mirrors!" (*PI* 113). This
seems to be a depiction of timeless joy, a closed world of infinite
sameness (the very image of the Lacanian Imaginary, undisturbed
by the Symbolic intruder), an infinity of sunlit hours like "the
reflections of a lamp in a perspective of mirrors."

Colette leads us into these "infantile adventures, fairylands of
love" (122) with incantatory prose: "Now let us enter, full of awe,
the fantastic atmosphere, let us shatter the imaginary barrier, let
us tread upon the meadows where the turf is as buoyant as a
cloud and as green as the green in our dreams, grazed by a 'silver
and purple ray' coming from no one knows where, laminated between two mountains" (119). Even the laws of nature are sus-
pended in this fairy story ("Above the cottage and its hill, did
there even exist a season of fine weather or a season of bad
weather? No. There was only Llangollen weather" 123); the animals and villagers alike are "spellbound in the vicinity of the cottage." Once upon a time. . . . The blissful monotony of this
"blessed and restricted universe," this "noble season of love"
(110), is evinced by countless entries in Eleanor Butler's journal,
reproduced by Colette, a diary that describes an infinite series of
days "of the most perfect and sweet retirement" (119). Unlike Renée Vivien's cruel and anguished sensuality, this female bliss has
little to do with physical passion and seems instead to be an innocent free-floating joy, an Eden beyond numbers, time, chronology: "The noble season of love, condemned by most people,
shows its nobility by disdaining unambiguous sensual pleasure,
by refusing to reflect, to see things clearly, and to plan a future"
(110).

Here the "impure" outside world is associated with clear vision,
with defined plans, with linear temporality, with goals—including physical ends such as orgasm ("Some will say that I give the
smallest role to the feverish pleasure of the senses, in this chapter
where women pass and pass again, two by two" 112–13). Impurity here is associated with difference, with the quantifiable differ-
ences of Don Juan's accounting mentality, with "Madame-How-
many-times." Impure heterogeneity is counterposed to an Imaginary parade of mirror likenesses, "passing two by two," without
the "insinuation" of difference: "The pudicity that separates two

lovers during the hours of repose, of ablutions, of illness, never insinuates itself between two twin bodies that have similar afflictions, and subject to the same cares, the same predictable periods of chastity . . . A woman marvels at herself, is thrilled by her resemblance to the woman she loves and pities" (111). Thus long before Luce Irigaray's lyric odes to her woman lover ("When our lips speak together"), Colette is describing an intimacy of reflection, the "deep peace of the harem," an eroticism apart from the intrusions of the alien other, where "the close resemblance even sets at ease sensual desire" (111).

Indeed Colette warns against the encroachment of an other who might seek to insinuate himself between the two reflections: "If, parted, the two shadows, replicas of each other—like the shadows of two balustrades, slender here, swollen there—allow an intruder to enter the space between them, it is enough to ruin the well constructed edifice" (112). This is a thinly veiled image of phallic violation, where the male intruder parts the symmetry of the curtained alcove, creating a space between its halves. So there are intimations of trouble in this fragile paradise: a male serpent may threaten this Eden ("Often it is a man who appears, faithful to his mission of enchanting and exhausting women merely by his dazzling difference" 112). Yet the "peace of the harem" is threatened not only by the sultan's visit, but by *any* change or difference that might destabilize this paradise of light: "The shadow projected on the intervening space need not be that worst intruder, a man. The most ordinary irruption can mortally change the steady hot-house warmth in which two women devote themselves to the cultivation of a *delusion*" (112, my emphasis).

Long before Kristeva's reflections on "Women's Time," Colette is pointing out the impossibility of a timeless Imaginary female realm—which tries to turn its back on the Symbolic, the temporal, the Real, to create a "delusion"—but where the womb is a veiled tomb.[20] The writer's veiled warning is actually an exposé; even while she cautions against the outsider, she herself intrudes to demolish "the deep peace of a harem," exposing it as an impossible dream. The narrator reveals that this is an idyllic but mon-

---

[20]Colette devotes a passage (121) to the journal's "veiled allusions" to the tomb that the two lovers plan to share, as stipulated in a sealed document.

strous life, stifling time by a force of will: "When could they lay hold of a sense of the future, those two enamored women who, at every moment, demolish and deny it, who envisage neither beginning nor end nor change nor solitude, who breathe the air only *à deux*, and, arm in arm, walk only in perfect step with each other?" (110).

In a later passage, the skepticism about this *ménage* becomes more pointed: even while admiring the "perfect transparency" of this life, Colette suggests that this idyll of "two foolish creatures, so intensely loyal to a delusion," is a mirage. Long before Foucault, Colette's extraordinary work explores all love relations as power relations, implying that even the most apparently transparent relation has the opacity of a mirror. Even in Eden Colette discerns the sexual politics between a conqueror and a victim: "What I would like to have is the diary that would reveal the victim, the diary that the younger of this couple, Sarah Ponsonby, might have kept. Eleanor, who speaks for both and wields the pen, has nothing to hide from us. The secret here is Sarah, who says nothing, and embroiders" (125–26). Colette thus sees difference in even this "identical" couple; she discerns one virile figure, the master who wields the pen, speaking for both (shades of Willy, who signed Colette's work with his name), and one female "Sempstress" figure who silently embroiders, busy exercising her female genius, dreamy, rebellious, and elusive.

La Femme cachée (1924; translated in *The Other Woman*) is the title of a collection of Colette's short stories—but it could title this chapter as well: Sarah belongs to a whole line of treacherous sempstresses, disloyal only in their thoughts, veiled by their industry. Like Bel-Gazou who sews under her mother's gaze while dreaming about sex (*My Mother's House*); like "the shadowy young ladies of the nineteenth century, stifled in the maternal shade and plying bright needles" while engaged in "dark diplomacy" (*Evening Star* 597); like Gabrielle herself as she sits at Sido's feet (*EP* 35)—this Sarah is a wily daughter of sorts who may hide a guilty desire. Yet again, the writer's urge to lift the veil is manifest as she gazes at Sarah: "What a light would be shed by a diary she kept; surely she would have confessed everything; now and then there would be the hint of a subtle and perhaps traitorous attraction . . . a wealth of sensual effusions" (*PI* 126). This scene harbors the restive sexuality of a harem, guarded from the outside, but brewing forbidden sexuality within.

Colette concludes this vignette with a reproach, as she herself becomes an interloper from the future, an intruder who steps in to confront Eleanor, the keeper of the journal:

> See here, stout-hearted Eleanor, you who were responsible for all the daily decisions, you who were so profoundly submerged in your Well-Beloved, were you unaware that two women cannot achieve a perfect union? You were the prudent Warden—the masculine element. It was you who measured the distance at which the real world must be kept [. . .] Your urbanity, which opened wide the cottage door to the wellborn passerby, knew still better how to shut it. (126)

We could say that this upbraiding of Eleanor challenges the dream of seamless identity sheltered from the Symbolic: no escape may be found from the principles of divisibility, of difference, the impulse of severance that founds enumeration and investigation. In fact the intrusive "male" factor is an essential element of the art of the "female genius," who creates a heterogeneous text or embroidery, a chain of discrete stitches that adds dimension to the flat surface, cloaking the too-naked truth. The text of the "female genius" thus suggests that difference and severance are only destructive when they are used to divide and conquer rather than to articulate and embroider; it also suggests that there is no "pure" masculine principle any more than there is a "pure" feminine domain. (Even Eleanor's watchful gaze is at once maternal/protective and masterly/invasive.) The essence of female genius is not purity, unity, transparency, but complication—a play *with* difference rather than a conquest or exclusion *of* difference.

The irony is that Eleanor—who most jealously excludes the male element and divisiveness of the real world beyond the cottage door—is also the representative of the masculine element, which measures, divides. The lesson of this Imaginary idyll is just that—that it is Imaginary, shadowed by the inevitable intercession of the Symbolic (which Colette calls the Warden). Why does Eleanor write? For whom? The writing itself is a concession to the existence of the other, that future judge, the reader who is first

Colette and then Colette's reader, who reads over her shoulder, in an opening of the cottage door across time. Eleanor's writing is a symptom of the impossibility of her despotic dream, yet it paradoxically maintains the monstrous illusion of closed symmetry.

But the page upon which Eleanor records her days with Sarah is doubled by that other silent page, the fabric upon which Sarah embroiders her ungrateful fantasies. It is doubled, and shadowed, but not mirrored; and the needle that pierces the fabric, going in and out of the embroidery hoop, suggests the intrusion of the other into the perfect sphere of the Imaginary construct. The sewing needle—like Eleanor's pen—is a discourse tracing the sexual difference that Eleanor would like to shut out, but that as Warden and Onlooker she unwittingly embodies. The sexless love of angels, the perfect symmetry of self with mirror image, is like Eden itself a myth. And as Colette herself learned—shut up by her "warden," Willy—writing will open the door of the most tightly sealed of prisons.

Of course Colette's tale is no diatribe against homosexuality: the problem with the Ladies of Llangollen is that they fail to recognize the *difference* between them, succumbing to the delusion of non-differentiation that can afflict any relation. What woman really "wants"—and here what she both desires and lacks—turns out to be something like what man "wants," although differently: she "wants" the other, not as ward or as possession, but as possibility of movement, as difference. The other is the third dimension through which the embroidery thread must pass as it creates its fantastic patterns; Scheherazade's work is one of *opening* the treasure trove, an opening made possible, paradoxically, by the closing off of some secrets from view.

The Poet's Secret

It was a question of merely pronouncing the magic
word, "Open sesame!"
—*The Pure and the Impure*

Thus Colette's vision may be read as a critique of a certain utopian essentialist vision, which, however attractive, is also impossible and even undesirable because imploded or regressive. It is at the same time a critique of the excesses of androcentric goal-oriented sexuality, caught up with possession, guardianship, voyeurism, knowledge, and "unambiguous sensual pleasure" counted as numbers of climaxes (the clinical aspect of *scientia sexualis*). But as Foucault shows, this dream of absolute knowledge of the other—the dream of *Discipline and Punish*—is also an Imaginary construct. Thus Colette's vision may be read, surprisingly, as an anticipation of Foucault's thought, in which discourse is revealed as enticement and excess, symptom of desire. Colette's *ars erotica* testifies that the "impurity" of the intrusive third term (for Lacan the Symbolic father's Law that grounds humanity; for Colette the veil that makes the mother inaccessible) cannot be simply shut out by an act of exclusion. The veil of difference will insinuate itself even in a mirrored female world, between mother and daughter, where no other interloper has materialized.

To cast the play of pure and impure in another way, in psychoanalytic and discursive terms, we might suggest that the unconscious itself is an interloper of sorts, which always menaces our "pure" reason from beyond. The "impure" intrusions of the unconscious in our speech, for instance, in a joke or a Freudian slip, open our reason to the play of difference and desire, effecting a textual inweaving of the conscious and the unconscious, signifying the incapacity of transparent language to mean just one thing, unequivocally. And of course the unconscious itself is plural and inscrutable, eluding the grasp of "pure" transparent reason. (This is perhaps in part what Lacan suggests by his famous dictum that "the unconscious is the discourse of the Other.") In this sense, "impurity" is desirable, an insemination of consciousness by the unconscious.

Thus Colette's "female genius" is a deployment of discursive sexuality, testifying that there is no such thing as non-discursive, unveiled sexuality. This is also the discovery of Freud, who sees sexuality as something always already "laid on to" biology, always already excessive, destined to be deflected from its object.[21] Colette's exposé reveals that "pure" sex has not existed since the

---

[21]The notion of *Anlehnung* or "laying on" of sexual desire to the biological process of feeding is discussed in *Three Essays on the Theory of Sexuality*.

first mythical fig leaf covered the first mythical body. In fact, Colette's view of sexuality is perhaps more radical than Foucault's, which seems to harbor the myth of something like natural sex, before the modern age of *scientia sexualis*. Colette's veiled woman, like Lacan's, has always been a modern.

Were Colette to confer with Freud concerning the technique of aesthetic veiling as a lure for the reader's desire and a cover-up of the writer's fantasy, she might point to the female genius of every writer, regardless of gender.[22] And she might not be surprised to find that Freud's definition of perversion as deflection from end, being sidetracked by decoys, is consistent with her own experience of writing, as a diversion that both fulfills and engenders desire. For who knows more than Scheherazade about putting off endings, substituting the forepleasure of the fetish (the tale) for the deadly pleasure of sacrifice, assuring that the storyteller lives on to enchant us for another evening? Colette's discursive sexuality stages a peep show in which the veil is no longer an alibi, but is rather the page of creativity. Female genius is not finally a question of gender—and certainly not of gender defined as what is missing, a nostalgia for what the veil veils—but of the profoundly human pleasure of the veil itself. Colette could probably tell Freud a great deal about what woman wants, rather than about what she lacks.

---

[22]In "Creative Writers and Daydreaming" Freud speaks of *Ankleidung* (veiling) as the means by which the writer's "egotistical fantasies" are made palatable to the reader—creating a "bribe" of literary pleasure which draws the reader into the literary process.

5

Wit and the Work of Mourning

Many emotions which are essentially painful may
become a source of enjoyment for the hearers of a
poet's work.
—Freud, "Creative Writers and Daydreaming"

And she laughed, sitting there in her mourning . . .
—*My Mother's House*

"Laughter": A Woman's Voice

We have seen that the veil figures as theme, image, and technique in Colette's fictional autobiographies. But one kind of veiling or costume is expressly repudiated in these autofictions: the widow's veils of mourning. This refusal of the veil of sadness is explicit in *My Mother's House*, in the chapter titled "Laughter," where we see Sido on the day of her husband's burial.

The vignette opens on a surprisingly bright note: we are told that throughout her years with "her beloved companion," Sido would use her sense of humor to counter the fear of separation, sternly forbidding him to die before she did:

> She would escape, as it were in one bound, from a painful reverie, and pointing her knitting needle at her husband would exclaim:
> "What! Just you try to die first, and you'll see!"
> "I shall do my best, dear heart," he would answer [. . .]
> "All I say is, let me see you try!" (119)

But this lighthearted exchange is abruptly undercut by a kind of tragic punch line: "He did try, and succeeded at the first attempt. He died in his seventy-fourth year, holding the hands of his beloved, and fixing on her weeping eyes a gaze that gradually lost its colour, turned milky blue, and faded like a sky veiled in mist" (120). Here a variation of the veil motif takes on a wrenching poignancy, with death coming to cloud the piercing gaze fixed on Sido, and severing the lovers. (In the original French, the sense of violation or separation is extremely strong, for the father's eyes are invaded [*envahi*] or overrun with the mist that envelops his view of Sido. Again, we find a resonance of Orpheus, whose beloved is swallowed by shadow.) In the moving passage that follows, Sido's veils of mourning emblematize the pain of her loss: "My mother accompanied him steadily to the grave's edge, very small and resolute beneath her widow's veil, and murmuring under her breath words of love that only he must hear" (121).

But immediately upon her return from her husband's funeral, Sido casts off her widow's weeds, her outward signs of grief ("Heavens! The heat of this black stuff! Don't you think that I might change now, into my blue sateen?" 120). This costume is the antithesis of the aesthetic veils of *The Pure and the Impure*; unlike those sheer layers that cloak and tantalize, the opaque widow's weeds are ostentatious badges of mourning, which blatantly display what is most private, and in so doing, repress and shroud the spirit that wears them. "But I simply loathe black!" Sido declares. "Don't let me ever see you in mourning for me! You know well enough that I only like you to wear pink, and some shades of blue" (121). This illogical statement is already a comic reworking of grief, since Sido blithely assumes that she will "see" her daughter in mourning, after her own death (perhaps this is even a comic forewarning of her intention to haunt her daughter). In any case, Sido characteristically will have nothing to do with imposed sadness, with socially enforced costumes that immodestly advertise private feelings.

In the closing passage, Sido commits another impropriety—forgetting for a moment the death of her husband, she bursts into laughter at the antics of a kitten: "A sudden and unexpected somersault landed him head over heels at our feet [. . .] And she laughed, sitting there in her mourning, laughed her shrill young girl's laugh, clapping her hands with delight at the kitten. Then, of a sudden, searing memory stemmed that brilliant cascade and dried the tears of laughter in my mother's eyes" (122). The chapter concludes with an elegy to Sido, and to her gift for survival, as she goes on "welcoming from every source the fleeting benediction of joy" (122), always easily moved to laughter, even given to "paroxysms of mirth" (119) in spite of her loss: "So she lived on, swept by shadow and sunshine [. . .] rich in children, flowers and animals like a fruitful domain" (122). In this tribute, a woman's laughter breaks through a veil of tears.

Even after Sido's death, the laughter of this merry maternal ghost resonates throughout Colette's work: "It is to her I sometimes turn for a youthful touch—though my laugh, now that I am in the seventies, is not so gay as Sido's humour was when she mocked at the little tombstones of burnished lead and beads, and their rural epitaphs" (preface, *MMH*). This legacy of laughter is one thing that consistently sets Colette apart from many other women writers of this century: her work is more often than not infused with infectious high spirits, an irrepressibly waggish comic voice. For although she shares the dark preoccupations of other women writing in France and elsewhere—writers such as Duras, de Beauvoir, Sagan, Yourcenar, Hébert, who recount stories of loss, of sexual victimization or frustration—there is no existentialist angst in Colette's work, no sacrificial tone, no sweeping tragic resonance. But even if Colette's voice lacks the self-importance of tragedy or the torment of angst, it is nonetheless imbued with a certain pathos and sense of nostalgia, and is profoundly wise, often ironic, echoing the layered perspectives of the writer's ghosts, her multiple identities.

The Comic Veil

We have seen, for instance, that in anecdotes concerning the parents, the narrative is haunted by a voice-over of sorts, which seems to be saying, "If only I knew then what I know now . . . loved ones die." This sort of dramatic irony—the irony of superior vision or hindsight—has a poignant effect; but Colette's irony frequently produces a comic effect as well, undercutting the apparent intensity of the remembered scene with a smiling wisdom ("This too shall pass") that, however gentle, pokes fun at the innocent or even naive world it depicts.[1]

---

[1]While volumes have been written about the literary uses of irony, for the purposes of this discussion I will adhere to Freud's simple and workable characterization of irony as a tension between two levels of meaning, a discrepancy between

But Colette's comic irony does more than provide distance, perspective, and comic relief in the family drama: it may also work to cloak disturbing underlying themes. In the example from "Laughter" cited above, for instance, the bantering tone distracts us, setting us up so that we are taken by surprise by a serious turn in the narrative (where Sido's playful admonition to the Captain is revealed, abruptly, as a dark prophecy: "'Only let me see you try [to die first]!' / He did try, and succeeded at the first attempt" 120). Thanks to the use of the comic veil as a diversionary device, the narrator passes here from comedy to pathos in one sentence, catching the reader off-guard and thus increasing the grim impact of the ensuing events (the Captain's death and burial). Conversely, Colette's comic irony may be used to soften a serious topic, lessening its menacing impact. For instance, Gabrielle's sexual initiation is treated humorously in such episodes as "The Abduction" and "The Wedding." Thus the comic veil may work in two ways: it may cloak a threatening topic that is perhaps too close to the bone to be treated seriously; or it may work to conceal a dark surprise until the moment of revelation, enhancing its impact. In addition to this game of obfuscation, Colette's comic irony may serve a more traditional function, *un*veiling hypocrisy or self-delusion of all sorts—as when the narrator comments wryly on the comic scenes she observes, from on high; or when her alter ego Sido criticizes the hypocrisy of social convention.

A Freudian perspective provides another way of thinking of the role of veiling/unveiling in Colette's comic irony. We recall Freud's suggestion that the joking process itself always veils the structure of play, since joking originates with the infant's play with words; and play in turn veils the death-drive (as described in *Beyond the Pleasure Principle*). Thus when Colette drapes her beloved ghosts in humor, is she perhaps giving play to a dark desire to join them in death, to be "at home," at rest?

what is meant and what is said. Freud writes, in *Jokes and Their Relation to the Unconscious*, 174: "[Irony] comes very close to joking and is counted among the sub-species of the comic. Its essence lies in saying the opposite of what one intends to convey to the other person, but in sparing him contradiction by making him understand—by one's tone of voice, by some accompanying gesture, or (where writing is concerned) by some small stylistic indications—that one means the opposite of what one says."

Perhaps. In any case, it seems that listening to Colette's comic voice through the veil of Freudian theory may aid in our search for the fantom subject behind the work, in the manner of some psychobiography. The Freudian analysis of comic technique in a literary text may be of interest for other reasons as well, contributing to a reading that emphasizes the writer's technique (as in the *textanalyses* practiced by Jean Bellemin-Noël), or focuses on questions of genre (as Peter Brooks's or Fredric Jameson's work often does), or centers on the text's reception by a reader or a group of readers.[2] For of course there are many varieties of psychoanalytic criticism, differentiated by the *object* of their analysis (author, character, theme, genre, text, reader).[3] It may be argued that Freud himself pioneered all of these methods, showing a particular interest in the effect of the text upon its reader, insisting that reading processes, like comic processes, are social transactions, creating bonds of identification. And even if Freud never broached the question of the specificity of the woman writer or the woman humorist, a Freudian reading of comic technique in literature raises questions of a "woman's place" in the transaction.

To be sure, any psychoanalytic reading of the comic process must refer to *Jokes and Their Relation to the Unconscious* (1905), Freud's seminal analysis of the processes of wit (*Witz*). The work is divided into several sections, cataloging the techniques of jokes (how they work); the purposes of jokes (what jokes aim to do); the pleasure mechanism in jokes (why jokes give pleasure); the social function of jokes (the conditions giving rise to the telling of the joke); the relation of joking to dreaming (the unconscious sources of jokes and of dreams); and the difference between jokes and "the comic."[4]

---

[2]Examples of psychoanalytic "reader-response" theory abound. See, for instance, Norman Holland's *The Dynamics of Literary Response* (New York: Oxford University Press, 1968) and Wolfgang Iser's *The Act of Reading* (Baltimore and London: Johns Hopkins University Press, 1978). For the technique of *textanalyse*, see Jean Bellemin-Noël's *Essais de textanalyse* (Presses Universitaires de Lille, 1988).

[3]For examples of these various types of psychoanalytic criticism, see Chapter 1, note 10.

[4]Freud attributes the difference between the comic and "jokes" proper to the number of parties involved in each process. The comic requires only two parties or poles (a laugher and an object) while a joke takes three (a joke maker, a joke receiver, and an object). Since all literary processes are triangular transactions

Significantly, Freud often refers throughout his work to the origin of joking in child's play, as the adult's way of recovering the lost joy of infancy. Still we have seen that in Freud's view, child's play is no joking matter, for not only is it linked to the repetition compulsion and the death-drive, but it also is charged with a serious mission of social adaptation.[5] Freud argues that play, like joking, is an act of reality-mastery, a way for the child to cope with an unpleasant situation, transforming it into a source of pleasure. Just what accounts for this transformation from "infantile" repetition in play to the imaginative adult activities of joking and writing, and joking *in* writing?

If Freud's theory may be of use in unveiling Colette's comic/literary technique, conversely Colette's text may elucidate the aesthetics of Freudian theory. Colette's work provides an excellent vantage point from which to watch the writer's comic sport, in which the poetic word itself is the sought-after object in a game of hide-and-seek between meaning and sound ("To catch up with it I find myself singing to its veiled homonyms" *ES* 160). We have seen that the writer's veil is often a shroud, which lends a haunting quality to the narrative; still the prevalence of Colette's wit suggests that she is able to replace the veils of mourning with a comic mask. By listening to Colette's comic voice in several key passages, we may hope not only to unveil another of the writer's visages, but also to hold up the mirror, to understand the impact of this writer on the reader. Indeed, Colette's work recasts Freud's *Jokes and Their Relation to the Unconscious* as *Writing and Its Relation to the Unconscious*; especially since this writer's fantom "I" seems to have a pronounced sense of humor.

Joke-Work as Text-Work:
The Comic Veil as Literary Technique

We may make use of Freud's joke theory briefly to address three related questions concerning Colette's autofictions: what is

---

(among an author, a reader, a character/text), then the category of the joke, as Freud understands it, is more appropriate than that of the comic for our analysis of literary processes.

[5] In "Creative Writers and Daydreaming" Freud writes that the child "takes his play very seriously and expends a great deal of emotion on it" (144). He even suggests that child's play is, in a sense, less "playful" than that of the adult.

her comic technique? (what are her preferred comic devices, and what do they contribute to her literary project of ghostwriting or veiling?); what is the purpose of her humor? (how does Colette's comic voice—as an aesthetic process aimed at producing pleasure—serve the larger literary process?); what is the social or intersubjective effect of her humor? (what kind of identification does Colette's feminine comic vision create among herself, her characters, and her reader?).

In the first section of *Jokes*, Freud outlines three general techniques of the joke-work—condensation, displacement, and regression—and argues that each of these techniques is similar to the workings of primary process in the dream (the *Träumarbeit* analyzed in the *Interpretation of Dreams* [1900]). Regression is perhaps the least comprehensible of these dream techniques; sometimes translated as representability, it refers to the fact that dreams are hallucinations and that "in order for it to be possible for the dream-thoughts to be represented in sensory form, their expression has to undergo far-reaching modifications" (*Jokes* 163). Freud considers concrete representation a regressive process in the adult, since it depends on infantile cognitive processes: the child's primary thought processes are couched in images, without verbal or conceptual constructs, and are concrete rather than abstract. (Freud cites the child's "confusion between words and things," the tendency to use words as playthings, as evidence of the child's incapacity to handle abstract concepts.) And Freud maintains that concrete imagistic thinking in the dream is regressive in a mechanical way as well: in dream, energy "regresses" inward, where it is discharged in hallucination, rather than progressing outward, to action:

> [The dream-work] takes the step from the optative to the present indicative; it replaces "Oh! if only . . ." by "It is." The "It is" is then given a hallucinatory representation; and this I have called the "regression" in the dream-work—the path that leads from thoughts to perceptual images [. . .] On this path, which is in the reverse direction to that taken by the course of development of mental complications, the dream-thoughts are given a pictorial character. (*Jokes* 162–63)

Thus Freud understands regression both in terms of process (internal hallucination) and in terms of content (concrete images);

but in both cases he emphasizes the capacity of regressive processes to fulfill desire.[6]

Freud goes on to compare the plastic quality of the joke scenario, a narrative often presented as a scene, to that of the dream-picture. He argues that some jokes make use of regressive *technique* as well, exploiting a word's sound rather than its meaning. (Freud cites the proclivity in wordplay or nonsense for *Zitterspräche* ["funny-sounding words" 125].) For this kind of wordplay allows the hearer the infantile pleasure of taking "words as things," as toys or objects, rather than as designators, transparent means to an end. (This is also, of course, a favorite device of poetry, as in the technique of the *ob-jeu* of Francis Ponge.) In an earlier chapter, Freud suggests that wordplay fulfills a social function as well, reflecting the joker's rebellion against the authority of reason:

> During the period in which a child is learning how to handle the vocabulary of his mother tongue [. . .] he puts words together without regard to the condition that they should make sense, in order to obtain from them the pleasurable effect of rhythm or rhyme. Little by little he is forbidden this enjoyment, till all that remains permitted to him are significant combinations of words. But when he is older attempts still emerge at disregarding the restrictions that have been learnt on the use of words [so that] a private language may even be constructed. (125)

Freud limits his observations to the relation between joking and dreaming, but it is interesting to extend this comparison to literary processes as well, which also may be said to make use of regression, since they transform concepts into scenic, imagistic representations, often painting scenes of regression in a literal sense, returning in memory to childhood.

In Colette's work, there is ample evidence of the use of regressive technique and imagery, both as literary device—when the entire narrative brings back the lost infantile past—and as comic

---

[6]Lacanians and more recent psychoanalytic aesthetic theorists, however, have shifted emphasis from the notion of content of the dream to its process, which "fulfills desire" regardless of what it depicts (thus dispensing with Freud's problem of how, for instance, a nightmare can be considered a "wish fulfillment"). See, for instance, Jean-François Lyotard's "Le Travail du rêve ne pense pas," in *Discours, figure* (Paris: Editions Klincksieck, 1971).

technique. We have already encountered a classic example of one regressive technique, in the vignette "The Priest on the Wall," where Gabrielle treats an intriguing new word as a plaything:

> Far from me the idea of asking one of my relations: "What kind of thing is a presbytery?" I had absorbed the mysterious word with its harsh and spiky beginning and the brisk trot of its final syllables. Enriched by a secret and a doubt, I slept on the *word* and bore it off to my wall. "Presbytery!" I would shout it over the roof of the hen-house and Miton's garden, towards the perpetually misty horizon of Moutiers. From the summit of my wall, the word rang out as a malediction: "Begone! You are all presbyteries!" I shouted to invisible outlaws. (*MMH* 31)

One could not ask for a better illustration of Freud's concept of the regressive confusion of concrete and abstract, whereby word-objects become a source of pleasurable play. We recall that Gabrielle enjoys this private game until she is set straight by Sido, who overhears her calling a snail a "presbytery," and insists that Gabrielle stop this nonsense and call things by their proper names. But Gabrielle rebels in her own way against the constraints of adult logic, in a manner consistent with Freud's suggestion that a spirit of rebellion continues to motivate wordplay even after it has been forbidden by reason: "Whatever the motive may have been which led the child to begin these games, I believe that in his later development [he finds] enjoyment in the attraction of what is forbidden by reason. He now uses games in order to withdraw from the pressure of critical reason. Even the phenomena of imaginative activity must be included in this activity" (*Jokes* 126). Gabrielle's capitulation is just as wily as that of Freud's rebellious child; in the face of her mother's criticism, she holds on to her word, making it the occasion of a new game: "And then I yielded. I was craven and I compromised with my disappointment. Throwing away the fragments of the little broken snail shell, I picked up the enchanting word and, climbing on to my narrow terrace, shaded by the old lilac trees and adorned with polished pebbles and scraps of coloured glass like a thieving magpie's nest—I christened it the Presbytery and inducted myself as priest on the wall" (*MMH* 32).

The intransigent child has the last laugh, refusing to bow completely to the dictates of adult sense. Furthermore, this passage attests that the adult continues to make use of her childhood game for yet another pleasure transaction, sharing her "last laugh" with her reader, delighting in her triumph over the adult's law—in a comic anecdote. For the reader's enjoyment here doubles that of the narrator, whose comic story permits us all to return to a common experience of childhood and to enjoy once more the license to ignore the strictures of meaning, to use the mysteries of language as a password to new wonders. This "regressive" comic anecdote may even be read as an emblem for Colette's own position as writer: perched on a wall between reality and fantasy, between her readers and her ghosts, she officiates in an aesthetic language-ceremony, pronouncing the magic words ("open sesame!") that permit us to pass through the veil of reality, transforming the disappointments of life into an occasion for pleasure.

Condensation: The Comic Thickening of Plot

Perhaps the most inclusive of the three dream-work techniques that figure in Freud's view of the joking process is condensation. (Interestingly, the German term [*Verdichtung*] evokes a thickening or layering and thus suggests yet another kind of cloaking; it evokes a connection with poetry [*Dichtung*] as well.) In dream or myth, Freud tells us, condensation is the tendency of primary process to compress two or more elements into a single symbol or image; the mythological sphinx is a good example—part bird, part cat, part human. The most obvious use of condensation in joking is in the double meaning of puns, the use of a single word to represent two distinct objects or ideas. The pleasure of this kind of joke, Freud tells us, is produced by the process of "bewilderment and illumination": the condensed term first baffles us, and then is cleared up in the moment that we "get" the joke. (A related technique discussed by Freud is "the rediscovery of something familiar": the delight in "getting" the joke, in discovering something familiar in its punch line, is compared to the joy of an infant who rediscovers a familiar face in a game of peekaboo. And this rhythm in turn recalls the joy of reunion in the *fort-da* game, when the child retrieves the "lost" parent/toy that has been hidden from sight.) In the same section, Freud treats the techniques of allusion, humor, and irony (all of which rely on oblique reference, or "representation by the opposite") as joke condensations of sorts, which depend on double meaning to produce their effect. For instance, irony requires a double vision (we must perceive that the speaker means the opposite of what she says: "That's a *great* idea!"). Humor consists in making fun of oneself, or of a scary situation, in order to rise above a threat, employing a double perspective to get outside one's predicament (the condemned man says on the scaffold: "This day is starting out great!").[7]

A similar observation may be made concerning the related comic devices of parody, satire, and caricature, which make fun of something lofty by exaggerating its defects or treating it in an offhand tone.[8] Here again these techniques make use of a kind of condensation, since their comic effect relies on a double perception, a comparison between the dignified object and its lowered treatment.[9] Freud does not extend these observations to the literary process; but structural linguistics has pointed out that figures such as metaphor are effects of condensation, thickening the nar-

[7]Specifically, Freud refers to this kind of somber double vision as "gallows humor" (*Jokes* 229). Thus gallows humor is nothing more than a joke pulled on oneself when the situation is frightening or menacing.

[8]*Jokes*, 200–202. Freud excludes parody, travesty, and caricature from the discussion of the joke-work on the grounds that they are conscious techniques. Still this distinction does not really hold. For "unconscious" techniques such as condensation, regression, and displacement may be consciously used in writing as well (as "figures" or tropes, or in the making of a metaphor), but this does not mean that their source is not to be found in unconscious thought processes (primary process); indeed, as Freud himself suggests, a great part of their impact may be attributed to this unconscious resonance. The issue here is the term "unconscious": can an artist make "conscious" use of primary process—as surrealist artists use dream images, for example—without "rationalizing" the effect? Freud argues elsewhere ("Creative Writers and Daydreaming") that this special access to the unconscious is the most important aspect of the poet's gift. In any case, these techniques (parody, caricature) figure prominently in Colette's work, where they seem to have an unconscious resonance for both writer and reader.

[9]Both images must be "condensed" and compared, held in view by the reader or listener, who must be simultaneously aware of both the real model and the caricature in order to "rediscover something familiar" in the image presented, and to derive pleasure from the resemblance.

rative line with underlying meanings.[10] These various kinds of condensation play a prominent role in Colette's highly metaphoric work, where parody, satire, caricature, allusion, and pun all contribute to the overdetermined vision.

A few examples (from *My Mother's House*): There is a decidedly satiric ring to the anecdote "My Mother and the Curé," where the venerable figure of the priest comes in for a devaluation, whereas the parodic tone of "Propaganda" pokes fun at the Captain's grandiose election campaigns, recounted in the deliberately inflated rhetoric of a military foray. And as an illustration of a more mechanical kind of condensation, on the level of simple wordplay or punning, we might cite the comic impact of "The Abduction": in this episode the humor derives from the double meaning of the French title ("L'Enlèvement")—from the verb *enlever*, which means both "to abduct" and "to carry away"—since the child is at once carried away by erotic fantasy and by the mother's loving arms.

As an example of another kind of double meaning, we could cite the irony of the title "'The Rage of Paris,'" the tale of several gullible village men who are duped into taking up needlework by a fast-talking actor from Paris (we understand that this fashion-plate is homosexual, by allusions to his speech and dress). The local menfolk, convinced that masculine needlework is the latest thing in Paris, form a sewing circle, until they are set straight by a neighbor who returns home to find the club at work in *his* parlor:

[His senior clerk was] counting his stitches on the tightly-stretched material of a tambour frame. The chemist's son, a ruddy-faced little rip, was embroidering a monogram on a tea-cloth, while Glaume, a portly and eligible widower, was filling in the design on a slipper with alternate squares of magenta and old gold wool. Even trembling old Monsieur Demange was trying his hand on a piece of coarse canvas. Standing before them, Monsieur d'Avricourt was reciting verses; an incense of sighs

---

[10]Roman Jakobson, for instance, refers to metaphor as a function of the vertical or "paradigmatic" axis of language, exploiting the layers of available meanings from which we choose our words and construct our sentences. See "Two Aspects of Language and Two Types of Aphasic Disturbances," *Fundamentals of Language* (The Hague: Mouton, 1956), 55–82.

rose from the circle of idle women upon whom his Oriental eyes disdained to rest.

I never knew exactly with what abrupt words, or possibly by what even more crushing silence, the Lord of the Manor withered "the rage of Paris" and brushed the scales from the eyes of those good folk who sat staring at him, needle in hand. (*MMH* 83)

Although the homosexual actor is caricatured in this vignette (Colette cites his manner of "walking, of bowing, of punctuating his crystalline laughter with little treble cries, of resting his hand on his hip as though on a sword-hilt" 82), it is not he who is the primary butt of this joke, but rather the naive townsfolk who ape the actions of "the Rage of Paris." In fact Colette underscores the ironic distance of her narrating voice by putting the title in quotes, with a sort of stylistic smirk.

Finally, as "'The Rage of Paris'" shows, caricature is a favorite comic effect for Colette, who delights particularly in drawing exaggerated cartoons of her familiars. We have seen that the Captain is the most frequent target of caricature: he is portrayed as an insanely jealous old man who carries a knife, who sings constantly, who taunts the neighbor woman with offers to initiate her sexually, for a price ("Sixpence and a packet of tobacco!" 47). Certainly the conventional dignified patriarch is demystified in this portrait.

Nor does Sido escape unscathed from her daughter's wit. In "Jealousy," for instance, both parents are seen as ridiculous old folks, engaged in a lovers' spat. When Sido is a few minutes late returning from her errands, she is confronted with a furious mate—"Here he comes, bristling, his beard tilted aggressively"— who accuses her of making eyes at the café owner's sons:

Her chin trembling with resentment, this little elderly lady is charming when she defends herself without so much as a smile against the accusations of a jealous sexagenarian. Nor does he smile either, as he goes on to accuse her now of "gallivanting". But I can still smile at their quarrels because I am only fifteen, and have not yet divined the ferocity of love beneath his veteran eyebrow, and the blushes of adolescence upon her fading cheeks. (*MMH* 19–20)

The final sentences of this passage present an interesting twist on the doubled perspective of the text: here the child, who is present at the scene, is amused, while the adult, who recalls the scene, declines to smile because she comprehends the full ferocity of jealousy in the aging parents who are now her contemporaries. Thus this caricature is a curious reversal of the adult narrator's smiling, superior stance in other comic episodes: here it is the *child* who dares to smile at the parents, while the adult does not see them as ludicrous, having come to share their point of view.

Finally, we might cite the technique that Freud calls "the rediscovery of something familiar"—related to "bewilderment and illumination"—as one of Colette's preferred comic condensations, perhaps because it reflects a larger tendency in her work, the yearning to come home to her childhood, rediscovering Sido. Colette uses this technique again and again—revealing that something alien and threatening is actually something familiar, masked or veiled by a changing light or the confusion of dream. This, for instance, is the technique of "The Abduction," where the nightmarish ravisher turns out to be Sido; this device is also used in "My Mother and the Books," where Sido's retelling of the familiar and beautiful version of childbirth brings the frightened daughter back to earth, when she has swooned reading Zola's unrecognizably graphic account of the same phenomenon. Likewise, in "The Wedding," the strangeness of the sacrificial bridal bedchamber glimpsed through the window at the peasant wedding is dispelled when the frightened little girl runs home to Sido, to the chaste circle of light, to the rediscovery of something familiar, an "illumination" following the "bewilderment" caused by a glimpse of adult sexuality.

But the obverse phenomenon is depicted in a tale such as "The Little One," where the garden is transformed by the coming of night from an Eden to an unfamiliar and hostile graveyard: here something familiar is made strange—and the effect, far from being comic, is alienating and terrifying. This is also the technique of "Toutouque," where the docile family pet becomes unrecognizable after she has furiously attacked another dog: "She attempted her kind, fostering smile, but she was gasping and the whites of her eyes, streaked with blood-shot lines, looked as if they were bleeding [. . .] I could find no other words in which to express my dismay, my alarm and my astonishment at seeing an evil power, whose very name was unknown to my ten years, so transform the gentlest of creatures into a savage brute" (95). Here the unmasking reveals an unsuspected layer and hints at the ferocity that may underlie Colette's gentle comic universe. This revelation suggests that comic condensation or veiling may be reversed— peeling off a layer of disguise—with a disquieting effect.

In any case, condensation, like regression, is not simply a technique of the joke or dream, but is a resource of the text-work as well, illustrating that primary process is an important component of what Freud calls "the poet's secret," the capacity to move and to astonish. Indeed, all the fictional autobiographies are condensed in a sense, overdetermined, since the narrating "I" always exists in at least two time frames, with at least two points of view, intricated in multiple webs of allusive imagery.

Displacement: The Artist's Sleight of Hand

The final joke technique that Freud considers to derive from the unconscious is displacement. In a dream, displacement consists of the shifting of the most significant portion of the dream's content to the sidelines of the dream scene, to elude censorship. Freud defines this process in the dream-work as "the selection of ideas which are sufficiently remote from the objectionable one for the censorship to allow them to pass, but which are nevertheless derivatives of that idea" (*Jokes* 171). He goes on to say that "among displacements are to be counted not merely diversions from a train of thought but every sort of indirect representation, and in particular the replacement of an important but objectionable element by one that is indifferent and appears innocent to the censorship, something that seems like a very remote allusion to the other one" (171).

In other words, displacement is yet another kind of costuming, which allows the objectionable idea to be sneaked past conscious censorship. In the joke, this kind of veiling is performed by means of a shifting (*Verschiebung*) of psychic emphasis from where it logically lies, allowing the joker to spring the punch line on the hearer, psychically pulling the rug out from under the listener and producing the surprise "punch" at the end. (Freud's example—"Have you taken a bath?" "What? Is one missing?" [49]—

depends on a shift of emphasis from "bath" to "taken," which cloaks the joke's point until it is revealed in the punch line.) In the category of joke-work displacements, Freud includes "psychic automatism" (the effect produced, for instance, by a Freudian slip, in an unintended punch line that our own unconscious springs on us). He adds that *irony* could be considered a case of displacement (as well as condensation), since it is a kind of dislocated double sense: "Its essence lies in saying the opposite of what one intends to convey to the other person, by making him understand—by one's tone of voice, by some accompanying gesture—that one means the opposite of what one says" (174).

One could make the same argument for parody and caricature, where an inappropriate tone is given to a familiar subject, in a shifting of emphasis that produces a comic effect. For instance, the technique of unification—the linking of two or more terms in an inappropriate coupling for the sake of comic contrast—could be considered a displacement of sorts, since it consists in the linking of unlike things with an "and" in order to produce a comic disparity. In "Propaganda," for example, the child is reduced to a bit of election "paraphernalia" by such a linkage: "The shabby victoria and the aged black mare were duly laden, when the time came, with the magic lantern, the painted diagrams, test tubes, bent pipes and other paraphernalia, the future candidate, his crutches *and myself*" (*MMH* 41, my emphasis).

Finally, the techniques that Freud calls the "rediscovery of something familiar" or "bewilderment and illumination" might be considered effects of displaced attention (where we are momentarily distracted or "bewildered" by the veiling of the point, in order to be "illumined" at the end). In this case, the techniques of condensation and displacement work in tandem: a familiar idea is veiled, disguised as an unfamiliar one—temporarily obscured by a kind of overlay, doubling, or condensation—and then subsequently revealed as familiar in the joke's conclusion. Thus this interplay of condensation and displacement is a game, performing a kind of psychic peekaboo that echoes the alternation of play, the *fort* and the *da*.

Similarly, in literary processes, a displaced attention or emphasis is the device that produces the shock of the twist or surprise ending, a source of great pleasure to the reader. A more theoretical interpretation of literary displacement may be found in structural linguistics (especially Jakobson's work as elaborated by Lacan), where there is an association of metonymy (or the related figure of synecdoche) with the horizontal syntactical axes of language. A displacement of emphasis or meaning occurs, whereby the function or attributes of an object are displaced onto "neighboring" ideas or objects ("crown" comes to stand for "king" in synecdoche; and in the metonymy "the kettle is boiling," "kettle" replaces "water").[11] In Colette's text displacement is more than a source of comic pleasure; it is also a preferred literary technique, manifest in such devices as the abrupt shift of tone to enhance affective impact ("He did try [to die first]; and succeeded at the first attempt"); or the surprise ending revealed in a "punch line" (the child in her own room calling, "Mother! Come quick! I've been abducted!" MMH 29).

In fact we have seen that all the joke techniques discussed by Freud (condensation, regression, displacement—similar to the techniques of primary process encountered in dreaming) are also at work in the text, as the stylistic veils that the author deploys, both consciously and unconsciously. Freud suggests (in "Creative Writers and Daydreaming" [1908]) that these similarities occur because the author is a dreamer of sorts. Freud's point seems to be that even when the poet consciously employs a literary device, he or she is taking a page from the book of the unconscious—using the veils of the dream-work as text-work, that is, both as an ornamentation and as a means of facilitating the expression of buried material, in order to enchant the reader, tapping the treasure trove of the unconscious ("open sesame . . . ").

[11]See Peter Brooks, "Freud's Masterplot: Questions of Narrative," in Felman, *Literature and Psychoanalysis*, 280–300, for a discussion of Lacan's "metaphoric" and "metonymic" categories. Lacan's transcoding of rhetorical terms into psycholinguistic terms uses Jakobson's concept of the horizontal axis of language, the syntax that connects words in a sequence, producing meaning (subject is linked to predicate, adverb to verb in a chain of meaning, displacing emphasis from one link to the next). In Lacan, this axis is termed the metonymic axis of *desire*: the drive to mean something moves us along the signifying chain, assuring that no one meaning is ever final, since meaning—an effect of interminable desire, the "motor" of human being—is always in reference to other meanings, diacritical, part of a signifying *chain*. Peter Brooks takes this chain of analogies one step further: he argues in literary terms that this kind of desiring displacement is the motor of plot, the forward impetus of the metonymic impulse of narrative.

Thus in Colette's work, the literary and the comic uses of primary process—in the joke-work/text-work/dream-work—are intertwined, infusing the most poignant observations with a dose of humor, even while shading the most burlesque anecdote with a kind of disquieting poignancy. Significantly, the specific technique of "humor" itself, in Freud's understanding, depends on just this kind of admixture of the painful or threatening with the lighthearted and amusing, the softening of the menacing side of life by the joker's hand. So we might say that humor is the dominant inflection of Colette's writing, as a pervasive but uneasy comic tonality: in Colette's text we can never be sure that the "rediscovery of something familiar"—or the illumination following an initial bewilderment—is not just the unveiling of one more mask, one more sleight of hand. Colette's comic voice, then, often actually lends a pathos to her work, rather than girding a stance of triumphant superiority. Like Sido, Colette smiles through her tears, "swept by shadow and sunshine": her humor is a sheer drapery, allowing us to divine a certain anguish, the pain of loss, veiled by the poet's hand.

The Purpose of Wit: Writer as Joker

> A tendentious joke calls for three people: in addition
> to the one who makes the joke, there must be a
> second who is taken as the object of the
> aggressiveness, and a third in whom the joke's aim of
> producing pleasure is fulfilled.
> —Freud, *Jokes and Their Relation to the Unconscious*

In what is possibly the most fascinating part of his work on joking, Freud discusses the aims of the joke, what it sets out to do, as an intersubjective transaction in a social context. Freud writes that there are two kinds of jokes, in terms of their purpose: "tendentious" and "innocent" jokes. In the first, a particular person or institution is the butt of the joke, whereas the second is not aimed at anyone, but is strictly a pleasure mechanism, a pointless "jest" (as in nonsense or wordplay), "an aim in itself" that does not serve a polemical cause.

But this distinction between tendentious and innocent jokes

cannot be strictly maintained, even in Freud's own account.[12] For, in the first place, Freud himself admits that all jokes are veiled transgressions ("all jokes have something forbidden to say" 106), softened and made acceptable by the joke-work, but never purely innocent or without aim. The difference between tendentious and innocent jokes is at best a question of degree: in the tendentious joke the target is easily identifiable, a person or an institution; in the case of "innocent" wordplay the target may simply be the constricting rules of logic. In fact, Freud himself doubts "if we are in a position to undertake *anything* without having an intention in view" (95), concluding that even innocent joking "should not, after all, be described as pointless and aimless, since it has the unmistakable aim of evoking pleasure in its hearers" (12). The joke, however aimless, always breaks rules, to serve the profoundly social aim of evoking pleasure in others.

Conversely—as Freud himself repeatedly suggests—even the most blatantly tendentious of jokes is not as purposeful as it seems, since it is primarily a pretext for pleasure rather than a conceptual vehicle. The joke, by definition, is the product of modified and attenuated desire, a substitute means of obtaining pleasure—not unlike child's play, which transforms an unpleasant reality into a pleasurable fantasy. Freud's work shows that all jokes are deflections of an original purpose or desire that has met up with an obstacle; even hostile or sexual jokes are always deflected from their first aims of actual seduction or physical aggression. In other words, if a joke is never completely innocent, neither is it ever completely tendentious: joking, a form of play, is an *aesthetic* activity: its hostile aims are always deflected. (Indeed, if a joke is too hostile, it will fall flat, eliciting a stern judgment from the hearer: "That's not funny.") In this deflection from purpose, jokes conform to Freud's own definition of the aesthetic, borrowed from Kuno Fischer: "The aesthetic attitude towards an object is characterized by the condition that we do not ask anything of the object, especially no satisfaction of our serious needs, but content ourselves with the enjoyment of contemplating it" (11).

In a later chapter, Freud states straightforwardly that the joke is

<hr />

[12]For my critique of Freud's distinction between innocent and tendentious jokes, see chapter 3 of *The Purloined Punch Line*.

always an aesthetic production, satisfying the condition "that in it we are not trying to get anything from things or do anything with them, that we are not needing things in order to satisfy one of our major vital needs, but that we are content with contemplating them and with the enjoyment of the idea" (95). This observation clearly has implications for the comparison of the joke-work and the text-work: both are aesthetic phenomena that are "innocent" or aimless insofar as they fulfill "none of the other [biological] aims of life" (95). In fact, jokes are a deflection of desire from real urges, stemming from biological interests: they are created by left-over *excessive* desire, channeled away from its original vital goals; in joking the aim of aggression or seduction has been modified into the "aimless" aim of aesthetic pleasure. In this respect, Freud's view of joking recalls his definition of perversion as a deflection of desire from biological aim, a detour of sorts from direct goals, a detour that makes the deflection of desire itself an occasion for pleasure.[13] It seems that the question of the "innocence" or "tendentiousness" of the joke is undecidable, since no joke is either entirely innocent or straightforwardly guilty of aim.

One thing is certain: in Freud's account the most important difference between joking and the private activity of dreaming—at least as concerns its purpose of producing pleasure—is that jokes are destined for an audience. In this regard, the "perverse" or "aesthetic" activity of the joker is less like that of the dreamer than that of the writer, whose text-work must share the pleasure produced with a complicit onlooker, the reader.

Jokes as a Social Process

This brings us to an important aspect of Freud's comic theory: his analysis of the social dynamics of the comic process, through the presentation of a paradigmatic joke scenario. Let us look briefly at Freud's narrative of "how the joke came to be," since

[13]In Part I, section 2 of *Three Essays on the Theory of Sexuality*, Freud writes: "Perversions are sexual activities which either (*a*) extend, in an anatomical sense, beyond the regions of the body that are designed for sexual union, or (*b*) linger over the intermediate relations to the sexual object which should normally be traversed rapidly on the path towards the final sexual aim."

this little tale has important ramifications for the understanding of the social function of any communicated narrative text.

In chapter 3 of *Jokes*, Freud tells the story of the origin of joking itself as a kind of comic anecdote, in which the joker overcomes a series of obstacles in order to produce the happy ending of the punch line ("Jokes make possible the satisfaction of an instinct— whether lustful or hostile—in the face of an obstacle which stands in its way" 101). Freud frames this story as a boy-meets-girl plot, with defined gender roles.[14]

"The one who makes the joke" (100), Freud tells us, encounters a desirable female object, to whom he addresses "wooing talk," which he hopes "will yield at once to sexual action" (98–99). But if the object resists, the frustrated wooer "turns positively hostile and cruel" and begins to deflect his desire into the substitute pleasures of "smut" or "sexually explicit speech" (98–100). Following this initial diversion of desire, a second male appears on the scene—a potential rival who further disrupts the little seduction maneuver ("The ideal case of resistance of this kind on the woman's part occurs if another man is present at the same time— a third person—for in that case an immediate surrender is as good as out of the question" 99). But our frustrated joking hero still "gets the girl" by exposing her to the other male in an obscene joke that is clearly exhibitionist in character.[15] For the woman is now dressed down before the second male, the listener who gets to enjoy her discomfiture (100). The pleasure game is played out between poles one and three, joker and listener, who share a laugh at the expense of the offended lady (who leaves the room, Freud tells us, "feeling ashamed"). In this scenario of male bonding the original goal of seduction is abandoned in favor of the fun of the dirty joke, shared between the rival-accomplices. Freud writes that the joker actually "calls on the originally interfering third party as his ally" (100), "bribing" the listener with "the effortless satisfaction of his own libido."

But interestingly, in a later section of *Jokes*, Freud points out the

<hr/>

[14]The following argument is made in detail in *The Purloined Punch Line*, where I analyze the joke as a paradigm for literary processes.

[15]Freud insists on the joker's triumph over his comic victim, who is "overcome" in the process: "By making our enemy comic, we achieve in a roundabout way the enjoyment of overcoming [her]" (*Jokes* 103).

aggressive nature of the capture of the listener's attention by the device of *ideational mimetics* (192–93). If the listener gets pleasure from the joke process, it is only because he is taken in by the joke-work, following the action, and is then caught off-guard by the punch line. We have seen, for instance, that Colette's humor works this way, when we follow along until the surprise revelation moves and amuses us. (In "The Abduction" the last line reveals that the "kidnapped" child is in her own room; in "Propaganda" we learn that the "propagandist" has only been electioneering as an excuse to spend time with his child; and so forth.) Moreover Colette's humor suggests that "the willing suspension of disbelief" (Coleridge's term for the pact between writer and reader), the entry of the reader into the writer's world, is the literary version of ideational mimetics, the device by which the reader follows along, led on by the writer until the pleasurable surprise ending.

Indeed, in *Jokes*, Freud points out the pleasure the joker takes in leading the listener on, "misleading and annoying his hearer," who "damps down *his* annoyance" by resolving "to tell the joke himself later on" (139n.) to the next victim in the joking chain. Thus the joking triangle is always a quadrilateral of sorts, a social chain in which the imaginary capture of both the joke's object (pole two) and its listener (pole three) is perpetuated with a changing cast of players. As Freud puts it: "A joke *must* be told to someone else . . . something *remains over* which seeks, by communicating the idea, to bring the unknown process of constructing a joke to a conclusion" (143). But desire will of course live to joke another day.

Now there are obvious similarities between this love triangle and Freud's oedipal drama, in which father and son, rivals for the female object, end up renouncing their rivalry in a complicit pact of identification. The passing of the Oedipus complex represents a turning from the tragic conflict to the comic resolution: the outcome is a comic happy ending, rather than a family tragedy. Similarly, in the joke scenario, the illumination at joke's end is no longer the exposure of a tragic crime, but the unveiling of some other forbidden "truth." For we recall that an important function of the joke-work is to disguise the joke's point until its timely revelation in the punch line, and even then to soften its punch by wrapping it in acceptable form (132). In this way, the joke-work behaves like the writer's text-work, which masks the writer's fantasies in order to make them palatable to the onlooking reader.

Like the literary process, the comic long-circuit is a drama of disguise, requiring at least three levels of layering. First, it must veil its own point, in order to surprise the listener at the joke's end. Second, it must wrap the point in good taste, in order not to offend the listener at the unveiling. Finally, as the superimposition of the oedipal triangle on the joking process suggests, the joke cloaks the primal urges of love and aggressivity motivating all human creativity. All of which demonstrates the importance of the listener in the joking scenario, as Freud himself is at pains to point out: "And this gives us a full impression of how indispensable the third person is for the completion of the joking process [. . .] Everything in jokes that is aimed at gaining pleasure is calculated with an eye to the third person, as though there were insurmountable obstacles to it in the first person" (155). Throughout *Jokes*, Freud insists on the social nature of the comic process, as a transaction that requires a witness, the onlooking other, without whom the joker could not pull off the artful sleight of hand, the transformation of obstructed desire.

And the joke is not only intersubjective and social, but contagious: "Laughter is among the highly infectious expressions of psychical states. When I make the other person laugh by telling him my joke, I am actually making use of him to arouse my own laughter" (156). Freud insists that the need to retell a joke is almost compulsive: "An urge to tell the joke to someone is inextricably bound up with the joke-work; indeed this urge is so strong that often enough it is carried through in disregard of serious misgivings" (143).

Freud's insistence on the social nature of this triangular comic process—where joking desire/pleasure is passed along like a contagion—suggests that the joking circuit has a great deal in common with another triangle: that of the reader, the character, and the writer. For when an author such as Colette uses the joke-work to produce pleasure, she is entering into a complex transaction, depending on the establishment of an identification (recalling the identification between father and son at the passing of the Oedipus complex—as well as the bond between joker and listener). In fact a similar bonding works in any literary process: the reader's attention is captured and held by the text-work and the promise of the exposure of the character's inner life, as well as the revelations of the plot's *dénouement*. As in joking, the writer gets a vicarious satisfaction from the fantasy thanks to the presence of the on-looking reader, who completes the circuit, furnishing the pretext for the writing of the tale, the public staging of the fantasy.

And insofar as the joke scenario is a replay of the old oedipal story—whereby a deal is made between reader and writer, establishing a pact of identification, as we readers see the world through the writer's eyes—then these local examples of Colette's humor are paradigms revealing how the work as a whole functions, even at those moments when it is not explicitly funny. For Colette's fictional autobiography often elicits a profound identification on the part of the reader (as in the moving scenes of childhood), as well as a "cathexis" with fascinating and sometimes prurient characters (as in *The Pure and the Impure*).

Of course Freud's joke scenario, however enlightening, is about as gender-biased as it can be: reading a woman humorist such as Colette leads us to wonder what happens when the joke's initiator is female. Is there any way that Colette's joke-work differs from this classic plot? When her voice tells the tale, what happens to locker-room humor? What does *this* woman want?

"She" Tells Her Story: The Priest on the Wall

Certainly one problematic aspect of Freud's work is the fixity of the gender categories in the tale he tells, where both teller and listener are males, enjoying a fantasy of sexual aggression aimed at the female object of "smutty" humor. But Lacanian readings of this paradigm, and of the oedipal scenario it echoes, have suggested that Freud's gender categories are not as inflexible as they seem. This, for instance, is one interpretation of Lacan's reading of Poe's "The Purloined Letter": in Lacan's account of the making of subjectivity and the circulation of desire, the role of subject or object becomes a matter of position rather than anatomy, in a desiring chain in which not only are all positions flexible and interchangeable, but the movement from position to position is both inevitable and obligatory. We will all take our turn as rogues and dupes in this intersubjective farce, as the letter is passed from holder to holder. In Lacan's fable, the letter, circulated from hand to hand, stolen from each successive possessor, initiates a comic game of tag; the "letter" is that which marks the subject as "it," the object of everyone else's schemes. Thus, paradoxically, it is at the moment of greatest power—when the subject has the letter— that "he" or "she" is most vulnerable, the next to be victimized by a theft, the next "dupe" of the sleuth Dupin.[16] In fact, in Lacan, the phallic position of agent and the feminine position of object not only inevitably succeed each other, but actually coincide in the same person, the holder of the stigmatized letter.

The same might be said of the androgynous position of the writer, for the activity of writing, like joking, both empowers and divests of power: the writer, like the joker, is dependent on the response of the onlooking third, whom she then "captures" by the entertainment. As for the object of desire in this triangle (the absent lady in Freud's joke scenario; the mother in the oedipal scenario; the ghost "Sido" in Colette's scenario), "she" too holds a great deal of power, because she is desired and because (at least in the joke scenario) she escapes the fray—actually leaving the room without responding to the other's advances. For Freud insists that the joking ensues only when the object makes herself unattainable; similarly, in Colette's psychic scene, the primary female object (Sido) eludes capture, as the spirit of many faces who may be arrested and portrayed only in her absence, after her death, and then only incompletely: "I am not at all sure that I have put the finishing touches to these portraits of her" (preface, *MMH*). Likewise, other objects of Colette's desiring scrutiny are figures of power and mystery: the silent sempstress Sarah, who "says nothing, and embroiders" (*PI* 126); the ghostly Renée, who carries off "more than one secret" beneath her purple veil (*PI* 97); the shadowy Charlotte ("How many shadows still conceal her . . . It is not for me to dispel them" *PI* 24); even the curiously absent father figure—all these spectral figures are transparent, eluding exposure, slipping away while they are still desired.

[16]This parable has been read by some feminists as a critique of the notion of biological sex as a factor determining psychic structure. For a feminist reading of Lacan's essay, see Barbara Johnson's "The Frame of Reference: Poe, Lacan, Derrida," in Felman, *Literature and Psychoanalysis*, 457–505.

Thus Colette's work, like Lacan's reading of Freud, suggests that any exposure or capture of the veiled ghostly object is an Imaginary one, like the infantile *fort-da* fantasy, an effect of unfinished desire, subject to infinite repetition. And Colette (like Lacan) also opens Freud to a reinterpretation of the notion of gender, even in the oedipal scenario, seemingly so gender-bound. For as Colette's own work attests, each position in the three-way literary circuit (reader, writer, character) is simultaneously a position of power and of vulnerability, a position of desire. Moreover, the seemingly powerful position of subject (of joker, of narrator, of desirer) is a question of role or locus, not of anatomy, and it is a position we all hold in turn.

But does this mean that the female subject, the female joker, the female writer, woman herself, has no specificity? Is there no such thing as a "woman writer"? Certainly recent theory has stressed the transactional nature of writing: regardless of the gender of writer and characters, the literary process will follow a desiring circuit, opening outward to an onlooking reader.

Yet even if the positions of writing subject, of character/object, and of reading recipient are open to both genders—just as are the traits of activity and passivity, even in Freud's account—there may still perhaps be a difference in what the female writer/joker holds up for pleasurable enjoyment, as well as a difference in how she exercises her powerful function of captor, when she is in the position of entertainer.[17] We have seen that Colette's role of writer vacillates between the coquetry of veiling and the straightforward activity of investigation and exposure; but even when she is in the active position of the one who exposes, her writing effects a complicated identification with her objects, lending a certain irony and multiplicity to her vision.

The same may be said of Colette's role as humorist. Certainly there is an aggressive component to her comic portraits, motivated by the desire to expose her objects to the reader's view. But Colette is not simply a locker-room joker, like the protagonist of Freud's joke scenario: Colette prefers the discretion of the allusive

---

[17]Freud himself suggests that the degree of activity or passivity of female behavior is culturally determined ("I need only hint at the elasticity and variability in the amount of exhibitionism that women are permitted to retain in accordance with differing convention and circumstances" *Jokes* 98).

nuance to the obscenity of straightforward reference. Indeed, we have seen that she shuns simple exposure of the sexual, opting for "impurity," the shadows of the ambiguous, over the glare of the "pure," except as "pure sound" (the ornamental sound of the word *pur* itself), a veil that obscures meaning and generates desire.

Even when Colette the humorist engages in tendentious joking—as when sexual matters figure in the joke—she prefers the technique of allusion to forthright revelation (we must guess that "the rage of Paris" is a homosexual; that Sido's jealousy of her exotic friend Adrienne is sexually motivated; that the little girl has had an erotic and perhaps orgasmic dream in "The Abduction"). Nuance and innuendo, rather than the kind of "smut" that generates Freud's tendentious joke, determine the tonality of Colette's comic writing. But of course, whether this "feminine" delicacy is simply a societally imposed inhibition or role, or whether it is part of an essential feminine nature, remains open to question, even in orthodox Freudian theory.[18] For Freud himself seems to suggest that it is perhaps only the repression of society that transforms the active sexual urge to a passive nature:

> The libido for looking and touching is present in *everyone* in two forms, active and passive, male and female [. . .] In women the inclination to passive exhibitionism is almost invariably buried under the imposing reactive function of sexual modesty, but not without a loophole being left for it in relation to clothes. I need

[18]Freud's infamous dictum—that anatomy is destiny—is qualified by many statements throughout his theory. In *Jokes* (98), in the *New Introductory Lectures* (117), and elsewhere, Freud argues that even the notion of anatomy does not coincide with the notion of a certain "nature" or even a set sexual inclination. And of course feminists have questioned his notorious concept of "penis envy," either rejecting the notion altogether, as a masculine projection, or rereading this "complex" as a symptom of societal conditions, the envy of the position anatomy confers in patriarchal society. Karen Horney and Ernest Jones were two of the first to do this revisionist work on the notion of female sexuality (see Janine Chasseguet-Smirgel's summary of their work and the work of the British school, in *Feminine Sexuality*. Further feminist reconsiderations of the accusation of "phallocentrism" in psychoanalysis may be found in Jane Gallop's *The Daughter's Seduction* and in Juliet Mitchell's *Psycho-Analysis and Feminism* (New York: Vintage–Random House, 1975). See also *Women and Analysis*, ed. Jean Strouse (New York: Grossman, 1974) and *Feminism and Psychoanalysis*, ed. Richard Feldstein and Judith Roof (Ithaca: Cornell University Press, 1989).

only hint at the elasticity and variability in the amount of exhibitionism that women are permitted to retain in accordance with
differing convention and circumstances. (*Jokes* 98)

In this account, what Freud calls the "male" libido is still the
active element, but it is open to question whether this active male
role is societal or essential (biological). (Elsewhere, of course,
Freud repeatedly claims that all libido is male, that is, active, and
that this male libido assigns the passive and objective role to the
female.) But this statement at least suggests that the woman is not
always a passive object/victim but is capable of staging her own
kind of active entertainment. For Freud argues here that the "feminine" urge to adorn—including the art of veiling as enhance-
ment—is a kind of exhibitionism, stemming from the transformation of the scopic urge, the urge to look, rather than from any
natural passivity, delicacy, or modesty. This complexity is certainly manifest in Colette's sinuous dance of allusion, as well as in
the delicacy of her humor, which both displays and hides: this
storyteller belongs to a long line of seductresses who set the
reader adrift on a magic carpet of innuendo ("I embark upon a
drifting souvenir of nights graced neither by sleep nor by certitude . . ." *PI* 25), spinning out unfinished tales for a thousand and
one sleepless nights, where the bare shock of the punch line has
been replaced by the ellipsis ("nights graced neither by sleep nor
by certitude . . ."). Colette's humor is the wit of the female genius, which displays without humiliating, and alludes without baring all.

The Fantom "I": Woman as Joker

But perhaps more interesting than the "femininity" of Colette's
technique is the question of Colette's objects, and her own relation to what is being told. About whom does she joke, and why?
We have seen that her preferred comic objects are none other
than Sido and the Captain, in scenes of family life: that is, the
ghosts with whom she most profoundly identifies.

In one whole series of anecdotes, Sido herself is the object of
the joke ("Jealousy," "The Abduction," "My Mother and the Forbidden Fruit," "Epitaphs"). Sido is gently caricatured in these loving portraits, but she also is portrayed with a large degree of iden-

tification; the adult daughter is at pains to indicate that she understands and sympathizes with her mother's point of view, if only in retrospect. At other moments, Colette's identification with the object of the joke is even more explicit: the protagonist of the anecdote, although portrayed comically herself, is also the heroine of the tale, in the first position of joker, the subject who exposes others to ridicule. For example, in such anecdotes as "My Mother and Morals," "My Mother and the Curé," "My Mother and the Books," we identify with Sido, as the narrator's mouthpiece who criticizes societal convention. Here, Sido is no longer simply the object of the tale, but is at the same time in the position of joke maker, thanks to a grafting of the writer's point of view onto that of her protagonist.

Indeed, we have seen that where her parents are concerned, the narrator is capable of realigning her identification, switching sides in midstream. The end of "Jealousy" is a case in point: after ridiculing her aging parents' passion, the narrator shifts positions, attributing the mocking tone of the vignette to the *child's* ignorance ("But I can still smile at their quarrels because I am only fifteen, and have not yet divined the ferocity of love beneath his veteran eyebrow, and the blushes of adolescence upon her fading cheeks" 20). Here the adult narrator lines up with her parents, on the side of the butt of the joke, identifying with their foibles against the mocking smile of her own younger self. This is an unexpected shift from caricature to humor—where the teller herself steps down from her superior stance to share the hot seat with the parents, splitting her "self" into object and onlooker. Thus we have a doubling of Freud's joke scene: the punch line here—the comic exposure of the parents' inappropriate jealousy—is undercut by a second "punch": a warning of sorts that if we laugh at the aging parents now, the last laugh will be on us when we grow old. This caveat changes the rules of the game: Colette, the joke's teller, abruptly backs out on the conventional complicity between joker and listener, lining up with her object and thus again taking the reader by surprise. She thereby adds a special twist to the comic transaction, implicating us as potential objects of the last laugh.

In another category of comic tale ("Epitaphs," "The Priest on the Wall"), the children are the butt of the joke, and Sido is the judge who exposes them to scorn or ridicule (scolding Gabrielle for thinking a "presbytery" is a snail; destroying her son Leo's imaginary graveyard). But here again Colette's scenario is a complication of Freud's version: this is a process of appeal, asking the reader to side with the accused, to adopt the child's point of view, changing the outcome of the trial, retrospectively putting Sido in the wrong and empowering the victim. By making her childhood self the target of a comic story, the narrator is rescued from a threatening situation, redeeming pleasure from what was initially a humiliating experience. (We have seen that this is the technique of "humor," according to Freud; but it is also the impulse behind a certain form of play in which children restage a humiliating experience, such as a visit to the doctor, but making *themselves* the all-powerful doctor in the replay, choosing a younger playmate as victim.)

To complete the familial triangle, we should again mention the group of anecdotes in which the father is the comic object (as in *Sido*, where he is pictured as a lovesick boy; or in "Propaganda," where he is revealed as an ineffectual electioneer). Such apparently straightforward exposures of the Captain's foibles are perhaps the most clear-cut instances of tendentious or aggressive joking in Colette, particularly given the rivalry between Gabrielle and the Captain for Sido's love: as rival for Sido's affection, Colette has an interest in laying bare her father's impotence and ridiculing his unrequited love, reducing him to the level of child. But we have seen (in Chapter 3) that this rival stance is undercut by the profound identification between the Captain and his daughter at the moment when Colette reveals her father's eerie secret—his lifelong dedication to hundreds of empty pages. With this revelation, the Captain's comic or parodic characteristics take on a heartbreaking quality: the buffoon is revealed as a tragic hero of sorts.

In other words, the exposure of the Captain's tragic impotence before the page casts a new light on his role as comic object, since as struggling writer he is an alter ego of the narrator herself. This new light also suggests that he too is an object of unrequited love, the love of his adult daughter, who comes to understand him "too late," after his death. The comic figure of the Captain is as overdetermined as any of the players in Colette's comedy: he is simultaneously cast as erotic object and object of hostility (pole two in the joking triangle); as audience for Colette, since he looks on and reads her writing, even from beyond the grave (pole three, the listener); and as the writer's model and alter ego (pole one, the subject/storyteller) since it is his name that has become "Colette's" own. In this comedy of shifting and mutually implicated identities, the dead father, shrouded in the paternal metaphor "Colette," has become the "spirit" of the daughter's work: and his shroud (the paternal name) has been transformed into a feminine adornment (the daughter's pen name), a veil cloaking and softening the daughter's irrecoverable loss. In a sense, Freud's comic theory permits us to reconsider this "woman's work" of transformation: this mourning-work, which at once bares and covers the father's lack, is a comic labor; and it is the work of the writer-weaver as well.

It is no doubt by design, then, that in Freud's account of the joking process, metaphors of clothing or disguise abound: Freud refers repeatedly to the joking *Verkleidung* (disguise) and *Entkleidung* (envelope or wrapping); he refers to the exposure of the joke's point as the revealing of its *Nudität*. All of these references to *Kleidung* (clothing, veil) in turn recall his other great metaphor for the writer's art as a kind of veiling (*Ankleidung*), in "Creative Writers and Daydreaming." What Lacanian theory adds to this gallery of veiled images is an interpretation of woman herself as "veiled phallus"—that is, as the ultimate object of desire, which can never be appropriated or totally revealed.[19] (Thus however phallocentric Lacan's imagery may be, it is not necessarily sexist: for the phallus is by definition the object that no one ever has.) Woman is Lacan's veiled metaphor for the inexhaustibility of desire, always overdetermined by others who occupy, or will occupy, the same place. The shifting nature of gender suggests that it is a veil to be cast off, then reassumed—even the all-powerful father is only a Symbolic function, rather than a historical person with a specific biological role. Colette's autofictions suggest that

[19]This is the focus of the seminars of the 1970s, especially "Seminar XX, Encore" of 1972–73, and the "Seminar of 21 June 1975," parts of which have been translated in *Feminine Sexuality*, ed. Juliet Mitchell and Jacqueline Rose. The introduction to this volume also contains an excellent summary of Lacan's controversial theories of femininity and of feminine sexuality as linguistic construct or category.

to work as a writer, perhaps especially as a woman writer, is to play with this veil of gender, unfolding its possibilities, comic and otherwise.

In short, what characterizes, and perhaps feminizes, Colette's voice as joker is a pronounced overdetermination of locus: the joking triangle exists in Colette's text, but as Lacan's work suggests, it is the scene of an ever-changing perspective, where one actor plays the different roles not just successively but simultaneously. Colette is the "Priest on the Wall"—the one who officiates at her own comic ceremony—but she herself is often the butt of these anecdotes, as well as the one who tells them and then rereads them, with the help of the onlooking other (we readers, her ghosts). She is in between—perched on the wall of gender, able to take either position and to communicate between both sides, as subject and object at once. The Priest on the Wall is powerless and powerful: like the child of the *fort-da* game, who casts away and retrieves her objects at will, the writer walks a thin line between agency and objectification, pleasure and pain.

As a woman writer—already a position of sexual indeterminacy in Colette's vision, since she wears the veil and wields the pen— Colette seems particularly adept at these shifts of position, doubling her voice with that of the other. In the case of her fictional autobiography, the fulfillment of desire afforded by the joke-work/text-work is never anything but ambiguous, since her exposure of the comic victim, with whom she identifies as one of her many "ghosts" or alter egos, always also reveals herself. In Colette's work, the motto of farce—"*à trompeur, trompeur et demi*"— has a masochistic twist: when she plays the role of rogue she herself suffers the consequences of dupe.

Nor is her reader excused from this chain. For we readers are the occupants of the third pole in the joking triangle, "bribed by an effortless satisfaction of [our] own libido" (as Freud insists), but at a price. Reading Colette, suddenly we too are the abandoned children, looking back into Eden, guilty children whose laughter is shadowed by sadness, who realize "too late" that our comic objects are lost. In Colette's comic web, the object of the joking hostility may be ourselves, caught in the web of textual others, that family that Colette has induced us to join. Above all, Colette's shifting text does not permit us to take an immutable stand, to assume a position of power or superiority over the objects of our prurient or comic interest. Colette's reader may be in the masculine position of one who looks, but "he" is implicated in the plight of the objects at which "he" laughs. And all of this cross-dressing is perhaps reason to smile, but at our own expense. As Freud knew, as Colette's work reminds us, when we lift the veil to see, to expose the butt of this joke, this veiled clown, we may find a mirror.

6

The Fantom Subject of Autobiography

> So it came about that both legally and familiarly, as
> well as in my books, I now have only one name,
> which is my own.
> —*Break of Day*

> The uncanny impression results [when] one identifies
> with another person, so that the self becomes
> confounded, or the foreign self becomes one's own.
> —Freud, "The 'Uncanny'"

Ghost Theory

We have seen that the veil is the canvas of the ghostwriter. Sometimes comic or ornamental, sometimes spooky, the veil is a multilayered surface that suggests other surfaces, a screen, a shroud, a blank page with invisible script underneath, which must be retraced in order to give form to the ghosts the veil envelops. The writer's activity mimes the undercover work of the unconscious as unveiled by Freud, deploying the resources of the text-work to perform the mourning-work. Thus Colette's text-work may be read as an unveiling of her own monument, inscribed with the epitaph "here lies Colette."

The effect of eerie familiarity in Colette's autofictions may even be described as uncanny, in Freud's sense of the term ("The 'Uncanny,'" 1919).[1] For Freud writes that "the uncanny leads back to something long known to us, once very familiar" (123). And he points out that *das Unheimlich* is itself an uncanny word, derived from *heimlich*, which can mean opposite things: either "familiar, cozy, homelike" or "unfamiliar, secret, hidden." Colette's autobiographical tales seem to be *heimlich* in both senses, where the most homey of situations and characters may take on a ghostly cast.

---

[1]"The 'Uncanny'" (1919), *S.E.* 17.123. The page numbers and citations given in this chapter are from the Alix Strachey translation, in the anthology *On Creativity and the Unconscious*, ed. Benjamin Nelson (New York: Harper and Row, 1958).

Freud specifies three categories of the uncanny, all of which figure in Colette's work: (1) infantile fantasies (Freud cites fears of the dark; fears of blinding or dismemberment, in tales of severed hands, ghostly dancing feet; and fantasies of intrauterine life, including horror tales of being entombed alive); (2) infantile omnipotence of thought or magic, when inanimate objects take on life; (3) the emergence of a double as a reflected image or a ghost, accompanied by "telepathy between beings," a "doubling, dividing, or interchanging of the self" (140). Finally, noting that an *unheimliches Haus* is haunted by ghosts, Freud observes that the uncanny sensation is most acute "in relation to death and dead bodies" (149). Freud speculates as to what these various experiences have in common: "The uncanny is in reality nothing new or foreign, but something familiar and old [that has] been estranged only by the process of repression" (148). According to Freud, all uncanny phenomena (magic, ghosts, bizarre coincidence, dismemberment) are the effects of the "return of the repressed," which comes back to haunt us from the "beyond" of the unconscious.

With its emphasis on the hair-raising effect of uncanny literature on the reader, Freud's essay is a forerunner of reader-response criticism. Freud attributes the uncanny effect in ghost or horror tales to the insertion of imaginary phenomena into a realistic narrative (when "something which we have hitherto considered imaginary becomes real" 152), producing a discrepancy, shock, or disorientation uncannily reminiscent of the surprise "punch" of comic phenomena. For the uncanny impression is produced, Freud insists, *only* by literature with a realistic cadre. Otherwise the tale becomes science fiction or fairy tale, where the rules of the game admit unreal or magical effects.[2]

Freud's essay is fascinating in its own right, but it has implications for Colette's autofiction as well. In Colette's portrait of the Captain, for instance, we have noted the images of castration and dismemberment (in the image of the father's severed hand, which rises up before the daughter, tracing an "invisible script"; and in

[2]Freud writes: "[The uncanny] retains this quality in fiction as in experience so long as the setting is one of physical reality; but as soon as it is given an arbitrary and unrealistic setting in fiction, it is apt to lose its quality of the uncanny" ("The 'Uncanny,'" 160).

the many references to blinding). And in *My Mother's House* and *Sido* we have seen incidences of intrauterine fantasy, in the theme of return to the maternal house and garden, while in *The Pure and the Impure*, the retreat of the Ladies of Llangollen is pictured not only as an intrauterine bliss, but also as a kind of tomb, a living death. In addition, Colette's tales of childhood abound with allusions to magic, to the animism of flora and fauna in Sido's enchanted realm; and this magic tonality recurs with a darker cast in the occult aura of *The Pure and the Impure*. Indeed, Colette's fictional autobiographies are an exercise in what Freud calls the infantile belief in omnipotence of thought, resuscitating the beloved departed ones by the sheer force of desire ("If only I could hear that voice again, I should weep for joy!" Colette exclaims in the overture to *My Mother's House*: and of course it is "that voice" that magically resounds between the pages/walls of her mother's house).

Of all the uncanny goings-on in Colette's textual haunted house, it is perhaps the occurrence of the double—as a kind of intermingling of the self and the other—that is most prevalent. Freud cites Otto Rank's study on the association of the double with "reflections in mirrors, with shadows, with guardian spirits," claiming that "the double was originally an insurance against the construction of the ego, an energetic denial of the power of death" (141). Thus the double is a guardian angel and an alter ego, a reflection of infantile narcissism.[3] But the double also has a threatening visage, especially in adult fantasy: "When this stage has been left behind the double takes on a different aspect. From having been an assurance of immortality, he becomes the ghastly harbinger of death" (141). Similarly, Colette's ghosts have two sides, menacing and benevolent: we have seen that her "reflections" are replete with mirrored images of ghosts and guardian spirits who both help and haunt, who drive her writing hand and who take that hand to lead her "home" at life's end.

Freud extends the notion of doubling to the general phenomenon of recurrence (as in the uncanny effect of coincidence or *déjà*

---

[3]Freud: "[Such ideas] have sprung from the soil of unbounded self-love which holds sway in the mind of the child" ("The 'Uncanny,'" 141).

vu). This sort of involuntary repetition in turn recalls the various kinds of repetition or rediscovery in the joke-work, itself doubled by the ghostly death-drive, the masked player in Colette's text-play. As for "uncanny" technique—the interweaving of fantasy with reality—one could hardly ask for a more apt example than the hybrid genre of fictional autobiography itself. The opening vignette of *My Mother's House* provides a striking example of this interweaving: the mother seems to wait at a real window, but we readers experience a strong sensation of the uncanny as we discover that the anxious mother is a ghost, waiting for her errant children to die, to come home, to return to the womb/tomb. (Interestingly, Freud cites the female genitals as a primal source of the uncanny impression of familiarity, as the "home" from which human beings go forth and to which they return, when they are buried in Mother Earth.)

Colette's uncanny text is fashioned with a warp and woof, participating vertically in memory and horizontally in lived experience, and shot through with the haunting cry—"Where are the children?"—that threads its way through the fabric of infantile memory (a memory that itself "veils" an ancient tale of love and loss, the guilty relation with the "murdered" parent). As spinner of texts, the writer performs an uncanny function, a weird sorcery, evoking the return of the repressed in veiled form, softening and covering the gaping wound of loss—or, as Lacan puts it, the "hole in the Real"—created by the death of a loved one. (We recall that for Freud, the activity of weaving itself is a cover-up of sorts, an activity that aims to hide the uncanny effect of female "castration."[4])

In this sense, all writing is a cover-up, an inweaving of the Real and the Imaginary in a Symbolic function. And all writers are ghostwriters, veiling their own primal wound in a diversion that skirts their own desire, shrouds their own *revenants* as new characters, recasts their private mythology as plot, weaving the fictional fabric in a motion that, like the shuttle on a loom, seems to progress forward, while always doubling back. As Colette weaves her text, the shroud in which she will lay her ghosts to rest, she drapes their memories in the loveliest of veils, which allow her at last to

[4]See Chapter 2, note 24.

see them ("So that's the real you? Now I see, I'd never understood you" *Sido* 186).

Thus the weaver-sorcerer does not reproduce real experience,
but performs a work of transformation and of healing. In Colette's
memory, Sido is constantly looking for her child, her refrain
pierced by gaps that signify her separation ("'Where . . .? Children . . . ?' / Nowhere" *MMH* 7). Thus Sido first searches for her
daughter and finds her—nowhere; but in Colette's replay the
daughter looks for the mother from whom she has been separated, and finds her—everywhere, a companion ghost. The spirit
of the lost parent returns to fill the gaping wound caused by
death, her veiled form mending the tear in the fabric of the Real.

Ghost Theory as Autobiography

In a fascinating essay on Freud's *Beyond the Pleasure Principle*
("Coming into One's Own"), Jacques Derrida treats the issues
that are at the core of Colette's ghostwriting: the fictional nature
of autobiography, the origins of play in grief and jealousy, the
need to recall one's ghosts as a way of assuring one's own identity. In a brilliant web of allusion, Derrida suggests that Freud's
theory of play and the repetition compulsion is itself an autobiographical game seeking to assure his own position as master of
psychoanalysis, his own name as "Name of the Father." Extend-
ing this web of references in her turn, Madelon Sprengnether has
reread Derrida's essay as a kind of confessional autobiography
("Ghost Writing: A Meditation on Literary Criticism as Narrative"), relating how she herself has sought to integrate autobiographical ghosts into her own work: "[But] while the language
I invent for them allows them to speak, it is not their native
tongue. They are liars and plagiarizers, borrowing my words for
their existence, compulsively telling their own story."[5] Both Derrida and Sprengnether are saying that the literary critic has no
outside superior stance vis-à-vis the text, that she is part of an
expanding chain of references, that even objective theory is a kind
of ghostwriting, that all writing is "simultaneously fiction and au-

---

[5]Madelon Sprengnether, "Ghost Writing: A Meditation on Literary Criticism as
Narrative," in *The Psychoanalytic Study of Literature*, ed. Joseph Reppen and
Maurice Charney (Hillsdale, N.J.: Analytic Press, 1985), 48.

tobiography."[6] Since Derrida's essay on Freud ("doubled" by Sprengnether) touches our concerns about Colette's ghostwriting, I would like briefly to retrace his reading of Freud's theory as an uncanny "return of the repressed," before doubling back to Colette's own ghost story.

In "Coming into One's Own," Derrida begins by asserting the fantom nature of Freud's main hypothesis in *Beyond the Pleasure Principle*—that the repetition compulsion is a manifestation of the death-drive. Derrida observes that like the child's toy in the *fort-da* game, Freud's strange hypothesis returns, haunting the essay, only to be cast away repeatedly, never coming to rest in a firm conclusion. Thus the structure of creative repetition observed by Freud in his grandson's play is also the structure of his own essay: his own theory haunts the text's shape, without ever finally being mastered, even as it serves as the occasion for a constantly renewed pleasure (the "play" of Freud's own theoretical speculation). After noting the uncanny insistence of Freud's shadowy hypothesis (of the death-drive), Derrida turns to the autobiographical nature of this text, wondering how such a highly subjective account can serve as the grounding of an institution, guaranteed by the name "Freud" itself. He notes in passing that autobiography, the use of the "I" and the signing of one's name, does not assure the reality of what "I" am claiming.

In other words, Derrida argues that Freud has written an essay that appears to be autobiographical and even homey (*heimlich*), but which is a sort of myth, true and invented at once. (The same may be said of Colette's tales of Sido: in both cases a family member is immortalized by the "familiar" onlooking "I" who records his or her actions.) Turning Freud on Freud, Derrida stresses the fallibility of Freud's own account of his familiars, uncovering Freud's investment in this "objective" reflection on death, repetition, and play.

---

[6]Sprengnether writes: "Thus literary interpretation strikes me as a refracted form of autobiography. The text of psychoanalysis itself—the product of a complex interplay of internal and external observation, informed with metaphor—may be read in this fashion. Derrida makes this point (among others) about Freud's *Beyond the Pleasure Principle* [. . .] Derrida reveals the melancholy undersong of this most melancholy book. We are by now becoming accustomed to reading Freud as a literary text. How long will it take for us to read Derrida in this fashion?" (45–46).

Derrida suggests that the child's desired object, the absent mother who has gone out for the evening (Freud's daughter Sophie), is also the object of Freud's own under-requited love, especially since at the time of the writing of *Beyond the Pleasure Principle*, Sophie had recently died: her absence to both her father and son had become irrevocable and permanent. Hers is the ghostly non-presence that haunts this narrative, causing the memory of little Ernst's trauma at being separated from his mother to be doubled by Freud's own grief at the loss of his daughter. Sophie is also an emblem of Freud's own mortality and the threat of the loss of his immortal name: as his married daughter, who no longer bears his name, she has failed to pass on the name "Freud" to her male child. There is thus (Derrida argues) a profound identification between the "disinterested" scientist-observer (grandfather Freud) and the baby who plays a game motivated by jealousy and resentment of his father (Freud's own son-in-law): it is this outsider who has stolen the mother/daughter (Sophie) from both of them, superimposing his name on the Name of the (grand)Father. Thus on a personal level, Freud strives to reassert his paternal rights, assuring his familial legacy. Derrida observes that little Ernst's father, Freud's son-in-law, is significantly removed from this text, never even mentioned ("the father is far away, *fort*" 128), while the grandfather Freud remains *da* ("as for the father of psychoanalysis, he's still there" 128). (There is a similarly complicated paternal absence in the work of Colette, for whom the living Captain is missing, *fort*, while the dead father is always *da*, in the very name "Colette.")

In fact Derrida suggests that Freud's whole theoretical project is anything but disinterested, reflecting the drive of every author who aspires to make a name, trying to assure that after the writer is gone (*fort*), he or she will still be there (*da*): "One gives oneself one's own movement, inheriting from oneself: it's set up so that the ghost, at least, can always collect" (121–22). Freud is writing his own ghost story, as the *Geist* of psychoanalysis.

Derrida then turns from the autobiographical nature of theory to the theoretical nature of autobiography, rehearsing the complications, in any work of fiction, of the distinction "between the 'I' of the narrator and the 'I' of the author" (122), a difference supposedly erased in autobiography. Yet in *all* writing, the narrating persona is a split personality of sorts, both inside and outside the textual world. We have seen evidence of just this sort of split between "Colette" and the "I" of her autofictions.

Derrida's mention of a split or multiple "I"—in a diversion of several pages—seems to elicit a brief excursion in our own "reflections" on Colette and Freud (the *"fort"* of this essay?). For in insisting on this kind of split subject, Derrida is "doubling" Freudian theory, which suggests that the ego itself is produced by a splitting (Freud's *Spaltung*) whereby the process of repression creates the unconscious, that part of the self that is always *fort*, alienated from consciousness.[7] Lacanian theorists have expanded on this idea as the "narcissistic creation of the ego," the result of a kind of doubling in which the subject's ego is created as a reflection of the internalized image of other beings, in the mirror stage.[8] All of these theories of the ego emphasize that the ego is not an original property of human subjects, a transcendental identity, but is rather an uncanny residue, a ghostly double of something else (the internalized image of the other; the alienated image of the self; the residue of the split between the conscious and the unconscious).

Derrida continues his own observation of Freud's family scene with a reflection on the role of the veil: the child casts the toy back and forth through the bed-curtains, suggesting that the "veil" is the frontier between *fort* and *da*, a dividing line between what is here and what is gone (like the veil of fiction, the page is the boundary at which the absent is made to reappear). Derrida concludes his essay with some reflections on the child's play with his mirror image as a formation of identity. (This conclusion suggests that the theoretical ghost who haunts this essay is Lacan—Derrida's own rival other who is quite pointedly left out—not unlike Sophie's husband in Freud's text, the missing rival father.[9] Nor

---

[7] Even earlier, in the essay "On Narcissism: An Introduction" (1914), Freud talks about the ego as the creation of "some new operation in the mind," suggesting that the ego may be the creation of a split between the unconscious and consciousness, through the process of repression.

[8] Lacan of course also insists that the subject's self-image—his or her recognition of "identity" in the mirror reflection, is always an alienation, the illusory recognition of an other as identical to self.

[9] Elsewhere Derrida aggressively confronts this "rival" (in "Le Facteur de la vér-

does Derrida make explicit reference to Freud's theory of the uncanny; yet his rereading of the *fort-da* game as a function of the
mirrored self-image certainly reflects Freud's notion of the uncanny double, an imaginary construct that confers a kind of immortality on the subject it "reflects."[10]) Colette might be said to
play a similar *fort-da* game with mirror identities: does "Colette's"
signature retrieve the missing father (*da!*), triumphing over the
absence of death, by forming the writer's identity in his image?
Do Colette's "reflections" on her father's pet name for herself
("Bel-Gazou . . . why did my father call me by it, long ago?" 30), a
name conferred in turn on *her* little girl, extend this chain of mirrors into the next generation?

But before reintroducing Colette into this game, let us reel in
our thoughts and return (*da!*) to Derrida's reflections on Freud.
After his speculations on mirroring as a version of the *fort-da*
game, Derrida reenters Freud's own hall of mirrors, overdetermining the place of each of the players in the familial tale (the
death of Sophie is repeated by the death of her second child, the
baby brother of whom Ernst—the *fort-da* child—is also jealous, in
a repetition of Freud's own jealousy of *his* younger brother, etc.).
In each of these instances of the death of Freud's posterity the
grief of the patriarch is doubled by fears about the possible demise of his own name. Significantly, in another text written at
about the same time, "Mourning and Melancholia" (1917), Freud
himself emphasizes that bereavement is a blow to one's narcissism—the loss of the mirror image with which one identifies, the
dispersal of one's integrated reflection in the mirror, the disappearance of one's model alter ego (*fort!*) with the subsequent shat-

ité," translated as "The Purveyor of Truth," *Yale French Studies* 52 [1975]: 31–113).
This essay, which deals with Lacan's treatment of Poe's "The Purloined Letter,"
forms part of an allusive web of theory: Derrida on Lacan on Freud and Poe, a
network later extended in Barbara Johnson's essay "The Frame of Reference" and
in my own work (*The Purloined Punch Line*).

[10]Derrida cites Freud's footnote concerning the child's game with his reflection:
"He had discovered his reflection in a full-length mirror which did not quite reach
to the ground, so that by crouching down he could make his mirror-image 'gone'
(*fort*)." Thus the child has doubled his game with the toy spool, with, as Derrida
says, "a replacement *bobine* for the replacement *bobine*, with his own *bobine* ('nog-
gin'), with himself as subject-object in the mirror and without the mirror" (Derrida, "Coming into One's Own," 132).

tering of one's image of self.[11] In fact, Freud suggests that grief itself is the effect of a residue of reflections and identifications, the result of having internalized the lost other. But Freud adds that after the blow to one's narcissism, the mourning-work ensues, as a process of healing performed step by step.

In the case of the family plot laid out in *Beyond the Pleasure Principle*, the relation between play and mourning is explicit and quite literal: for the mother who is the object of desire, the "toy" of the *fort-da* game (Freud's daughter, Sophie) does indeed disappear while her child is young, dying shortly after the birth of her second child, leaving her father, her husband, and her two little boys to untangle their web of grief and jealousy. Interestingly, Freud observes that the *fort-da* child does not appear to mourn—because the "dead woman is easier to keep for oneself" (140)—suggesting that the ultimate possession of the object is facilitated by its complete destruction (presumably since the child is able to lay hold of the mother's memory in death, in the final possessive move of the *fort-da* game). Does Colette do otherwise? She tells us that she did not weep at her mother's passing, and repeatedly remarks on how the dead may be fixed in time: "After death they take on a firmer outline and then cease to change" (*Sido* 186). Derrida suggests that writing (as a form of adult play) may indeed be part of this process of mourning and reality mastery: "Repetition is bequeathed: the legacy is repeated [. . .] The legacy and jealousy of a repetition [. . .] are not accidents that just happen to the *fort:da*: they pull its strings, more or less strictly. And they assign to it an auto-bio-thanatohetero-graphic writing scene" (146). Every written page is thus an elegy, every theory a ghost story, just as every reading of the text is haunted by our own desire.

The Ghost of Theories Past

In Derrida's "ghost rewriting" of *Beyond the Pleasure Principle* we may discern the return of a much earlier work, *Jokes and Their Relation to the Unconscious*—with its emphasis on play and repetition, on mastery and desire—as well as shades of Freud's early writing about writing itself ("Creative Writers and Daydreaming,"

---

[11]"Mourning and Melancholia" (1917), *S.E.* 14. All quotes and page numbers in this essay refer to the Joan Rivière translation, in the anthology *General Psychological Theory*, ed. Phillip Rieff (New York: Collier-Macmillan, 1963). Hereafter *MM*.

"The 'Uncanny' "). The observation of the uncanny unexplained effect of the joke is repeated, with darker resonance, in the later work on play and repetition, haunted by compulsion. For even the most pleasurable of comic experiences is already haunted by its uncanny double, the death-drive, and is already "beyond the pleasure principle." Indeed each of these texts shadows the others, rehearsing the same ghost-plot. In all of these works—on writing, on joking, on play—Freud suggests that desire engendered by loss is diverted into a creative labor, in which loss is veiled by acts of substitution, compensation, and disguise.

Before taking up the recurring thread of this work, returning to the question of the fantom subject of Colette's text (*da!*)—I would like to engage in one more excursion, unwinding one more skein of literary theory. I would like to refer briefly to the two great treatments of ghost story by the fathers of psychoanalysis themselves—Freud's own "Delusion and Dream in Jensen's *Gradiva*" and Lacan's "Desire and the Interpretation of Desire in *Hamlet*"— since both essays implicate the theorist as a reader of ghost stories and as a maker of ghost theory.

Freud's text analyzes a gothic novel of sorts—Wilhelm Jensen's *Gradiva*—which tells the story of a young archaeologist. While on a dig at Pompeii, Norbert Hanold sees the ghost of a beautiful Roman girl, presumably buried in the eruption of Vesuvius centuries before, who is the very image of an excavated fresco that has long fascinated him. Eventually he discovers that this apparition, who rises spookily out of the ruins in the heat of the noonday sun, is in fact a real girl. Moreover, her uncannily familiar air comes not from the fresco Hanold has been studying, but from the fact that she is actually his long-forgotten childhood sweetheart, whose memory has been buried, repressed in the interests of the scientist's work. Reawakened to love, he rediscovers his own childhood "ghost" and lives happily ever after.

This novel, Freud tells us, presents the paradigm of a certain neurosis, in which repressed material gives rise to metaphoric symptoms (the fresco "stands in for" the forgotten girl). It also demonstrates, by analogy, the process of analysis, whereby one's ghosts may be dispelled by unearthing their real origins, uncovering the repressed signifier, by mining the unconscious. (Significantly, Hanold is an archaeologist.) Freud goes on to draw an analogy between Hanold's activity and that of the writer, who rediscovers "buried" material. This connection returns our digression to Colette, who has just such a mania for delving, uncovering "what no eye before mine has gazed upon." The emphasis, both in Freud's analysis of *Gradiva* and in Colette's observation on her own creative vision, is on the vertical retrieval of material from the unconscious, as well as on the relation of repression to literary processes such as metaphor (since metaphor in a sense "stands in for" what it has occulted and buried, and serves as a ghostly double of the excluded term).

In Lacan's ghost story, the essay on *Hamlet*, the fantom is a delusion, as in Freud's reading of *Gradiva*; but in *Hamlet*, as Lacan reads it, the return of the slain father after death is not a simple case of the "return of the repressed."[12] Here it is a case of the return of the *insufficiently* repressed, the insufficiently internalized. For Lacan sees Hamlet's paternal ghost as a psychotic production, an image or hallucination produced by "foreclusion" (Freud's *Vorwerfung*). Foreclusion is the casting out of the truth of "castration" (as the unavoidable encounter with loss and human desire) in a gesture of expulsion reminiscent of the first move of the *fort-da* game, rather than its repression/internalization, symbolized by the adoption of the Paternal Metaphor. This casting out creates a hole or void out there in the Real, which is subsequently filled by hallucinations seemingly materializing in the external world.[13] In other words, in Lacan's "return to Freud," *Vorwerfung* is an expulsion of loss, a refusal properly to mourn the slain father, to internalize and assume his Law, to accede to the pact symbolized by his name. It is also the paradigm of psychosis, resulting in loss of contact with the Real.

In its outward emphasis, projecting "castration" outside the subject, this kind of psychosis seems to operate along a horizontal metonymic axis, becoming the paradigm of unfulfilled desire, of dalliance, of procrastination, an alibi that seeks to put off the end of the inexorable chain of events, even while it puts these events

[12]For another Lacanian perspective on *Hamlet*, psychoanalysis, and ghostwriting, see Nicolas Abraham, "The Phantom of Hamlet or the Sixth Act: Preceded by the Intermission of 'Truth,'" *Diacritics* 18.4 (1988): 2–19.

[13]Lacan's notion of foreclusion is drawn from Freud's case history of the Wolf Man ("From the History of an Infantile Neurosis" [1918], *S.E.* 17) who dreams of wolves in trees, which Freud interprets as an externalized image of the threat of castration.

in motion. In Lacan's reading, Hamlet is cured of his delusion, but he dies in the process of reestablishing his contact with the Real, paying up his Symbolic debt by acknowledging "castration" or loss, as well as guilt (his own oedipal complicity in his father's murder), and by suffering his own "castration" or bereavement (loss of Ophelia, loss of the mother, death by the sword).

Thus Freud's ghost story is one of repressed neurotic desire (the vertical grounds of metaphor), while Lacan's is one of projected psychotic desire (the horizontal grounding of metonymy, the syntactical axes). Freud's ghost shows the subject the resting place of his buried desire; Lacan's ghost exhorts the subject to put his desire into action, rejoining reality in a chain of events. Hanold's delusion is not psychotic since he actually sees a real girl, whom his neurosis causes him to mistake for something else. Hamlet's is a genuine psychosis, doubled by Ophelia's madness. Read together, these two ghost stories are like a warp and woof of psychoanalytic pathology: two axes joined at the crossroads between horizontal and vertical. They may be seen as the warp and woof of textual processes (metaphor and metonymy) and as allegorical enactments of the dual axes of illness, the doubled destiny of haunting desire.

How do all these ghost stories relate to Colette's autobiographical work? I want to return to two reflected questions: how does Colette shape her text; and conversely, how does the text shape "Colette," as the fictional product of her own writing? In addressing these questions, we can read Freud's own "autobiographical" ghost theory (*Beyond the Pleasure Principle*) as a paradigm of autofiction, where content mirrors form: Freud's text discusses the activity of play as repetition and as identity formation—driven by the death impulse—at the same time that it performs these activities. Just so, Colette's veiled text mimics the haunting it describes.

Shaping the Text: Vertical Memory and the *Bildsroman*

> Now fills the air so many a haunting shape . . .
> —Goëthe; Freud's epigraph to *The Psychopathology of Everyday Life*

In many ways Colette's work seems to be shaped by the time-honored tradition of the *Bildungsroman*, the novel of education and experience, and the related genre of the *Künstlerroman*, the story of an artist's formation. But how does Colette's "ghostwriting" differ from this tradition? In their manual *Literary Terms: A Dictionary*, Karl Beckson and Arthur Ganz give these definitions of conventional genres of education and formation:[14]

> *Bildungsroman*: (*Bildung*, "formation"; *roman*, "novel") [. . .] a portrait of the youthful development of a central character. Examples are Dickens's *David Copperfield*, Mann's *The Magic Mountain* and Samuel Butler's *The Way of All Flesh*.

> *Künstlerroman*: a novel which traces the development of the artist, usually from childhood to his maturity. Generally, the pattern of these novels is similar; a sensitive young man, artistically inclined, finds that he must struggle against the misunderstandings and bourgeois attitudes of his family, which is unsympathetic to his creative desires. Attempting to preserve his "artistic integrity," he leaves home, determined, like Stephen Dedalus in James Joyce's *A Portrait of the Artist as a Young Man*, to fulfill his destiny as a creative artist.

One other definition from the same source is of interest for Colette's project:

> *Autobiography*: The author of an autobiography presents a continuous narrative of the major events (and sometimes the minutiae) of his past. The autobiography differs from the diary or journal which lacks continuity and is kept for the author's private purposes.

These definitions, however useful, illustrate the shortcomings of conventional genre studies for unconventional writers, including many women writers. In the definition of autobiography, for instance, the traditionally female genre of the diary is dismissed out of hand, as something belonging to the private rather than the public sphere and lacking in continuity. In the companion definitions of the *Bildungs/Künstlerroman*, the bias is even more obvious: here male authors tell the story of male youths, engaged in a positive process of self-realization. Equally problematic are

---

[14]Karl Beckson and Arthur Ganz, *Literary Terms: A Dictionary* (New York: Farrar, Straus, and Giroux, 1976).

the terms of these generic definitions: what is meant by "education," "destiny," "central character," "youthful development"? Do these apparently gender-neutral terms—which purport to depict "the way of all flesh," even when the "flesh" is that of "the artist as a young *man*"—tell the story of female education? These terms suggest a linear narrative of completion, a voyage of achievement. Youth is a prelude, which sends a central Subject forth to his predicate, his triumphant narrative destiny.

Feminist scholars (among them Nancy K. Miller and Linda Howe) have recast these terms, discussing and analyzing the female *Bildungsroman* as a narrative of survival, or even of suffering, often portraying a maladjustment to society or a compromise with its restraints, rather than a process of self-discovery *thanks to* contact with society.[15] Miller and others have argued that if the female *Bildungsroman* has often centered in the bedroom, it is because sexual politics have had everything to do with a woman's survival. To be sure, much of Colette's work seems to be just this kind of female *Bildungsroman*, providing a "portrait of the artist as a young woman" (particularly *My Apprenticeships*, which shows Colette's early formation as a writer through her disastrous relationship with Willy). And certainly Colette's fiction abounds with stories of women who learn to survive the wreckage of love, often by unusual choices and decisions (*The Vagabond, Chéri, The Other Woman*).

But Colette's autofiction is much more than a tale of survival, for it presents an alternative life-vision that is also an alternative vision of narrative and of the self-made woman who writes her own history, creating a fictionalized "I" in the process. So even the revisionist notion of a female *Bildungsroman* seems inadequate to describe Colette's autofiction: the traditional elements of the *Bildungsroman* need to be completely recast for us to appreciate the complexity of Colette's vision.

Subject and Predicate: The Axes of Bildungsroman

One way of thinking of the linear development in the conventional *Bildungsroman* is by analogy with the linguistic construction

---

[15]See K. K. Ruthven's *Feminist Literary Studies* (Cambridge: Cambridge University Press, 1984), 120–21.

of meaning. I have already repeatedly referred to Roman Jakob-son's theory of language as the interworking of two axes, the paradigmatic (vertical) axis of selection, and the syntagmatic (hor-izontal) axis of combination.[16] Jakobson considers these two axes to be, respectively, metaphoric (vertical, paradigmatic, substi-tutive, poetic) and metonymic (horizontal, linked, syntagmatic, prosaic).[17] These categories provide a way of contrasting the hori-zontal linearity of the *Bildungsroman*—as it unfolds along a devel-opmental plot line—with Colette's metaphoric memory, which operates in depth, along a vertical axis.

Whereas the traditional *Bildungsroman*, for instance, relates the experience of a protagonist (analogous to the grammatical "sub-ject" in a linear phrase, the first element of the syntagmatic line), Colette's work shows no such traditional central character: the "I" of her works is situated somewhere between the fictional status of the *Bildungsroman* protagonist and the "real" status of the conven-tional autobiographical subject. Moreover, in these tales, the cen-trality of the narrating subject is put into question—the "I" has become marginal, an onlooker (in *The Pure and the Impure*) or an orbital character (in the childhood fictions) who focuses the reader's attention on another center. And the identity of the nar-rating "I" is plural, shifting, overdetermined with multiple ages and perspectives. The narrator herself warns us that her authen-ticity is questionable ("Are you imagining, as you read me, that I'm portraying myself?").

Nor does Colette's work display the developmental "predicate" of the *Bildungsroman*, the chronologically linear events that re-count the youthful development of the central character, initiated by a break with the family and a contact with society. In Colette's work the subject's growth is depicted as a lifelong process, con-tinuing in old age (where, if anything, the discoveries seem to become more acute). And even the account of her early artistic

---

[16]Roman Jakobson, "Two Aspects of Language."

[17]In the first volume of *Ecrits*, Lacan in his turn extends these notions to the classification of psychic disorders: "metaphoric" symptoms—like neurosis—are produced from repression, where the symptom stands for the buried or occulted term; "metonymic" symptoms—like perversion or fetishism—are the product of a horizontal excessive desire which displaces attention from the original object to another nearby object, in a kind of diversion.

"apprenticeship" to Willy (to use Colette's own ironic term) is a story of subjugation rather than initiation, in which the adolescent girl is not so much guided as coerced (her first "fumbling attempts at writing" are done under lock and key, under orders from her husband).

This then is an artist without a sense of creative destiny; rather than striving for artistic recognition, she mounts a sullen resistance, both to the society she encounters and to the perverse demands of a husband who has wrested her from village and family. The transition from child to woman—here signified by marriage (unlike the passage to manhood in the *Bildungsroman*, marked by travel and social experience)—is not a liberation or an apotheosis or even an exhilarating contact with the outside; it is a confinement, entailing the eclipse of the mother's given name (Gabrielle-*Sidonie* Colette becomes Colette Willy) and the exile from the maternal circle of light. One must look to the "portrait of the artist as an *old* woman" to find a heroine who comes into her own, by returning—rather than progressing—to an essential knowledge, by rediscovering the lessons learned at her mother's side. "Colette" finds her identity only when she abandons the effort to adapt to society, unlearning the lessons of the outside.

Thus our reading of Colette's fictional autobiography can only be impoverished by conventional notions of development and plot, so important in the *Bildungsroman* or *Erziehungsroman*. *Erziehung* means a drawing out, *Bildung* means an extended construction; neither is applicable to Colette's "rediscovery of something familiar" (to again borrow Freud's term for the pleasure of repetition); for this rediscovery is not the result of an extension of experience, a progress through time, so much as it is a kind of vertical piling up of associations, an overdetermination of the "I" that permits several selves to coexist in the same subject, and to share and substitute their vision, to see through other "I's." We might say then that Colette's autofictions are less *Bildungsromans* than *Bildsromans*, picture-novels, which give access to overdetermined images, with the help of a vertical metaphoric memory sifting down through layers of accrued experience.

For Colette's "family plot" is a garden and a graveyard. In *Break of Day*, for example, the writer's memories are characterized as precious deposits to be mined; and it is the function of the writer's insight to unearth these treasures, to bring these forgotten secrets to light. But this process cannot be completed too abruptly: the precious kernels of memory, like buried seedlings, must be incubated, nourished, worked, and allowed to blossom into fictional flowers, from seeds of truth. The treasure of Colette's writing is the layered vertical memory that blooms into fiction and thus brings to light those beloved ghosts who, Colette finds, now dwell within the writer herself.

What, then, are the characteristics of the *Bildsroman*, and how may it be distinguished from the conventional *Bildungsroman*? First, these introductions to life are experienced at home, in childhood rather than in adolescence. This initiation consists in lessons passed from mother to daughter, lessons in *looking* at life and nature, which for the most part have little to do with achievement or making one's way in the outer world. The narrator refers repeatedly to her mother's acute powers of observation, her ability to read nature's portents, the attentiveness of all her senses to the changes in her domain ("Sido's great word was 'Look!'" *EP* 38). The bond between mother and daughter is a bond of the senses and of intuition, especially since Sido enjoins her daughter not only to *see*, but to uncover what is unseen, to look below the surface. Colette passes this injunction on to her own daughter, Bel-Gazou ("Oh, look at those yellow cowslips! And the unicorn tips of the lords and ladies are showing!" *Sido* 132). Indeed the seer's attentiveness is the mother's haunting legacy: "Certain omens, dimmer since her death, haunt me still . . ." (*Sido* 160). In the *Bildungsroman*, knowledge is acquired by the individual, while in the *Bildsroman* knowledge is transmitted among generations.

The second major distinction between the *Bildungsroman* and the *Bildsroman* concerns the story line. The most vivid of Colette's picture books (*My Mother's House*) follows only the barest of chronological developments; but we have seen that it is organized vertically, associatively, around an overdetermined image: the circle of light, the halo, the Eden inhabited by Sido. The mother is at the center of a series of concentric circles—light, house, garden, village—a series of rings that blossom to circumscribe all the elements of the novel. And a similar association shapes *Break of Day*, where the "central image" (the circular cactus rose, with its concentric petals) informs the rest of the novel, itself centered on

Colette's house, haunted by the spirit of Sido. The gravitational center of the *Bildsroman* is the maternal beacon at the center of "a Mariner's Chart of gardens, winds and rays of light" (*Sido* 158).

The *Bildsroman* does not follow a forward trajectory; the notion of progress is replaced by the periodic cadence of orbit, of sally and return to the maternal "Evening Star": this is the progress of the planets across the sky, in a movement of eternal return. Indeed, in this *Bildsroman*, the central character of conventional tales of formation has been decentered, placed in orbit around another emotional center: this is decentered autobiography, more love poem than memoir. Similarly, in *The Pure and the Impure*, the "central characters" are the shadowy others waiting in curtained alcoves, marginal characters to whom the narrator is drawn. (And there is a kind of symmetry in these two groups of tales: in the childhood stories, Gabrielle is drawn spellbound to the light; while in the adult *ars erotica*, Mme Colette is drawn to shadow.)

Thus while the conventional *Bildungsroman* is driven along a metonymic axis of outward experience and contact with the world, the *Bildsroman* is metaphoric in its organization; its circular and overdetermined (paradigmatic) layered images are associated semantically, not syntactically, by virtue of their similarity of meaning. We have seen that Colette's central images are to a degree interchangeable and superimposed: rose, evening star, maternal body, circle of light, buried treasure, embroidery hoop—these are piled up as equivalent metaphors. The direction in this text is circular and downward, rather than linear, upward, and onward (the goal-oriented destiny of the *Bildungsroman*). Colette's treasure hunt—uncannily reminiscent of grave-robbing—delves into the unconscious and unearths layers of metaphor, mined at the site of infantile meaning (the grave of the parents? the womb?); like an archaeologist, Colette uncovers and restores artifacts of the past, be they tangible (like Sido's letters) or intangible shards of memory.

To be sure, we cannot claim that this vision is exclusively female—Proust, for example, uses a similar technique of archaeological uncovering, and his novel "blooms" out of his cup of tea. But we may at least assert that this uncanny vision poses an alternative to the male-centered *Bildungsroman* of exploration, development, conquest, and experience *out there*. The *Bildsroman* is not about severing ties; it emphasizes the importance of roots and memory. In this vertical vision, familial ties are the source of one's identity, a mooring to be reinforced rather than severed in search of a personal triumph "beyond."[18] The mother provides the point of gravity or orientation, marking the site of memories to be exhumed and elaborated: hers is the stabilizing and grounding impulse, to remain in one spot and to explore its depths, vertically. (Characteristically, Sido refuses to budge from her home, feeling she can never exhaust its riches: "Leave my village? Why ever should I?" *Sido* 147.)

Of course Colette's work is not simply vertical; it is a fabric woven of vertical *and* horizontal threads, warp and woof: if the maternal axis is the vertical axis of metaphor, the paternal is the diverted axis of metonymy, of unrequited love, of desire. The writer's very identity is a text woven from the past, in an intergenerational lacing: "I disentangle [*j'épèle*] the things in me that come from my father, and those that are my mother's share" (*Sido* 178). (In the French, the verb *épeler*—to spell out, to unwind—reinforces the relation of the textile act of "disentanglement"—of a skein, a *peloton*—with the horizontal unwinding of words in narrative, by the writer.) Thus in spite of its metaphoric/maternal emphasis, there is also a linear thrust in this tale, provided by the father who dreams of military expeditions in far-off lands. This horizontal thrust is felt as the *fort* of the *fort-da* rhythm, in the lines of cursive script that retrace the Captain's hand.

But this linear movement of the writing hand is also a circular one, looping back to begin each line anew. Again, we may look to Freud's *fort-da* game as an allegory of writing. For the toy describes both a circular orbit and a back-and-forth trajectory, with the child as center, string as radius. Colette's writing describes this same movement, both circular and linear, with an emphasis on the return to the center of the circle (the jubilant *da!* of reunion, which rewrites the "sentence" of exile) rather than on the voyage outward. Like the embroidery hoop invaded by the hand of the sempstress, Colette's writing takes place within an en-

---

[18]See Carol Gilligan, *In a Different Voice* (Cambridge: Harvard University Press, 1982), for a discussion of female vision as a function of connectedness. For a psychoanalytic discussion of this difference, see Nancy Chodorow's *The Reproduction of Mothering*.

chanted circle, inscribing the past across the fabric of the page. It
is the mother's hand that trains her daughter to embroider, to
reach into the depths, vertically, in order to embellish the surface;
it is the father's hand that guides his daughter's hand across the
page/fabric, retracing the invisible shapes of his desire. And since
the father is an outsider of sorts, it is he who transforms the
mother-child relation, opening the closed dyadic reflection into a
true solar system, a circle of light. Thus if there is a paternal horizontal axis in the *Bildsroman*, it is not one of development, but of
metonymic desire, the intermittent progress of the chain stitch
that links generations, circling below the work's surface in order
to progress.

Indeed, Colette's *Bildsroman* may be read as an exploration of
the author's own stores, a mining of the author herself as the site
of treasured memories. For Colette herself has become a haunted
house inhabited at life's end by the fantoms she has incorporated.
As the writer sifts down, delving into the unconscious, lifting veil
after veil from these shapes, the shape of the text takes on the
ghostly outline of "Colette" herself.

Shaping the Self: Identification and the Text-Work

While psychoanalysis holds that the self takes shape, and
changes shape, by a process of "identification" (*Identifizierung*), no
term in Freud's body of theory seems less stable. Freud uses the
term to mean many things throughout his writing, beginning
with the relatively simple identification described in *Jokes* (1905),
in which the listener identifies with the teller as they share a
laugh aimed toward their common victim. Freud expands this intersubjective notion of identification to the larger process of group
identification in *Totem and Taboo* (1912), where he claims that the
sons of the primal clan identify with the slain father first by actual
cannibalism, by ingestion of the father and incorporation of his
powers, and later by ingestion of the totemic animal who symbolizes the father. In this instance—as in the joking triangle—the
identification is a kind of pact between "fathers" and "sons," who
agree never again to come to conflict. This primal myth is expanded in *Moses and Monotheism* (1939), which describes how the
Hebrew people come to identify with the patriarch Moses, whom

they have slain in an uprising; here again this identification is solidified by adherence to the father's Law, which guards against a repetition of the patricide ("Thou shalt not kill"). Group identification is also the theme of *Group Psychology and the Analysis of the Ego* (1921), which examines the identification of groups or whole nations with a charismatic father figure. All of these social identifications gird the social order and are reinforced by repetition, often ritualistic in nature.

In addition to these readings of identification as group dynamic, Freud treats identification as a formative process in the individual. The mimetic characteristics of this process are pointed out in the *New Introductory Lectures* (1933), where the "metamorphosis of the parental relationship into the super-ego" is preceded by "the assimilation of one ego to another one, as a result of which the first ego behaves like the second in certain respects, imitates it and in a sense takes it up into itself."[19] Freud continues: "It is a very important form of attachment to someone else, probably the very first, and not the same thing as the choice of an object. [. . .] If a boy identifies himself with his father, he wants to *be like* his father; if he makes him the object of his choice, he wants to *have* him, to possess him" (56).[20] Although the difference between object of love and object of identification is clearly drawn here, Freud's own work shows that many forms of object love do in fact depend upon a kind of identification.

In fact many of Freud's works stress the narcissistic aspects of identification as a component of sexual or object love. In the 1924 essay "The Economic Problem of Masochism," for instance, masochism is described as an inverted sadism, in which the masochist identifies with the sadist's pleasure. Similarly, in "Mourning and Melancholia" (1917), Freud argues that in grief one mourns an internalized object, which has been assimilated to one's own ego.

[19]*New Introductory Lectures on Psychoanalysis.* This quotation is from page 56 of the paper edition (New York: W. W. Norton, 1965); all page numbers in this chapter refer to this edition.

[20]This distinction between "identification" and "object choice" is the clarification of an earlier hypothesis ("On Narcissism") concerning two types of object choice—anaclitic (the child wants to *have* the nurturing parent) and narcissistic (the child wants to be *like* the protecting parent). In the earlier essay, the narcissistic model applies to self-love, or to the love of what one would like to be (the ego ideal) or what one once was (one's children), as well as to homosexual love.

Depression is also a kind of mourning, focused on the part of the ego identified with the lost object: but because this object now elicits anger, one part of the ego "rages against the other," causing feelings of low self-esteem.

In all of the aforementioned identifications—social, formative, or pathological—it is a question of an incorporation or internalization that provides the model that fashions "identity." Whether this kind of modeling is considered a necessary and largely positive stage of development—as it is in Lacan's theory of the mirror stage—or the source of a pathology, as in Freud's account of masochism and melancholia, it is clear that the individual's mimetic processes of identification closely parallel the group processes that ground societal law, taboo, and social code. In the *New Introductory Lectures* (1933), Freud makes this connection explicit, insisting that the child's internalization of the parent as "Law" is the basis for the formation of the superego, which socializes every human subject. And the self is overdetermined by other figures as well, and even by later perceptions of the parent, as the child matures: "In the course of the development the super-ego also takes on the influences of those who have stepped into the place of parents—educators, teachers, people chosen as ideal models [. . .] Nor must it be forgotten that a child has a different estimate of its parents at different periods of its life; [these parental figures] make important contributions to the formation of character" (*NIL* 57). Above all, Freud insists that the superego is an actual structure of the psyche, something that gives shape to the self.

In his later work, Freud expands and transforms the concept of the superego into the notion of the ego ideal, which is "the vehicle by which the ego measures itself, which it emulates, and whose demand for ever greater perfection it strives to fulfill. There is no doubt that this ego ideal is the precipitate of the old picture of the parents, the expression of admiration for the perfection which the child then attributed to them" (*NIL* 58). Thus the ego ideal seems to be a mingling of "parental precipitates" and other cultural models—myriad shades of one's past, including one's lost love-objects. Freud stresses the intergenerational quality of this modeling as well (*NIL* 60): "Thus a child's super-ego is in fact constructed not on the model of its parents but of its parents' super-ego" (which is of course constructed on the model of *their* parents' superego, and so forth). The identifications that shape our ideals, our guilts, our sense of self are part of an extended social chain, formed in part by the ghosts of our past.

The Dissolution of the Oedipus Complex

Freud's late work repeatedly discusses the superego as a residual effect of the Oedipus complex, the result of the identification between rival "fathers" and "sons" (the subject agrees to become *like* the father rather than trying to *be* him).[21] Elsewhere Freud suggests that this identification with the father entails an internalization of Law, enforced by the paternal superego: "The superego deals with the ego like a strict father with a child" (*The Question of Lay Analysis*, 1926).[22] Even as early as the *Introductory Lectures* (1917), Freud insists that this identification with the father is "the great task" that every human being must perform in order to "cease to be a child and to become a member of the social community" (*IL* 337).[23] Freud later continues to insist on the social importance of a properly developed superego, which can only be gained by surmounting the Oedipus complex: "The super-ego is stunted in its strength if the surmounting of the Oedipus complex is only incompletely successful" (*NIL* 57).

But Freud warns that the superego can become positively tyrannical and cruel, if it remains *too* connected with the *historical* person of the father, rather than with his internalized Symbolic function (the Law): "This super-ego can set itself against the ego. It

---

[21]This process is described in "The Dissolution of the Oedipus Complex" (1924), *S.E.* 19; and it is again discussed in *New Introductory Lectures* (1933), which also contains an attempt to describe female sexuality as an effect of the girl's insufficient resolution of the oedipal complex. Freud returns to the effects of the passing of the Oedipus complex in *The Ego and the Id* (1923), *S.E.* 19, and *An Outline of Psycho-Analysis* (published posthumously in 1940), *S.E.* 23.

[22]*The Question of Lay Analysis* (1926), *S.E.* 20, chapter 5.

[23]Characteristically, Freud emphasizes the situation of the male child: "For the son this task consists in detaching his libidinal wishes from his mother and employing them for the choice of a real outside love-object, and in reconciling himself with his father if he has remained in opposition to him" (*Introductory Lectures* 337). In the 1939 essay *Moses and Monotheism* (*S.E.* 23, section III, chapter 2), the emphasis is less on reconciliation than on identification as a prelude to constructing the superego: "In the course of the individual development a part of the inhibiting forces in the outer world becomes internalized; a standard is created in the ego which opposes the other faculties by observation, criticism, and prohibition."

can treat it as an object, and often uses it very harshly." Freud goes on to say that "it is very important for mental health that the super-ego should become sufficiently depersonalized. It is precisely this that does not happen in the case of a neurotic, because his Oedipus complex does not undergo the right transformation" (*Question of Lay Analysis* 198–99). Thus the result of oedipal identifications that are "stunted" or remain too personal is illness.

Further complicating this story, Freud suggests that an insufficient resolution of the Oedipus complex may result not only in illness, but in another kind of "deficiency": femininity. In the *New Introductory Lectures* and elsewhere, Freud tries to account for "the insufficiently moral" feminine character as the symptom of an improperly formed and internalized superego. Freud's sorry account is by now familiar: the little girl's passage to femininity is a turning from the mother, and a turning to the father, with whom she desires to have a child, preferably a male child, as compensation for her own anatomical lack. As a result of her desire for the father, the girl enters into her own oedipal complex, as a rival to the mother, becoming "truly feminine." Thus her infantile desire for the mother is transformed first into a rivalry and then into a kind of grudging identification. But Freud cannot explain why the little girl renounces her father as love-object (it cannot be because of castration anxiety, as in the boy's case, since she has "nothing to lose"). Freud gets around this difficulty by suggesting, in a particularly outrageous formulation, that the girl never really does get out of the oedipal complex: because she has no penis, she never internalizes the Law based on the threat of castration, thus never develops a proper superego (reserved for boys only) nor becomes a fully human being. Moreover the girl's feminine identification with the mother—more or less equivalent to the grudging acceptance of her own female state—remains tainted by resentment for having inherited her mother's "castration" ("the attachment to the mother ends in hate" *NIL* 108).

In light of this assessment, the girl's final identification with the mother is at best an uneasy compromise, the result of a failed love relationship: the daughter, no longer able to love her mother as sexual object, is resigned to being like her. There is nothing in Freud's hypothesis that suggests a making of peace with the mother, as occurs in the passing of the male oedipal complex, where the son's pact with the Symbolic father grounds the social order.

Freud does speak on occasion of a more positive mother-daughter identification: but it is a *pre-oedipal* identification, before the rivalry between mother and daughter ensues. Already in the *New Introductory Lectures*, in fact, the girl's pre-oedipal attachment to the mother is acknowledged as of primary importance ("we get an impression that we cannot understand women unless we appreciate this phase of their pre-Oedipus attachment to their mother" *NIL* 105). Interestingly, as an example of pre-oedipal identification, Freud cites the girl's play with dolls, which "serves as an identification with her mother with the intention of substituting activity for passivity. She was playing the part of her mother and the doll was herself: now she could do with the baby everything that her mother used to do with her" (113). This view of doll-playing suggests an intriguing comparison with the *fort-da* game: both are acts of reality-mastery, reenacting real events on the child's terms; but in the girl's case the play is based on identification with the mother rather than on *desire* for her. We might even infer that thanks to this pre-oedipal play, the girl-child is able to identify with the positions of both child and mother, toy and agent, occupying the roles of subject and object at once (much as Colette does in her creative "play" of identification).

The Stages of Identification: Freud on Colette

Leaving aside for the moment Freud's speculations on the "special case" of female development, let us try to bring some order to his complex and varying definitions of identification. Perhaps the most cohesive treatment of the notion is found in *Group Psychology and the Analysis of the Ego*, where Freud posits three categories of identification—formative, regressive, and libidinal: "First, identification is the original form of emotional tie with an object; secondly, in a regressive way it becomes a substitute for the libidinal object tie, as it were by means of the introjection of the object into the ego; and thirdly, it may arise with every new perception of a common quality shared with some person who is not an object of the sexual instinct" (*GPAE* 39–40).

The first category might be construed to include all the kinds of

identification based on modeling, mirroring, and the internalization of the other's image (as emphasized in Lacan's notion of the
Imaginary order). The second category, regressive identification,
would include all those instances where identification plays a role
in pathology: the lost object has been internalized, resulting in a
kind of splitting of the ego, with subsequent illness: masochism,
melancholia, even hysteria, in which the patient mimics the
symptoms of the love-object with whom she identifies.[24] The third
category would include the late identifications with all the components of the ego ideal (parents in later life, friends, teachers, role
models).

In the *New Introductory Lectures* (1933), Freud again posits three
types of identification in the life of the individual, but this time he
differentiates between three developmental and even chronological *phases* of identification, rather than coexisting *types* of identification. In this genetic account, he suggests that identification
works first as a mimetic shaping of the self (pre-oedipal); then as
the final moment of the Oedipus complex itself (the identification
between father and son); and finally, as a way by which the su-
perego/ego ideal is formed (as a post-oedipal residue of sorts).

Freud's developmental paradigm seems to fit Colette's textual
self, at least as concerns the first and last stages of identification
(pre- and post-oedipal). For we have noted that the making of
"Colette" seems to start with a strong pre-oedipal identification
with the mother, when Sido is the model internalized by her
daughter, in mimetic gestures, both conscious and unconscious
("I used to imitate her way of talking, and I still do" *Sido 167*).
Similarly, something like Freud's final stage of identification
seems to be part of the adult woman's formation (the identification with the internalized image of the parents as superego/ego
ideal). For there is an evolution in Colette's relation to the parents
and particularly the mother: Sido seems to evolve from the larger-

---

[24]Freud discusses the hysteric's identification with the loved one by mimetic
symptom in the *Introductory Lectures on Psychoanalysis* (1916–17), *S.E.* 16: 427–28.
But this mechanism of mimetic identification clearly overlaps with the other kinds
of identification mentioned by Freud: as in the case of the "oedipal" identifications
of *Totem and Taboo* and *Moses and Monotheism*, where there is an internalization
of the paternal image/Law by an entire tribe or people, which results in the constitution of the character of this people, its collective identity.

than-life Imaginary model of Gabrielle's childhood to the Symbolic role of Colette's adult companion, the friendly ghost of *Break of Day*, who "frequents" her grown daughter (as in the French *fréquenter*) rather than "haunting" or dominating her. It is almost as though Colette needs to lose her love-object in life to get out of the Imaginary relation, transforming the mythic deity ("My Mother") into "Sido"—friend (on a first-name basis), companion, role model. (Freud himself insists that the parents must lose their mythic status to become the friends of their children in later life.)

The problem with Freud's paradigm, of course, is that it posits no real second step between the pre- and post-oedipal stages for the female: since the "passing of the Oedipus complex" is reserved for boys, Freud's account leaves the little girl stuck in her oedipal hostility toward the mother. We have noted that Colette does have something like a classic oedipal rivalry with Sido at some point, when the mother gets in the way of the relation between father and daughter. But no marked hatred or rivalry persists into her later life (as Freud would suggest); in fact her conflict seems to be resolved in favor of the mother-daughter relation, in something like a feminine post-oedipal identification with the mother. Indeed, Colette's work repeatedly displays this paradigm of resolution between female rivals; this is the outcome, for instance, of *The Other One*, that extraordinary novel in which two rival women decide to share their man, preferring their friendship to the expendable relation with the man who has divided them. If anything, Colette's testimony would seem to suggest that the mother-daughter identification may be more profound than the kind of post-oedipal gentlemen's agreement that is established between fathers and sons.

Colette on Freud: Replaying the Game

Thus a reading of Colette alongside the text of psychoanalysis may propose a revision in Freud's text: Colette suggests that the outcome of mother-daughter conflict need not be an uneasy peace or grudging acceptance of femininity. *This* daughter's overriding impulse is to lay claim to the mother's likeness and to pass on "all that [Sido] has bequeathed" to her (preface, *MMH*). Throughout

Colette's work, there is ample evidence of a successful resolution of the female Oedipus complex, resulting in an intermingling of selves.

So while the various identifications that Freud traces may help us to understand the making of "Colette," it nonetheless appears that the father of psychoanalysis has failed to imagine anything like the depth and importance of the female pre- and post-oedipal identifications to which this creative girl-child bears witness. Reading Colette with Freud suggests that Freud himself is stuck in the oedipal complex, remaining blind to the possibility that the mother may provide a paradigm for the female superego. In other words, as feminists have argued, he does not take enough account of femininity as a positive category. On the other hand, he may take too much account of femininity (and he is joined by Lacan) as an impassible barrier, which means that woman must be treated as a special case, outside experience that shapes our common humanity.

And rereading Freud through Colette suggests that the traditional paradigms of psychoanalysis are of limited usefulness for other reasons as well. I have argued, for instance, that the oedipal paradigms (of Freud) and the Symbolic and Imaginary categories (of Lacan), while discernable in Colette's experience, show more flexibility in her autofiction than in the conventional psychoanalytic scenario. For here the roles of nurturer/object and lawgiver/obstacle are not gender-bound. Consequently, Colette's complex identifications with her parents are not delimited by gender, but are rather a web of shifting possibilities. In fact, the superego, a largely patriarchal figure in Freudian theory (and from which Lacan's Symbolic father is derived), is more often than not a *maternal* figure in Colette's self-narrative; even while retaining the father's Symbolic role in some contexts, Colette also evokes a powerful Symbolic mother, suggesting that the matriarch may be internalized as both the (judgmental) superego, and the (friendly) ego ideal. Both aspects are seen in Sido's ghost in *Break of Day*, who seems at first to judge, but then reveals herself as a nonmenacing kindred spirit. In this sense, the identification between the writer and the ghostly mother is doubled by that between writer and reader. For the reader is also a fantom of sorts, an overseer (as internalized critic, reading over the writer's shoulder) and a ghostly interlocutor, the invisible companion to whom the writer speaks.

Finally, there is no paradigm in Freudian psychoanalysis for the kind of profoundly formative Symbolic relation between father and daughter that Colette's work portrays. For that we must turn to Lacanian theory, which stresses the importance of the Name of the Father in the child's access to humanity. Of course even in Lacan's account there is an androcentric bias, with the insistence on the Phallus as the signifier of signifiers, the sign of desire that marks the subject's entry into the Symbolic order. Still Colette's work helps us to hold sight of the most radical aspect of Lacan: the Symbolic father is the *dead* father, who must be internalized as wound, in the assumption of the humanizing Symbolic debt (in Lacan the Phallus—as mark of desire—is always missing; which means that to be human is to be lacking, bereaved). The passing of the oedipal conflict, then, is an act of mourning. As the bearer of the father's stigma, Colette assumes the human wound of incapacity and makes of it the space in which she may write her text, her monument to the father and to his "Sido."

Text as Self: The Fantom Subject of Autobiography

All that is to live in endless song,
Must in life-time first be drowned.
—Schiller, quoted by Freud in *Moses and Monotheism*

Thus Colette's text is a work of mourning that transforms the parents from real external objects to internalized parts of the self, burying the parental alter egos within the unconscious, and taking the name "Colette" as the metaphoric monument to mark their passing—and their permanence. In this way, the act of writing shapes the writer herself, transforming "Gabrielle" into "Colette." For as Freud suggests in *The Problem of Anxiety* (1926), grief is a kind of healing process: "Mourning originates under the influence of reality testing, which demands categorically that one must part with the object because the object no longer exists. Now it is the task of mourning to carry out this retreat from the object in all the situations in which the object was the recipient of

an intense cathexis. The painful character of this separation ac-
cords with the explanation just given" (121).

As Freud understands it, mourning is a process that unties the
bonds to the external world, now emptied of the object. Lacanian
theory adds that when the longing is too intense to accept the
lack of the object in reality, actual hallucinations can result,
whereby the mourner continues to see the lost object "out there,"
in reality (in other words, the mourner sees a ghost). In Lacan's
version of this psychosis, the illness/hallucination is the result of
the mourner's failure to internalize the loss, to incorporate it, undoing the real ties and assimilating or "burying" one's ghosts
within.[25] If we apply Lacan's reading of this phenomenon to Colette, we see how the text-work, the mourning-work, and the construction of the subject "Colette" coincide: it is a question of first
undoing the intense Imaginary ties to the lost objects, and then of
transforming the relation to a Symbolic one, internalizing the objects, finally *becoming* the lost parents. Thus the daughter's
mourning-work is paradoxically both a letting go and a way of
holding on.

In "Mourning and Melancholia," Freud insists on the similarity
of symptoms between mourning and depression, which "contains
the same feelings of pain, [and] loss of interest in the outside
world" (*MM* 164–65). But Freud notes an important difference: in
depression, there is a loss of self-esteem. He then suggests that
this loss probably occurs because in the case of melancholia the
object is not usually dead, but simply absent: the object has abandoned the person. ("Melancholia [stems from] all those situations
of being wounded, hurt, neglected, out of favour, or disappointed, which can import opposite feelings of love and hate into
the relationship or reinforce an already existing ambivalence"
[*MM* 172]. Freud gives the example of the proverbial bride
stranded at the altar.) Freud credits this particular kind of pain to
an identification: here again the subject internalizes the lost object, as in the mourning-work, making the object part of the ego:

[25]This idea is the core of Lacan's notion of foreclusion as a kind of psychosis, in
which hallucinations fill the "hole in the real" created by the lost object. In "Desire
and the Interpretation of Desire in *Hamlet*," for instance, Lacan suggests that the
mourning-work consists in *internalizing* the lost object (the dead/castrated father),
and completing his work of vengeance.

but then the bereaved subject turns the profound rage of abandonment against that part of the self identified with the faithless object.

In other words, melancholia results from a division in the ego: "One part of the ego sets itself over against the other, judges it critically, and, as it were, looks upon it as an object. The self-reproaches are reproaches against a loved object which have been shifted onto the patient's own ego" (168–69). This conflict "casts a pathological shade on the grief, forcing it to express itself in the form of self-reproaches, to the effect that the mourner himself is to blame for the loss of the loved one, i.e. desired it" (172). (We again think of Colette's self-characterization as "the happy little vampire that unconsciously drains the maternal heart" *MMH* 25.) Interestingly, these passages seem to anticipate Freud's later concept of the overly harsh superego of the neurotic, which has remained too connected with an actual person, the historical parent, and which becomes tyrannical, berating the ego and causing feelings of misery (*The Question of Lay Analysis*, chapter 5). In fact, we may already discern the ghostly shadow of this harsh superego in the earlier essay on melancholia, although Freud does not yet give it a name: "Thus the shadow of the object fell upon the ego, so that the latter could henceforth be criticized by *a special mental faculty* like an object" (*MM* 170, my emphasis).

Moreover this passage suggests that the pain of the condition might be the result of *more* than one split in the ego. For the superego is produced by an earlier division in the ego, as the residue of the oedipal parents, while the ego itself is the product of an even earlier internalization of an alien object (the nurturing parent), after which it models itself. No wonder depression leaves the ego "shattered": the poor ego is a battleground, where the residue of at least one primal other "rages against" the internalized image of an earlier lost love-object.[26]

---

[26]"Mourning and Melancholia" (174): "The complex of melancholia behaves like an open wound, drawing to itself cathectic energy from all sides [. . .] and draining the ego till it is utterly depleted." Freud also writes (172): "The loss of a love-object constitutes an excellent opportunity for the ambivalence in love-relationships to make itself felt and to come to the fore," allowing the negative feelings for the love-object to emerge. In melancholia, this negative affect may be turned on the self: "If the object-love, which cannot be given up, takes refuge in

In any case, Freud seems to suggest that the difference between the healing process of successful mourning and the illness of melancholia may be linked to the status of the object: in the case of mourning, the object is really dead and gone, whereas in the case of melancholia, the object has simply abandoned the subject, giving rise to feelings of intense rage: "Melancholia is related to an unconscious loss of the love-object, while in mourning there is nothing unconscious about the loss" (*MM* 166). To put it simply, the positive side of the ambivalence that characterizes any love relation can win out when the object has been lost in death, whereas the negative side will prevail when the object has simply "absented" itself.

The difference between mourning and melancholia is also a question of the outcome—in mourning, there is no morbidity, but simply an absorbing work, from which the subject emerges "whole," or at least mended, knitted together, while in melancholia, the split subject tears itself apart, unable fully to incorporate or forgive the lost object against which it feels such rage. But this healing does not lead to a single, unified, transcendental ego: on the contrary, mourning overdetermines the self with plural "I"dentities. In other words, successful mourning seems to result in an identification that heals the ego, assimilating and integrating the fantoms that haunt it, while melancholia exacerbates the split in the ego, the internal warfare among ghosts, fraught with guilt and anguish. By putting one's ghosts to rest, the process of successful mourning prevents the lost other from becoming a menacing double—as either the spooky hallucination seeming to return from beyond, because it has not yet been internalized; or as a hypercritical superego, the too-personal ghost of the real parents, who have not been "buried" or depersonalized, and who thus continue to "haunt" the self with guilt.

We might say that melancholic identification is still in the realm of mimetic, Imaginary identification, whereby the ego internalizes

---

narcissistic identification, while the object itself is abandoned, then hate is expended upon this new substitute-object, railing at it, depreciating it, making it suffer and deriving sadistic gratification from its suffering" (172). So Freud suggests that this severe self-punishment is not without its masochistic pleasure, since it provides "a gratification of sadistic tendencies and of hate [which] have been turned upon the self."

the model of an alterego who is resented and feared. But whereas melancholia stays in the realm of Imaginary identification, with pathological results, mourning achieves a Symbolic identification, allowing the incorporation and assimilation of the functions and vision of the lost object (whereby the children of the object become parents in their turn).[27] In the Symbolic identification, the loss is accepted (this loss is perhaps what Lacan calls Law) and the child makes peace with her fantom selves, as allies who look on and counsel, in self-dialogues and reflection.

The vicissitudes of mourning might be summarized thus: (1) when mourning is avoided, the ghost may remain a spook, a ghoulish hallucination, resulting from the incapacity of the subject to decathect from the object and to internalize it; (2) *during* the mourning process, the ghost is an Imaginary construct (the work of mourning, however, tests reality and discovers that the object is no longer out there, in a series of painful proofs that allow the subject finally to accept that the lost object is now merely a figment of the imagination; this internal "work" frees the subject's libido to rejoin the external world, and to return to external work); (3) *after* the completion of the mourning-work, the ghost may become a residue of sorts, a Symbolic *Geist*, a kindred spirit-companion; part of a composite ego ideal. The mourning-work, instigated by loss, thus becomes the means by which a new identity takes shape.

What I want to suggest, then, is that Colette's work effects a passage from melancholia—with the attendant feelings of guilt and anger—to a genuine mourning, in which the subject "overdetermines" her self with the selves of her lost others. In so doing, she assumes the father's unfinished work, she sees again with the mother's eyes—and she makes peace with her own plural self. Whereas *My Mother's House* rings with nostalgia and self-incrimination ("too late! too late!"), *Break of Day* is replete with a sense of refinding, of return—not in the sense of infantile regression, but as a Symbolic healing by which the subject claims the lost parents as her own. The daughter's burial of the parents allows her to exorcise the menacing spooks and to incorporate their spirit as the *Geist* of her work, her muse.

[27]Freud also speculates on the role of just this kind of identification in religious communion as a kind of participation in the body of the lost object ("The Future of an Illusion" [1927], *S.E.* 21) and a pact with that object.

What the writer's work adds to the work of mourning is the social dimension, calling on the reader to complete the process. The critical faculty of the superego has been passed to an outside other; what was first gleaned from others is returned to them, in the mourner's return to the world—that is, to work. Thus Colette becomes "spinster" of comic tales replacing one kind of identification by another, undoing the regressive Imaginary cathexis to the object by substituting fictional (Symbolic) objects for the real lost parents. This is at once a work of mourning (the untying of certain bonds) and of play (the "casting on" of new ties, the subject controlling the game). It is the passage from passivity to activity, moving from the role of the haunted victim to that of the active "medium" who calls forth and shapes one's *own* ghosts, animating the shades of the past. It is a passage from the Imaginary narcissism of the Captain's closed study, where the fixation on Sido *prevents* work—to the outward address of the Symbolic, in which the book is opened to the gaze of the other, and the inspiration of an internalized Sido *fosters* work. Sido the Imaginary object makes way for Sido the Symbolic interlocutor, conversing with a writer named "Colette."

The Name of the Father as Maternal Metaphor

I now have only one name, which is my own.
—*Break of Day*

In Lacan's version of the human tragedy of desire, it is of course the Name of the Father, as emblem of one's place in the social chain, that serves as metaphor for the process of entry into social being.[28] As is always the case with metaphor, the *nom du père* is associated with the process of repression (*Verdrängung*): for

---

[28]Lacan writes: "It is in the Name of the Father that we must recognize the support of the Symbolic Function which, from the dawn of history, has identified his person with the figure of the Law" ("The Function of Language in Psychoanalysis," trans. in Wilden, *Speech and Language in Psychoanalysis*. Feminist appropriations of Lacan, however, have chosen often to stress this Paternal Metaphor as a kind of stigma signifying the inexhaustibility of desire, the universality of something like "separation" from the parents and other love-objects, rather than a symptom of the confrontation with the threat of castration.

as all metaphors do, the paternal metaphor both stands for and occludes a missing term, which it both represents and "buries."[29] Hence for Lacan the Paternal Metaphor is also a kind of headstone—marking the spot where the repressed meaning lies (the trauma of castration—but more specifically, the hostile feelings toward the historical father). Of course, this kind of generational conflict is at the center of Freud's account of the origin of Law: once upon a time, the rebellious sons of the tribe slew the father; the incest taboo was then instigated in order to protect the family from a repetition of this primal upheaval. The Law is then the sign of a repressed guilt, and a kind of tribute to the dead tribal father of *Totem and Taboo*, whose *nom* (name)—and whose *non* (interdiction, pronounced like *nom* in French)—will henceforth be borne by the social group. Thus the human generational conflict is both a stigma and a legacy, at once repressed and represented by the name bestowed by society, a tribute to the surmounting of the deadly conflict, a testimony of the subject's submission to the humanizing Law (of loss, of "castration") that enables contact with others. The Name of the Father is a tombstone, a monument acknowledging those who have gone before, making our own humanity possible; a testimony to their loss and their continued presence.

But can woman play a role as protagonist in the human drama, other than merely sealing the pact between men?[30] Or is she relegated to the role of object of exchange—who will exchange one emblem of belonging and submission (the Name of the Father) for another (the name of the husband) when she is "given away" at the altar? (In the traditional scenario, the son's wife becomes in a sense the property of her *husband's* father, since she assures that *his* name will be carried on by *her* children.) This identification, signified by the exchange and labeling of women as peace offer-

---

[29]For example, the simile "the sun is like an apple" expresses two paradigmatic terms; but renaming the sun "the apple" in a metaphor ("the apple rose in the sky") removes the original term, even while standing in for the excluded term.

[30]This is the question that motivates Luce Irigaray's well-known Marxian-feminist reading of *Totem and Taboo*, criticizing the notion of the cultural exchange of women among tribes (in *This Sex Which Is Not One*, trans. Catherine Porter with Carolyn Burke [Ithaca: Cornell University Press, 1985]; published in French as *Ce sexe qui n'en est pas un* [Paris: Editions de Minuit, 1977]).

ings, is doubtless important for fathers and sons, and for society (as Lévi-Strauss has argued, after Freud). But can the masculine terms of subjectivity (castration, Name of the Father) be feminized? What of the daughter who opts to keep her "own" name (like Colette, years before feminists made the practice fashionable)? If we end our search where it began, with a search for the fantom subject of autobiography, we must acknowledge that the clue to this elusive fantom has been out in the open all along—the name "Colette" is the clue in full view, which need only be picked up and read.

The female writer, who turns to the Symbolic order to write her own story, must come to terms with the question of her relation to the paternal name. One solution, of course, is to invent one's own name (as feminists sometimes did in the seventies, adopting a single name; thus Colette was ahead of her time).[31] A variation of this option, for women writers at least, has been to adopt a pen name (here again, Colette led the way). In any case, Colette was one of the first to grapple with the problem of owning her name, making "Colette" a metaphor for her work. But the Name of the Father offers her no simple solution: the family name must undergo many transformations on the way to becoming "Colette," reflecting transformations in the self it designates.

Purloined Paternity

What, then, is the Name of the Father for Colette?

First, we should note that the term itself—the "Name of the Father"—has a certain linguistic duplicity: it may refer to the family name, of course; but it also may be read as the Captain's pet name *for* his little girl (the "fairy tale" name Bel-Gazou, which reemerges years later when it is passed on to Colette's own daughter). In this sense, the *nom du père* returns out of the mists of time to reclaim the daughter's daughter (whose last name is not "Colette" but de Jouvenel), reasserting the paternal legacy when the patronym is obscured.

Of course, the more familiar face of the *nom du père* is the family name, also transmitted from the Captain to his daughter, but sig-

---

[31]During the late seventies, the feminist writer Monique Wittig, for instance, was known simply as "Theo."

nificantly *not* abandoned in marriage, as convention demands. At the time of her first marriage Gabrielle-Sidonie Colette drops the *mother's* appellation ("Sidonie") and takes on the family name as given name, becoming Colette Willy; at her second marriage, she again retains the *nom du père* as her given name, becoming Colette de Jouvenel. And with her final marriage, she eschews the conjugal label altogether (she never took Maurice Goudeket's name), adopting a single name, both "given" and "taken"—the given name Colette is taken in place of her husband's name, in an act of self-nomination, forging a new identity, which nonetheless bears traces of old loves and desires.

"Colette" as manifesto of independence declares a new social status, a new relation to patriarchal law, indicated by her own proud statement that marital status will no longer be the determining factor in her identity: "This day forth I will have but one legal name." In addition to this conscious personal and legal choice, I have argued that there is also, in the classic Lacanian sense, a Symbolic identification, which incorporates the slain father: like the tribal sons of *Totem and Taboo*, Colette identifies with her father's role and her father's unfinished task, taking up his pen and filling the empty pages already dedicated to their mutual love. But this choice perhaps also indicates an identification with the mother, since, as it turns out, Sido was the first one to use their surname in place of a given name: "I hear my mother's words of indulgent reproof, calling my father, as always, by our surname: 'Oh, Colette! Colette!'" (*MMH* 46). (Interestingly, Colette too will call her first husband, Gauthier-Villars, by his adopted surname—and Colette's own first pen name—"Willy.") So the conscious assumption of the father's name is overdetermined by unconscious desire: not only does it indicate an identification with the father, but it also harbors the desire to be in the place of the one who names him "Colette," the desire to *be* her mother, beloved of the father; conversely, her self-naming (making her "Colette" in her turn) indicates the desire to *be* her father, beloved of Sido.

Indeed the novel *Sido* is written from the father's place, with his pen and his voice. The title itself is an implied quote, since the Captain is the "one person in the world" who calls the mother "Sido" (160); thus the title signifies that the daughter has identified with her *father*, "the one person" to use the mother's intimate name. In other words, writing an elegy to Sido signed by the father's name, the daughter too becomes "Colette," but differently, in her own womanly way.

Nom de plume—a Feather in Sido's Nest

We have seen that in this androgynous family name-game of shifting multiple identities, nothing, including gender, is simply what it seems: the "phallic" pen is an emblem of the daughter's femininity, her "female genius"; and the "feminine" veil actually shrouds the father, in the feminized metaphor "Colette." The label "Colette" is itself a fiction of sorts, a veil of feminine and intimate appearance—with its ornamental second syllable and its resemblance to a woman's first name—but it cloaks an identification with Captain Colette and with his writer's calling. From the time of Colette's first marriage, the name takes on this androgynous metaphoric quality, reflecting both parents and both genders: in the name Colette Willy the father's name eclipses the maternal given name (Gabrielle-Sidonie), taking the feminine place in the chain of nomination. But it is the name of the father shorn of its patriarchal value, removed from its proper place and worn as feminine adornment.

By the time this name comes to stand alone, it has taken on the full weight of metaphor, standing for many things: it is a declaration of autonomy, of freedom from men, but it also signifies an access to the man's world of words (a world in which, ironically, both impotent male models—the Captain and Willy—were unable to function). As a metaphor, it is overdetermined by multiple identities: a pen name (a traditionally male attribute) that is also *nom de plume*—a feather from Sido's nest. For the writer inherits two parental legacies: her father's will to write (the horizontal metonymic desire) and Sido's "gifts of acute perception and trenchant observation" (vertical metaphoric memory). To multiply the complications in this familial drama, the primal triangle is always a foursome (as in Lacan's Schema L of analysis); the reader looks on, implicated in each term simultaneously and successively. As a result, the experience of the real woman is mediated not only by that of her fictional "I's," her ghosts, but by that of her readers, in an aesthetic act that surpasses the actual experience: "Everything rushes onward, and I stay where I am. Do I not already feel more pleasure in comparing this spring with others that are past than in welcoming it? The torpor is blissful enough, but too aware of its own weight" (*EP* 132). To be thoroughly savored, the pleasures of the real woman must be filtered through the overdetermined "I's" of "Colette," the writer.

Thus "Colette" is perhaps a Paternal Metaphor of sorts, but it is a purloined paternity, no longer imposed upon the daughter, but borrowed as a sign of identification with *both* missing parents. For in *Break of Day*, where "Sido's" voice shares the narration—through the use of real letters and imagined conversations—it is clear that the maternal "I" has thus become another facet of the plural "Colette" (she sees through Sido's eyes, speaks with her voice). But in writing *Sido* (a name coined by her father), she has also become the Captain, signing "Colette" with his hand.

Still she is able to become "Colette" only after the dreaded separation has become real: after the actual death of both parents. Only then does she pass from melancholia—unresolved feelings of anger and loss of self-esteem, accompanied by a silence, a writer's block concerning her family—through true mourning. This mourning/internalization permits her to chase away the menacing "forecluded" ghosts who haunt her, the too-personal parental figures who continue to inspire her with guilt. By actually living and assuming her loss, she can move from the passive position of victim of hostile ghosts, to the active position of ghost-writer, transforming her parents from scary spooks of the past to benevolent companions in the present and hopeful spirits of the future.

Thus Colette's autofiction reveals the affirmative aspect of the human tragedy of desire: if the sexual divide of which Lacan speaks ("there is no sexual relation") may be taken as an allegory of separation, of the permanence of desire, enacting estrangement and alienation, it must also be understood as a divide that creates a space, making room for human activity. For it is this inexhaustible difference—perhaps of male from female, but also of subject from object, of parent from child—that enables us to create, moving the hand across the page, deploying the *parental* metaphor in all its richness.

The making of "Colette" is a work of self-assembly: like a dream, which the unconscious assembles from "daily residue," this name contains scraps of her actual life: the maiden name, the married names, the pen name. Col-ette: the very syllables of that name, assumed after such suffering, evoke the ghostwriter's work—*col* suggests a glue (*colle*), performing the patchwork reassembly of the dismembered patriarch, re-membering the blinded Oedipus, by borrowing the "I's" of his lost love (Sido). And *col* also evokes a narrow passage, a neck—out of the womb, out of "my mother's house," into the "break of day," the birth as a writer. But it is only thanks to the feminized syllable, the stigmatic "ette" that makes the patronym usable as a woman's first name, that the daughter becomes herself, a woman writer. Thus this work of assembly and identification also divides and proliferates the subject—making of "Colette" the ultimate "shifting" pronoun, designating mother, father, and child. After "Colette," the name of the father will never be the same.

What does this woman want? Who is the subject of this ghost story? Not the real Colette, any more than "Colette" is a real name. The textual Colette herself is a metaphor, fashioned from remnants of her life, moving like her own ghost in this extended dream. Nor is the true subject of the autobiographical works the real mother, or father, or family, for Colette reserves the right to fantasize, even to err: "If I am mistaken, leave me to my delusion," she tells her reader (*Sido* 166). The subject of Colette's writing is the history of that writing itself, as a metaphor for human life, which sweeps on not only in spite of its encounter with death, but because of that encounter. The writer strives to complete the mourning-work by an act of playful restitution, in order to bring to light "something that no human eye before mine has gazed upon" (*MMH* 163). What is this treasure, to be exhumed at Sido's grave? The bounty so eagerly sought is an entire cast of fictionalized shades of the past. As Colette puts it, writing what might serve as her own epitaph (*My Apprenticeships* 17): "I cannot do better than to use the plural pronoun and take my place modestly in the crowd." Perhaps what this woman wants is nothing more nor less than to reunite her ghostly throng under a single headstone, bearing the name "Colette."

Select Bibliography

Since the Colette literature is vast, the following bibliography is limited to references that I have found particularly helpful. The listing of primary source works by Colette includes (in date order) only those texts with which this book deals; where possible, I have used the Farrar, Straus, and Giroux translations, which at the time of writing were the most generally available. The publication of the definitive edition of the *Oeuvres complètes* of Colette was begun in 1984, by Gallimard, in the *Pléiade* series. The secondary sources given are those cited in the text or notes, with some additions of particular interest for a psychoanalytic reading of autobiographical texts. Finally, I have included general theoretical works either cited in this book, or of general interest for a psychoanalytic/feminist approach to autobiography.

Colette Works Cited

Colette. *La Retraite sentimentale.* Paris: Mercure de France, 1907. *Retreat from Love.* Trans. Margaret Crosland. New York: Harcourt Brace Jovanovich, 1980.

———. *Les Vrilles de la vigne.* Paris: Editions de la Vie Parisienne, 1908.

———. *La Maison de Claudine.* Paris: J. Ferenczi et Fils, 1922. Trans. in *My Mother's House and Sido.* Trans. Enid McLeod and Una Vicenzo Troubridge. New York: Farrar, Straus, and Giroux, 1978.

———. *La Femme cachée.* Paris: Flammarion, 1924. In *The Other Woman.* Trans. Margaret Crosland. New York: Signet, 1975.

———. *La Naissance du jour.* Paris: Flammarion, 1928. *Break of Day.* Trans. Enid McLeod. New York: Farrar, Straus, and Giroux, 1979.

———. *La Seconde.* Paris: J. Ferenczi et Fils, 1929. *The Other One.* Trans. Elizabeth Tait and Roger Senhouse. New York: Farrar, Straus, and Giroux, 1979.

———. *Sido.* Paris: Editions Krâ, 1929. Trans. in *My Mother's House and Sido.* Trans. Enid McLeod. New York: Farrar, Straus, and Giroux, 1978.

——. *Ces Plaisirs.* . . . Paris: Ferenczi et Fils, 1932. Title changed to *Le Pur et l'impur*, 1941. *The Pure and the Impure.* Trans. Herma Briffault. New York: Farrar, Straus, and Giroux, 1966, 1980.

——. *Mes Apprentissages.* Paris: Ferenczi et Fils, 1936. *My Apprenticeships.* Trans. Helen Beauclerk. New York: Farrar, Straus, and Giroux, 1957.

——. *Journal à rebours.* Paris: A. Fayard, 1941. *Looking Backwards.* Trans. David Le Vay. Bloomington: Indiana University Press, 1975.

——. *De ma fenêtre.* Paris: Aux Armes de France, 1942. In *Looking Backwards.* Trans. David Le Vay. Bloomington: Indiana University Press, 1975.

——. *L'Etoile vesper.* Geneva: Editions du Milieu du Monde, 1946. *The Evening Star.* Trans. David Le Vay. In *Recollections.* New York: Macmillan, 1986.

——. *En pays connu.* Paris: Manuel Bruker, 1949. Sections in *Places.* Trans. David Le Vay and Margaret Crosland. New York: Bobbs-Merrill, 1971.

——. *Le Fanal bleu.* Paris: J. Ferenczi et Fils, 1949. *The Blue Lantern.* Trans. Roger Senhouse. New York: Farrar, Straus, and Giroux, 1963. Also in *Recollections.* Trans. David Le Vay. New York: Macmillan, 1986.

——. *Le Voyage égoiste.* Paris: Le Fleuron, 1949. *Journey for Myself.* In *Recollections* (Journey for Myself and *The Evening Star*). Trans. David Le Vay. New York: Macmillan, 1986.

——. *Lettres à Marguerite Moreno.* Paris: Flammarion, 1959.

——. *Earthly Paradise: Colette's Autobiography, Drawn from the Writings of Her Lifetime.* Ed. Robert Phelps. New York: Farrar, Straus, and Giroux, 1966.

——. *Letters from Colette.* Ed. and trans. Robert Phelps. New York: Farrar, Straus, and Giroux, 1980.

Secondary Sources on Colette

Beaumont, Germain, and André Parinaud. *Colette par elle-même.* Paris: Seuil-Ecrivains de toujours, 1951.

Biolley-Godino, Marcelle. *L'Homme-objet chez Colette.* Paris: Klincksieck, 1972.

Bray, Bernard, ed. *Colette: Nouvelles approches critiques.* Paris: Nizet, 1986.

Cahiers Colette 3/4. "Colloque du Dijon 1979." Paris: Flammarion, 1981.

Colette: Catalogue de l'exposition de 1973. Paris: Bibliothèque Nationale, 1973.

Cottrell, Robert D. *Colette.* New York: Ungar Press, 1974.

Crosland, Margaret. *Colette: The Difficulty of Loving.* New York: Dell, 1973.

Davies, Margaret. *Colette.* New York: Grove Press, 1961.

D'Hollander, Paul. *Colette: ses apprentissages.* Paris: Klincksieck, 1978.

——. "*La Naissance du jour* et *Mes Apprentissages*, ou la recherche d'un temps perdu." Bray 37–44.

Eisinger, Erica, and Mari McCarty, eds. "Charting Colette." Special issue, *Women's Studies* 8.3 (1981).

Forestier, Louis. *Chemin vers 'La Maison de Claudine' et 'Sido.'* Paris: Société d'Edition d'Enseignement Supérieur, 1968.
Giry, Jacqueline. *Colette et l'art du discours intérieur.* Paris: La Pensée Universelle, 1981.
Goudeket, Maurice. *Près de Colette.* Paris: Flammarion, 1956. *Close to Colette.* Trans. Harold Nicolson. New York: Farrar, Straus, and Cudahy, 1957.
Jouve, Nicole Ward. *Colette.* Bloomington: Indiana University Press, 1987.
Ketchum, Anne. *Colette ou la naissance du jour: Etude d'un malentendu.* Paris: Minard, 1968.
Lottman, Herbert R. *Colette: A Life.* Boston: Little, Brown, 1991.
Marks, Elaine. *Colette.* New Brunswick, N.J.: Rutgers University Press, 1960.
Mitchell, Yvonne. *Colette: A Taste for Life.* New York: Harcourt Brace Jovanovich, 1975.
Richardson, Joanna. *Colette.* London: Methuen, 1983.
Sarde, Michèle. *Colette, libre et entravé.* Paris: Stock, 1978. *Colette: Free and Fettered.* Trans. Richard Miller. New York: William Morrow, 1980.
Stewart, Joan Hinde. *Colette.* Boston: G. K. Hall, 1983.

Freud Works Cited

Freud, Sigmund. *Character and Culture.* Ed. Phillip Rieff. New York: Collier-Macmillan, 1963.
——. *Delusion and Dream and Other Essays.* Ed. Phillip Rieff. Boston: Beacon Press, 1956.
——. *General Psychological Theory.* Ed. Phillip Rieff. New York: Collier-Macmillan, 1963.
——. *On Creativity and the Unconscious.* Ed. Benjamin Nelson. New York: Harper and Row, 1958.
——. "The Splitting of the Ego in the Process of Defense" (1938). Trans. James Strachey. *The International Journal of Psychoanalysis* 22 (1941). (Unfinished essay not included in the *Standard Edition.*)
——. *The Standard Edition of the Complete Works of Sigmund Freud.* 24 vols. Trans. James Strachey. London: Hogarth, 1955, and New York: W. W. Norton, 1961.
Beyond the Pleasure Principle (1920). Vol. 18.
"A Childhood Recollection on *Dichtung und Wahrheit*" (1917). Vol. 17.
Civilization and Its Discontents (1930). Vol. 21.
"Creative Writers and Daydreaming" (1908). Vol. 9.
"Delusion and Dream in Jensen's *Gradiva*" (1906). Vol. 9.
"The Dissolution of the Oedipus Complex" (1924). Vol. 19.
"The Dynamics of Transference" (1912). Vol. 12.
"The Economic Problem of Masochism" (1924). Vol. 19.
The Ego and the Id (1923). Vol. 19.
"Female Sexuality" (1931). Vol. 21.

"Fetishism" (1927). Vol. 21.
"Fragment of an Analysis of a Case of Hysteria" (1905). Vol. 7.
"From the History of an Infantile Neurosis" (1918). Vol. 17.
"The Future of an Illusion" (1927). Vol. 21.
Group Psychology and the Analysis of the Ego (1921). Vol. 18.
The Interpretation of Dreams (1900). Vols. 4–5.
Introductory Lectures on Psycho-Analysis (1916–17). Vols. 15–16.
Jokes and Their Relation to the Unconscious (1905). Vol. 8.
Leonardo da Vinci and a Memory of His Childhood (1910). Vol. 11.
"Medusa's Head" (1940 [1922]). Vol. 18.
Moses and Monotheism (1939). Vol. 23.
"Mourning and Melancholia" (1917). Vol. 14.
"Negation" (1925). Vol. 19.
New Introductory Lectures on Psychoanalysis (1933). Vol. 22.
"On Narcissism: An Introduction" (1914). Vol. 14.
An Outline of Psycho-Analysis (1940). Vol. 23.
The Problem of Anxiety (1926). Vol. 20.
The Psychopathology of Everyday Life (1901). Vol. 6.
The Question of Lay Analysis (1926). Vol. 20.
"Repression" (1915). Vol. 14.
"Some Psychological Consequences of an Anatomical Distinction be-
    tween the Sexes" (1925). Vol. 19.
Three Essays on the Theory of Sexuality (1905). Vol. 7.
Totem and Taboo (1912). Vol. 13.
"The 'Uncanny'" (1919). Vol. 17.
"The Unconscious" (1915). Vol. 14.
——. *Three Case Histories*. Ed. Phillip Rieff. New York: Collier-Macmillan,
1963.

Theoretical and Critical Works of Interest

Abraham, Nicolas. "The Phantom of Hamlet or the Sixth Act: Preceded
    by the Intermission of 'Truth.'" Trans. Nicholas Rand. *Diacritics* 18.4
    (1988): 2–19.
Abraham, Nicolas, and Maria Torok. *L'Ecorce et le noyau*. Paris: Flam-
    marion, 1987.
Beckson, Karl, and Arthur Ganz. *Literary Terms: A Dictionary*. New York:
    Farrar, Straus, and Giroux, 1976.
Bellemin-Noël, Jean. *Essais de textanalyse*. Lille: Presses Universitaires de
    Lille, 1988.
——. "Textoanalysis and Psychoanalysis." *Sub-Stance* 59, 18.2 (1989): 102–
    12.
——. *Vers l'inconscient du texte*. Paris: Presses Universitaires de Fance,
    1979.
Benstock, Shari, ed. *The Private Self: Theory and Practice of Women's Auto-
    biography*. Chapel Hill: University of North Carolina Press, 1988.

Bersani, Leo. "Artists in Love." *Baudelaire and Freud*. Berkeley: University of California Press, 1977.

Bettelheim, Bruno. *The Uses of Enchantment*. New York: Knopf, 1976.

Brooks, Peter. "Freud's Masterplot: Questions of Narrative." Felman 280–300.

——. "The Idea of a Psychoanalytic Literary Criticism." Rimmon-Kenan 1–18.

——. *Reading for the Plot: Design and Intention in Narrative*. New York: Knopf, 1984.

Chase, Cynthia. "Transference as Trope and Persuasion." Rimmon-Kenan 211–32.

Chasseguet-Smirgel, Janine. *La Sexualité féminine*. Paris: Payot, 1964. *Feminine Sexuality*. Ann Arbor: University of Michigan Press, 1984.

Chodorow, Nancy. *The Reproduction of Mothering: Psychoanalysis and the Sociology of Gender*. Berkeley: University of California Press, 1978.

Cixous, Hélène. "Castration or Decapitation." *Signs* 7.1 (1981): 25–36.

Davis, Robert C., ed. *Lacan and Narration*. Baltimore and London: Johns Hopkins University Press, 1984, 1986.

de Beauvoir, Simone. *Le Deuxième sexe*. Paris: Gallimard, 1949. *The Second Sex*. Trans. H. M. Parshley. New York: Knopf, 1953.

de Man, Paul. *Blindness and Insight: Essays in the Rhetoric of Contemporary Criticism*. New York and London: Oxford University Press, 1971.

Derrida, Jacques. "Coming into One's Own." Trans. James Hulbert. Hartman 114–48.

——. "Le Facteur de la vérité." *Poétique* 21 (1975). "The Purveyor of Truth." *Yale French Studies* 52 (1975): 31–113.

Feldstein, Richard, and Judith Roof, eds. *Feminism and Psychoanalysis*. Ithaca: Cornell University Press, 1989.

Felman, Shoshana, ed. *Literature and Psychoanalysis: The Question of Reading: Otherwise*. Baltimore and London: Johns Hopkins University Press, 1982.

——. "Paul de Man's Silence." *Critical Inquiry* 15 (Summer 1989): 704–44.

——. "Rereading Femininity." Gaudin et al. 19–44.

Flieger, Jerry Aline. *The Purloined Punch Line: Freud's Comic Theory and the Postmodern Text*. Baltimore and London: Johns Hopkins University Press, 1991.

Foucault, Michel. *La Volonté de savoir*. Paris: Gallimard, 1976. *The History of Sexuality: Volume I: An Introduction*. Trans. Robert Hurley. New York: Vintage–Random House, 1980.

Gallop, Jane. *The Daughter's Seduction*. Ithaca: Cornell University Press, 1982.

Garner, Shirley Nelson, Claire Kahane, and Madelon Sprengnether, eds. *The (M)other Tongue: Essays in Psychoanalytic Interpretation*. Ithaca: Cornell University Press, 1985.

Gaudin, Colette, M. J. Green, L. Higgins, M. Hirsch, V. Kogan, C. Reeder, and N. Vickers, eds. *Feminist Readings: French Texts/American Contexts*. Special issue of *Yale French Studies* 62 (1982).

Gilbert, Sandra, and Susan Gubar. *The Madwoman in the Attic*. New Haven and London: Yale University Press, 1979.

Gilligan, Carol. *In a Different Voice*. Cambridge: Harvard University Press, 1982.

Girard, René. *Le Violence et le sacré*. Paris: Grasset, 1972. *Violence and the Sacred*. Trans. Patrick Gregory. Baltimore and London: Johns Hopkins University Press, 1977.

Hartman, Geoffrey H., ed. *Psychoanalysis and the Question of the Text*. Baltimore and London: Johns Hopkins University Press, 1978.

Holland, Norman N. *The Dynamics of Literary Response*. New York: Oxford University Press, 1968.

———. *5 Readers Reading*. New Haven: Yale University Press, 1975.

Irigaray, Luce. *Ce sexe qui n'en est pas un*. Paris: Editions de Minuit, 1977. *This Sex Which Is Not One*. Trans. Catherine Porter with Carolyn Burke. Ithaca: Cornell University Press, 1985.

———. *Speculum de l'autre femme*. Paris: Editions de Minuit, 1974. *Speculum of the Other Woman*. Trans. Gillian C. Gill. Ithaca: Cornell University Press, 1985.

Iser, Wolfgang. *The Act of Reading*. Baltimore: Johns Hopkins University Press, 1978.

Jakobson, Roman. "'Two Aspects of Language and Two Types of Aphasic Disturbances." *Fundamentals of Language*. Ed. Roman Jakobson and Morris Halle. The Hague: Mouton, 1956.

Jameson, Fredric. "Imaginary and Symbolic in Lacan: Marxism, Psychoanalytic Criticism, and the Problem of the Subject." Felman 338–95.

———. *The Political Unconscious: Narrative as Socially Symbolic Act*. Ithaca: Cornell University Press, 1981.

Jardine, Alice. *Gynesis: Configurations of Woman and Modernity*. Ithaca: Cornell University Press, 1986.

Johnson, Barbara. *The Critical Difference*. Baltimore and London: Johns Hopkins University Press, 1980.

———. "The Frame of Reference: Poe, Lacan, Derrida." Felman 457–505.

Kofman, Sarah. *L'Enigme de la femme: La Femme dans les textes de Freud*. Paris: Galilée, 1980.

Kristeva, Julia. *Desire in Language: A Semiotic Approach to Literature and Art*. Ed. Leon S. Roudiez. Trans. Thomas Gora, Alice Jardine, and Leon S. Roudiez. New York: Columbia University Press, 1980.

———. *The Kristeva Reader*. Ed. Toril Moi. New York: Columbia University Press, 1986.

———. "On the Melancholic Imaginary." Rimmon-Kenan 104–23.

———. *Polylogue*. Paris: Editions du Seuil, 1977.

———. *La Révolution poétique du langage*. Paris: Editions du Seuil, 1977.

Kurzweil, Edith, and William Phillips, eds. *Literature and Psychoanalysis*. New York: Columbia University Press, 1983.

Lacan, Jacques. "Desire and the Interpretation of Desire in *Hamlet*." Felman 11–52.

——. *Ecrits*. 2 vols. Paris: Editions du Seuil-Points, 1966, 1971.

——. *Ecrits: A Selection*. Paris: Tavistock Publications, 1977.

——. *Le Séminaire livre XX: encore*. Paris: Editions du Seuil, 1975.

——. "Le Séminaire sur 'La Lettre volé.'" *Ecrits* I, 19–75. "Seminar on the Purloined Letter." Trans. Jeffrey Mehlman. *Yale French Studies* 48 (1976): 39–72.

Lang, Candace D. *Irony/Humor*. Baltimore and London: Johns Hopkins University Press, 1988.

Laplanche, Jean. *Vie et mort en psychanalyse*. Paris: Editions du Seuil, 1976. *Life and Death in Psychoanalysis*. Trans. Jeffrey Mehlman. Baltimore: Johns Hopkins University Press, 1976.

Laplanche, Jean, and Jean-Baptiste Pontalis. *Vocabulaire de la psychanalyse*. Paris: Presses Universitaires de France, 1967. *The Language of Psycho-Analysis*. Trans. Donald Nicholson-Smith. New York: W. W. Norton, 1973.

Leclerc, Annie. *Parole de femme*. Paris: Grasset, 1974.

Lejeune, Philippe. *Le Pacte autobiographique*. Paris: Editions du Seuil, 1975.

Lévi-Strauss, Claude. "The Structural Study of Myth." *Structural Anthropology*. New York: Vintage–Random House, 1963.

Lyotard, Jean-François. *Discours, figure*. Paris: Klincksieck, 1971.

Marks, Elaine, and Isabelle de Courtivron, eds. *New French Feminisms*. New York: Schocken Books, 1981.

Miller, Nancy K. *The Poetics of Gender*. New York: Columbia University Press, 1986.

Mitchell, Juliet. *Psycho-Analysis and Feminism*. New York: Vintage–Random House, 1975.

Mitchell, Juliet, and Jacqueline Rose, eds. *Feminine Sexuality: Jacques Lacan and the Ecole freudienne*. Trans. Jacqueline Rose. New York: W. W. Norton, 1982.

Montrelay, Michèle. *L'Ombre et le nom: sur la féminité*. Paris: Editions de Minuit, 1977.

Olney, James, ed. *Studies in Autobiography*. New York: Oxford University Press, 1988.

Reppen, Joseph, and Maurice Charney, eds. *The Psychoanalytic Study of Literature*. Hillsdale, N.J.: Analytic Press, 1985.

Rich, Adrienne. *Of Woman Born*. New York: W. W. Norton, 1976.

Rimmon-Kenan, Shlomith, ed. *Discourse in Psychoanalysis and Literature*. New York: Methuen Books, 1987.

Ruthven, K. K. *Feminist Literary Studies*. Cambridge: Cambridge University Press, 1984.

Schor, Naomi. "Female Paranoia: The Case for Psychoanalytic Feminist Criticism." Gaudin et al. 204–19.

Skura, Meredith Anne. *The Literary Use of the Psychoanalytic Process*. New Haven and London: Yale University Press, 1981.

Spence, Donald P. *Narrative Truth and Historical Truth: Meaning and Interpretation in Psychoanalysis*. New York: W. W. Norton, 1982.

Spivak, Gayatri. "French Feminism in an International Frame." Gaudin et al. 154–84.
Sprengnether, Madelon. "Ghost Writing: A Meditation on Literary Criticism as Narrative." Reppen and Charney 37–49.
Strouse, Jean, ed. *Women and Analysis: Dialogues on Psychoanalytic Views of Femininity.* New York: Grossman, 1974.
Suleiman, Susan Rubin. "Nadja, Dora, Lol V. Stein: Women, Madness and Narrative." Rimmon-Kenan 124–51.
Watson, Julia. "Shadowed Presence: Modern Women Writers' Autobiography." Olney 180–89.
Weber, Samuel. *The Legend of Freud.* Minneapolis: University of Minnesota Press, 1982.
Wilden, Anthony. *Speech and Language in Psychoanalysis.* Baltimore and London: Johns Hopkins University Press, 1981. First published as *The Language of the Self: The Function of Language in Psychoanalysis.* New York: Dell, 1975.
Yaeger, Patricia, and Beth Kowaleski-Wallace, eds. *Refiguring the Father: New Feminist Readings of Patriarchy.* Carbondale: Southern Illinois University Press, 1989.

Index

Reading
WOMEN
Writing

A SERIES EDITED BY SHARI BENSTOCK AND CELESTE SCHENCK

brary of Congress Cataloging-in-Publication Data

eiger, Jerry Aline, 1947–
    Colette and the fantom subject of autobiography / Jerry Aline
  Flieger.
      p.   cm. — (Reading women writing)
    Includes bibliographical references and index.
    ISBN 0-8014-2692-8 (cloth : alk. paper). — ISBN 0-8014-9980-1
  (paper : alk. paper)
      1. Colette, 1873–1954—Criticism and interpretation.   2. Women and
  literature—France—History—20th century.   3. Psychoanalysis and
  literature.   4. Self in literature.   5. Autobiography.   I. Title.
  II. Series.
  PQ2605.028Z664   1992
  848'.91209—dc20
                                                          91-55557